⊘ the life a

handbook
for
life

Also by Caroline Righton and available from Mobius

The Life Audit

the life audit
handbook
for
life

Caroline Righton

HODDER
MOBIUS

The information in this book has been obtained from reliable sources. However, it is intended as a guideline only. While every effort has been made to ensure its accuracy, no responsibility for loss, damage or injury occasioned to any person acting or refraining from action as a result of information contained herein can be accepted by the publishers or author.

The nutrition information on pages 177–186 was originally published in the *Good Nutrition Guide*, 1994, by Geddes and Grosset of David Dale House, New Lanark and is reprinted with permission.

Copyright © 2006 by Caroline Righton

First published in Great Britain in 2006 by Hodder & Stoughton
A division of Hodder Headline

The right of Caroline Righton to be identified as the Author of the Work has been asserted by her in accordance with the Copyright, Designs and Patents Act 1988

A Mobius Book

1

All rights reserved. No part of this publication may be reproduced, stored in a retrieval system, or transmitted, in any form or by any means without the prior written permission of the publisher, nor be otherwise circulated in any form of binding or cover other than that in which it is published and without a similar condition being imposed on the subsequent purchaser.

A CIP catalogue record for this title is available from the British Library

0 340 83937 6

Typeset in Stone by Servis Filmsetting Ltd, Manchester

Printed and bound by
Clays Ltd, St Ives plc

Hodder Headline's policy is to use papers that are natural, renewable and recyclable products and made from wood grown in sustainable forests. The logging and manufacturing processes are expected to conform to the environmental regulations of the country of origin.

Hodder & Stoughton Ltd
A division of Hodder Headline
338 Euston Road
London NW1 3BH

Contents

Introduction: Welcome to the Handbook for Life

Do you ever feel stuck in a rut? Or that life is whizzing by, nothing is happening and you are wasting time and missing opportunities? Or perhaps you feel paralysed by the huge number of choices you have, so much so that you end up doing nothing special with each day and the future stretches ahead of you like one big yawn. Do you want to make changes but feel fearful?

If only life came with a Handbook, complete with guidelines and boxes to tick for all the achievements that go to make up what most of us might consider to be a good and happy life. Things like, **Make good friends – tick. Fall in love with the right person – tick. Be optimistic – tick. Get a fulfilling job – tick. Be healthy – tick. Make the most of your money – tick. Be a good person – tick.** You get the idea – all this along with, **Know how to iron pillow cases the best way – tick** and **Find the definitive casserole recipe.**

Although it doesn't always feel like it, most of us do have a great deal of freedom to make choices in our lives. This means there is enormous scope to get things wrong, at least once, before we get them right, which seems to me to be a tremendous waste of time. From big things such as marrying the wrong person, being a rubbish parent or pursuing the wrong career, to having a chaotic linen cupboard (may not matter to you but has driven me mad for years, until now!) there are a lot of pitfalls to avoid and things to learn about life.

This book sets out to be a place where you can find received wisdom, best practice and basic advice along with ordinary people's observations, preferences and experiences to help you make up your own mind and to accompany all aspects of life's random learning. There's something on just about everything, from how to be a good friend, to how to dump a bad one; how to have that difficult conversation about your job; your debts, your fears, your sex life, all the way to death – yours or that of someone dear to you. It also addresses, quite unashamedly, the more mundane things, the domestic nuts and bolts that make for happy days.

Last year I wrote *The Life Audit*. It is a plan that helped me sort through a period when, despite on the surface seeming to have it all, I was uncertain and unhappy about what I *really* wanted out of life and what would *really* make me happy. The premise of *The Life Audit* is – take control of your life and audit it as you would a business; stocktake the hours and minutes of your day; analyse how you use the time and think about what you would prefer to be doing with it, where and with whom; then, armed with all your personal data – make informed and strategic changes. Within days of auditing my life I felt happier, more optimistic and more content, and knew what aspects of my life I wanted to nurture and what I wanted to audit out. I still audit my life on a regular basis. It's become an ongoing maintenance job and as I ruminate and write down the hours I've spent de-crumbing the cutlery drawer or striding purposefully to the pub each week, there's no stone unturned in confronting the good and bad that makes up my life.

This handbook has come about as the direct result of writing *The Life Audit*, because every time I addressed a new aspect of life (my life, everyone's life) – such as Mortality – I really wished there was a manual that could help me out with finding some answers, point me in some right directions and explain what *really* happens as you die (for instance). And in other areas, what exactly does BMI stand for and when should I start worrying about my creaking ankles? How does a sabbatical work and how might I be a better citizen? And what does Citizenship mean anyway? I wanted answers and advice, but more than anything

I wanted to know I was on the right track to figuring things out myself.

Put a jumper on and get over it!

I may sound a little brisk but this book should become a hypo-thetical jumper ... it should make you personally more resourceful and responsible in trying to solve your own life's dilemmas. You feel a bit shivery? Well, before you book an appointment to see the doctor, or worry yourself sick that you're coming down with pneumonia, first try putting on a jumper and seeing if that does the trick and warms you up. Just get over it (being cold) and on with it (life). Likewise, hit a crisis or need to make a decision? Don't immediately look to someone else to solve your problems or ignore the situation and stick your head in the sand. Pick this book up and try in the first instance to be informed about your options and see if there are solutions or choices that you can make work for yourself.

I feel sad hearing people being knee-jerk needy and looking to someone else to be told what to think rather than working a bit harder themselves to be more accountable for their own problem-solving. I think a lot of life's problems don't have to turn into 'big issues' if you look for your own *simple* solution first. Feeing out of control and that only someone else has the answers, is very disabling. Find your own answers. Be informed. Make your own decisions.

Having said all that, remember that in reality, of course, you are not *totally* alone. One of the basic tenets of life-auditing is identifying your own resource pool of people, skills and things. This book should become a reference book within those resources and accordingly swell the volume of wisdom to which you have instant access. Writing it and talking to both professionals and ordinary people has made me realise just how much wisdom *everyone* has to offer in something.

While there are many specialist manuals that deal with

different subjects from car maintenance to writing your will, this book takes a broad-brush approach to life and covers the same areas that I tackled in *The Life Audit*.

Relationships – partners, family, friends, acquaintances, colleagues, children, pets, professionals and support services
Soul – identity and nurture
Work and Leisure – how to make your job work for you, change career or start a business and how to relax
Health – well-being, fitness, diet and weight loss
Money – income and expenditure, saving, spending and making, total worth
Citizenship – responsibility and concern
Home – bricks and mortar, contents, housework and maintenance
Image – clothes, grooming and style
Mortality – what happens and how to deal with it

We are often spoilt for choice when it comes to making decisions and less and less is there *one* right way to do anything. Whether we like it or not, we don't have the social and moral corsetry that in the past gave us boundaries and restrictions for what was and wasn't acceptable. And gone are the days when everyone bought into certain codes of behaviour and woe betide the person who didn't match up to them or, even worse, didn't know them in the first place. So, because one size rarely fits all and often there really isn't just *one* right way, there are alternative views and opinions. It's now up to you to decide whether fish knives or fellatio are your bag or not; and who's going to say you are wrong or right because, to be frank, just about anything goes. Which means that it is up to the individual to decide what works for them. Scary, isn't it! And could be a bit lonesome too? No! Not at all! The one great thing about this freefall free-for-all is that we are all pretty much in the same boat, we're all alone together, muddling through with trial and error, trying to work out what's best to do. So we are really not alone at all. We just need to take responsibility and share a bit more and listen a bit better to make sure the choices we make are as well informed as possible. It's in this spirit I offer you the *Handbook for Life*.

What do I know . . . ?

Since writing *The Life Audit* I have heard the stories of hundreds of people, both by meeting them and via The Life Audit website *www.thelifeaudit.com*. We've talked about everything under the sun, from how to avoid answering the phone when you suspect it's a person you don't want to talk to, to whether pure linen bed sheets are worth the money they cost (a lot and no, not on most budgets). Many of their experiences of 'finding their right jumper' are featured in this book. In fact their concerns and questions, their common sense and good advice, along with those of my family, friends and colleagues, have all informed my opinions, of which there are plenty – well, it is my book! None of us, as far as I know, and certainly not me, have got 'ologies' or certificates to say we have completed a course in any of the subjects covered to prove we are 'qualified' to give you the benefit of our experience or opinions. But we have all lived a little, and often quite a lot, and I have made judgments that what is offered here is wise, true, valid and relevant. I need you to know that – so blame me if you don't like what you read. Having said that, the collective, subjective stuff is balanced by some very specific information from individuals. I've talked to some named experts who offer unique advice, and I've backed the whole lot up with a great deal of research, in particular on the worldwide web. Years of journalistic training came in very handy.

Of course there is a huge mass of information out there and for almost every endorsed, strongly advocated process or recommended procedure, there is another way, recommended by another body, with just as much integrity. So can I emphasise that all the research, the opinions, the ideas contained in the

Handbook for Life are *my* call on what appears to be the consensus view of what works.

Members of *The Life Audit* website who have contributed hail from all over the world as the first book is selling in many countries from China to Kenya, Australia to Japan. So my chapter on parenting, for example, drew on the observations from lots of far-flung people including mothers and fathers in Sydney, South Africa and Ontario as well as people who live in my tiny village in Devon in the UK. Parenting may have a *universal* best practice – but the legal ramifications attached to the paperwork for adopting a child, for instance, are different all over the world so some things are culturally specific. That presented a bit of dilemma. To keep the book useful and focussed, international and flexible and to ensure it stays current as long as possible, I've packed it with *general* principles, experiences and the best advice I can give. So read it and then, wherever you see this ⊘ symbol, if you want to find out more, get the small print or talk to a specialist, go to *The Life Audit* website (www.thelifeaudit.com) where you will find a comprehensive list of contacts and support organisations for *your* country, whether that's the UK or South Africa. I'm also very happy to hear any source recommendations from you which I'll check out and post up too, if appropriate.

This is a book for reading and dipping into, it doesn't demand that you follow a programme or work incredibly hard. But I hope you will find it useful and inspiring. And although it's not based around exercises to do, I think that you should take an active role in being responsible for finding and testing your own solutions and learning to research well. I am eternally thankful to the editors and producers I have worked with during my journalism career who taught me *how* to look for information. The basic principles are to be clear about the questions you have, to be comfortable with the credentials of the sources you choose and to make up your own mind about whether the answers are the ones you are looking for. All my signposts point to the web for information as most of us have access to a computer now, even if it's at the local library. With the web, the sources available to you are endless, but cultivate discernment about which offer valid and accredited advice and, most of all, don't forget those familiar sources closer to home, such as your family, friends and, of course, this book. Now, onward! We're going to start with the big one, the topic that has got people talking, more than any other . . . Relationships.

Relationships

The most discussed section of *The Life Audit* has been Relationships. The whole idea of auditing your relationships, whether they are with friends, lovers or family, is like a giant taboo – rather shocking yet somehow, it appears, rather appealing and compelling. Holding relationships up to the light for intense scrutiny is stirring stuff and while the audit process doesn't necessarily mean getting rid, it would seem we all have people we want to reposition in our affections and indeed, with some, OK, audit out! This happens because, (in the main, I hope) there are others we wish to cherish more and spend more time with. But whatever the case, relationships are pivotal and these are the questions that arose most commonly amongst Life Auditors:

What makes a good relationship?
I'm lonely, how can I make friends?
How can I meet someone special who will care about me?
How will I know true love when it comes along?
How can I make people do what I want them to?
How do I audit a destructive relationship out of my life?

One technique to help you answer these questions is to trace back all your key relationships and place them, according to their importance, in a circle of concern, time and need radiating out from you at the centre. In this section of the handbook we'll look at the categories of significant others, family, friends and the professionals and support services you have in your life.

Relationships with colleagues are covered in the 'Work' section. (See page 100.)

The quality of our waking hours can be measured by the company we keep and the way we conduct the encounters we have with everyone from our significant other to the receptionist at the sports club. Bad relationships sap our souls, knock our self-confidence and make us feel rubbish and inadequate. Being betrayed by a lover, a friend, a parent or a child is killing and takes enormous getting over, while good relationships and good love make life fantastic and worth living whatever pain is going on elsewhere. Every step of every stage of every relationship is charged with full-on and potentially exhausting emotions, because that's what good relationships are all about – emotional investments that require nurture and time. The more love we invest, the bigger the loss if things go wrong. Many of us are frightened of addressing our relationship issues because we have high, often unarticulated expectations of those we care for and we expect the partnership – whatever sort it is – to operate with minimal intervention, to work instinctively.

So, although it can initially seem a little daunting, take a pragmatic approach to marshalling your thoughts about the people in your life. Concentrate on things such as learning to read the spontaneous reactions you have to the sound of a voice on the end of the phone, the sight of a name in the email inbox, and properly understanding the life-enhancing or well-poisoning nature of the engagement and what its sum worth is in their life and yours. Each and every relationship has issues and presents dilemmas and these need to be identified and addressed for it to stay properly secure and enriching.

It's possible some of the advice offered here won't be appropriate or relevant to you but it's all worked at some time for someone else and is offered in that spirit. Before we get into the specifics of particular relationship types, there are some basics that apply to everyone and all encounters.

Relationships are crucial

Communication

Communicating effectively is at the root of all good relationships, regardless of who they are with. Even the briefest encounter can be improved by good communication. Life Auditors constantly report that it is the passing exchanges with strangers or acquaintances that life their spirits or dash them down, solely by how they are conducted. With more significant relationships, of course, it's even more important to ask yourself some honest questions.

- When you talk to someone, do you really listen and hear what they're saying?
- Do you think before you respond and consider whether they want your opinion, advice or shared experience or whether they would prefer just a sympathetic ear?
- Can you bear to hear painful truths?
- Are you able to speak painful truths yourself and handle the potential fallout?

Think about the quality of your communication. Do you actually make a point of turning the telly off and talking to your family, friends, partner, child? Do you really talk and really listen and feel a proper exchange has taken place? There are things you can do to improve communication.

- Don't just make your feelings clear with words – your face, smile, eyes and body language all add to the total expression of what you are saying.
- Always make eye contact with everyone you talk to. Not doing so makes you look shifty or a bit thick. If you struggle with this, suppress a tendency to move your eyes away by concentrating on *theirs* and watch the emotions and reactions they are conveying.
- Listen actively. Nod as someone is talking to you, not like a mad person, but attentively. Spot the interested

question you can ask or the conversational tangent that crops up and can take the encounter down a different avenue.

- Watch your body language: folded arms can seem unfriendly, leaning against a wall can seem bored and touching your face sends out a message that you are nervous.
- Cultivate a decent handshake. If you are a parent, train your children in this early on to avoid limp flabby paws being extended in later life.
- If you find yourself in a situation where you just don't know what to say, be honest 'I don't know what to say', is often all the encouragement someone needs to continue talking.
- If you are nervous about making conversation – think in threes. Have three subjects that you feel comfortable talking about, such as films, a local issue, a story in the news. Think of three things related to those subjects that might be topical. Think of three opening comments and questions you could express or ask someone.
- If this seems too difficult, stick to occupation or family and ask open-ended questions starting with what, where, when and who; these will encourage longer, more detailed answers than 'are' and 'do' questions which will only get you one-word 'yes' or 'no' responses.

Don't forget to pay attention to how you use other forms of communication as well, especially if personal contact is difficult or undesirable. The telephone, mobiles, texts, letters and emails are all communication tools that can be used to greater or lesser effect, each with its own rules of etiquette, the most important of which is to bear in mind how the missive or message is going to be received at the other end. Without eye contact you must be clear how what you are saying at arm's length is going to come over.

- Take the hint if people mention you have a downbeat phone manner or often ask during calls on either a mobile or land line if you are all right. It means you are being ungenerous in your communication and you need to lift your voice and avoid abrupt responses. Try smiling and either look in the mirror at your own expression or create a mental picture of the person you are talking to.
- Texting has its own language and comes down to personal preference. Unless you know the recipient is as conversant as you with the intricacies of making punctuation symbols speak volumes, keep them brief; and sign off with your name unless you know for a fact it will appear when the message is delivered.
- Texting is a great medium for peacemaking. It allows brief, unemotional contact after a low or a rift, which gives the relationship something to build on.
- Email as an instant but non-interactive form of communication is fraught with potential to get it wrong.
- The trick is to treat it as a type of electronic postcard.
- Remember it might get posted up on a noticeboard, or forwarded on, so never send anything intimate, secret, inflammatory or libellous.
- It should have some formal structure, as in the recipient's name and a sign off, but doesn't necessarily need all the other formal inclusions of a letter.
- Never use capitals because they indicate you are shouting.
- Follow a sender's lead about whether to use Dear or just the name or even just the text body of the message on its own.
- Be disciplined about leaving answerphone messages. Almost all of us are guilty of leaving long rambling messages sometimes, but *everyone* I know finds this irritating, especially when it's clear that all that's actually required is for the call to simply be returned.

Confrontation

'Better out than in' or 'Least said soonest mended' were the infuriatingly contradictory tactics my very wise late mother-in-law would randomly advise about confrontation.

And she was right, there are times to speak out and others when biting your tongue is the better policy. So if you think something really tough has to be said about someone's behaviour and the way something makes you feel, try to be considered about your approach. As yourself these questions:

- Why do you feel it is so important to be frank?
- Can you understand what might have been the other person's motivation for their 'bad behaviour' as you see it, if that's the issue?
- Are you being frank to make *you* feel better about an injustice, in which case are you sure it will and can't you just quietly get over it?
- Or is it to reprimand them, in which case why do you feel it beholden on you to do so?
- Have you considered what the fallout from the confrontation might be? Do you care?
- Might it cause lasting damage, in which case are you prepared to take that risk?
- Or do you feel it is important to be frank to keep a relationship you value healthy and honest?
- Consider setting and timing. For example, addressing a sensitive issue with a teenage child often works well when the two of you are in the car. They don't have an escape route so they're pretty much a captive audience and the lack of eye contact can allow for embarrassing or difficult things to be said with minimal drama.

Sometimes, especially if the confrontation is with someone you care about, it's better to say something more in sadness than anger and to choose you timing so the recipient can mull over what you have said and have the chance to be more considered when they respond. For example, Antonia was increasingly fed up with her new husband's habit of going out for drinks with colleagues several nights a week after work and turning up home two hours later than he'd promised, ruining their supper together at the same time. Rowing about it hadn't seemed to change his behaviour and their overall relationship was deteriorating until one morning, as she left for work, she said with great seriousness and sadness that she needed him to know that his behaviour made her feel as though he had little respect for either her or their marriage and that she found it difficult to accept treatment that she would not be prepared to put up with from a casual acquaintance, let alone the man she loved and had married. There was no time for it to develop into an argument and he was left to ponder. That evening he was home on time and although he still went out drinking with his mates he made sure she knew his plans and he kept to them from then on.

I think respect actually is an undersold part of good relationships. It doesn't matter how close you are to someone, there should always be 'respect' in the way you treat them as a person and the way you are treated too. You shouldn't ever be prepared to just put up with bad behaviour from anyone.

If a situation seems intractable but you have got nothing to lose, sometimes it's important for you to just keep *trying* to find the right words to communicate how you feel. A friend of mine insists that if you have tried everything else, *talk* and *talk* and *talk* until you are exhausted and *their* ears are bleeding. This doesn't mean going round and round in circles, just make sure you have said what needs to be said and that they have heard those words, even if they still refuse to listen.

Arguing

You won't always get the model of good behaviour described in the paragraph above, in which case you could be heading for an enormous and potentially unhelpful row. When confrontation gets noisy try these tactics:

- If someone is really angry with you about something, don't interrupt them, however unfair their tack is.
- Let them have their rant and run out of steam and then try to put your side of the story, starting with: 'I understand what you are saying but I feel this way . . .' If they bluster in again indignantly, pause again until they fall silent and try again.
- If you are in the wrong, however unreasonable or excessive their anger, say so quickly. Don't end up having a row about the row.
- If you are the angry person – don't go into the fray all guns blazing. Know a solution that would make you feel better and say it as soon as you can. One that leaves the other person with some dignity is most likely to be taken. If you reach an impasse, suggest a cooling-off period and that you both try to sort out the problem later.
- If they won't agree to this, remove *yourself* from the situation, especially if the argument is getting really out of control or overemotional. Take a shower, have a walk, say *you* need to reassess and calm down, even if they don't.
- Never *storm* out. It solves nothing and your return will inevitably be sheepish. It is impossible to *storm back* with any dignity.
- Analyse an argument. Is the headline bone of contention really the issue or are there underlying problems that need addressing?
- Sometimes an angry person won't want to let go of the rowing or stormy sulking and will seem to want it to go round and round in circles and on and on. If you feel a continuing row is pointless and that there really is nothing more you can say or do that is going to stop it, think yourself into a happy place by visualising something lovely or a favourite moment from the past. Let their rage or angry silence wash over you and with any luck it'll burn out at the same time, although possibly not until after

your carefree demeanour has confounded and infuriated them. This is not as difficult a thing to do as you might think. The moral high ground has some great views.

- And remember that arguing is not necessarily about winning the point. Sometimes an argument does have a value in giving views a good airing, often about a wider issue. For that reason, arguments can sometimes be a good opportunity for communication, especially if you listen well, and can contain useful information about the real depth of emotions or problems.
- If the argument fails to resolve the issue and it's not a complete deal breaker for the relationship, try to see what came out of the exchange from everybody's point of view and move on.
- If there are taboo or touchy subjects that start rows time and time again, front them out, talk about them lots to disarm their potency.
- Hanging on to the anger or frustration is a negative and wasteful emotion. It is possible to agree to disagree.

Significant others

Significant others are your most important core relationships, yet perversely are the ones often most vulnerable because it's just so easy to take them for granted. Also, because they are so intimate, there are many sensitive and deeply personal flashpoints for hearts and minds to fall out over and they are often intricately interwoven with day-to-day elements of living that need them to function on a practical and financial level as well. Of course, your significant other may currently be your Burmese kitten, your child or a parent but for the purposes of this chapter I am assuming it's your partner.

Good relationships

Let's start by defining what we're looking for in our partnership with our significant other. The qualities of good relationships are easy to define – and all sound admirable! Of course, they are not necessarily as easy to put into practice to make for a lasting partnership! But let's all repeat together . . .

- A good relationship is when you feel you are truly soul mates and supportive, looking out for each other and functioning as an interdependent team.
- When you are in it for the long haul and can put your head down and grit your teeth knowing you *will* get through the stormy times. It isn't a faulty purchase you can take back to the shop and swap.
- When you manage to retain your individuality within the couple.
- When you have mutual respect for each other's individualities and you don't feel threatened by the other's interests, skills or friends.
- When you never resort to contempt, or criticism, bullying or sulking to get your own way or to put the other down.
- When neither of you ever feels a victim.
- When you are still passionate and interested in each other.
- Good relationships have easy compromise and instinctive ways to resolve altercations. They have reciprocity about giving and taking and it never matters who starts something and who finishes it.
- There is shared understanding that the relationship operates on different levels and that these often demand you both to be different types of people with different dialogues and attitudes, some emotional and some practical and functional. You will each play to different strengths at different times.
- You both believe and trust that the whole is bigger than either one of you on your own and can't be threatened by the paralysis or faltering of its components.

Looking for love

All so easily said, I know, and of course you need that special someone in the first place. If you are looking for a relationship, don't cling to the comfort zone of friends in the same position. How often have you seen a clutch of thirty-something women out together, not a bloke to be seen, and the conversation you overhear is about the lack of decent men in their lives? The same applies to a group of lads out on the pull looking for fit, friendly girls. Keeping each other's company may be good at reassuring them they are not alone in their single plight but they're unlikely to meet someone of the opposite sex if their social life revolves around same-sex friends. (See below.)

Divorced, bereaved or older people need to choose the company they keep with particular care, first because the opportunities to socialise may be less, due to children or other commitments, but also because it's all too easy to just look for comfort, seeking and sharing life experiences with similar people, and so never move on beyond current sadness enough to meet someone completely new. Don't feel too 'damaged' by your bad time or, for that matter, put off by others'. It's often the people who have had the most knocks who have the maturity and life experience to make wonderful relationships and make the compromises that a lasting partnership needs.

Don't put all your expectations on your *social* life. Be ever ready all the time – not as in wearing your best pants, but as in you just might meet a likely candidate anywhere and at any time, at the supermarket, bus stop, walking the dog. Present a pleasant, upbeat and friendly persona to the world and be open-minded and interested in everyone and everything. Apply the basics about how to make new friends (see page 66) but be more strategic and seek out events and interests where members of the opposite sex might be. Golf clubs, wine or food associations, motor sports events, community activities and campaigns, arts, craft and literary events and certain sports at certain venues can all tend to be one-gender dominant, although by no means exclusively, and as long as you have a genuine interest, are worth pursuing. For how to find out about these activities, see Leisure and Citizenship chapters.

Wendy was divorced and Martin a widow when they met at a local Wine Society tasting. 'I was interested to know more about wine and the tastings meant there was a social aspect with a built-in subject to talk about,' said Wendy, while Martin, a bit of a connoisseur, had gone along mainly to be sociable as he felt shy and awkward meeting new people but the 'wine' aspect made it feel like familiar territory. They hit it off straight away.

Being genuinely curious or engaged by an activity is important. Bear in mind that the biggest turn-off is someone who lets it be seen they are *desperate* to get involved with someone else. Be wise to all opportunities to meet new people of the opposite sex and don't just look for the good-looking candidates. You may find your wish list changes and where an ex or a dream lover was once a benchmark for every new person to be measured against, you suddenly discover a different set of criteria. You know what it's like when you meet new people? You notice everything about them, their looks, their build, likely income, etc., and then, the better you know them, so those things fall away and the real characteristics of a great sense of humour, sharp intellect or witty conversation become the reasons you are pleased to see them. Anyone who has been in love will tell you that amazingly quickly you stop actually 'seeing' the physical characteristics most of the time and love the person they are. A cliché but true.

If you decide to try **dating agencies**, the onus is on you to check that they are good. A higher free for joining doesn't necessarily mean you're going to get a better service. You really need to ask questions about their vetting procedures and also how vigilant they are about protecting *your* identity – not all agencies automatically withhold your personal contact details. The best thing is to get a personal recommendation, but if that's not possible then make sure you go in and have a proper meeting face to face and steer clear of any agencies which only use postal questionnaires. You might want to ask if the agency is a member of an accredited association and be wary of any which aren't entirely upfront about their fees.

There are masses of dating agencies out there – loads on the web and if you look through your local phone book or newspaper, there will be lots locally too. When you are matched with someone, there are some basic codes of practice it might be sensible to stick to.

- First and foremost – be careful. It's a good idea to build up some sort of relationship, either by email or over the phone, before you arrange to meet someone. Follow your instincts and, without being cynical, be wary. Does this person sound too good to be true? If you think you're being spun a line, chances are you're right. Listen out for inconsistencies and anything which in your mind constitutes a double take.
- When you're first in contact with someone, withhold your full identity. Don't give someone your last name, your private email address, home address or number. Just take your time and wait until you feel sure this person is to be trusted. If someone is pressurising you to give them those details, back right off. It's not polite or a good sign of their intentions.
- If and when you do meet, then tell a couple of friends where you're going and who you're meeting. Meet in a public place, make your own way there and back. The most important thing is to know you're in control of the situation and if you decide you want to back out at the last minute or leave early, then you can and should.
- Always trust your gut instinct about someone.

Samantha had arranged to meet a man called David on a bench near a public memorial. 'I went quarter of an hour earlier and sat on another seat where I could watch him arrive. He wasn't bad-looking. But he was talking very intimately to someone on his mobile phone and it felt all wrong. I went home. The next time I did the same thing with Gerry and he seemed fine. So I went up and said hello and we had a nice time.'

There is also **internet dating**, which is responsible for many international marriages between people who, after corresponding on the ether for months, sometimes years, finally – terrifyingly – fly halfway round the world and meet in the flesh; but, by this time, they know each other so well that invariably the physical coming together is just fine and they go and get married. Or it could be that, quite unbeknownst to you, you've been emailing someone who lives round the corner.

Choose your site carefully. There are specialist ones that cater for different interests and types. Be strategic with the profile of yourself you are going to post up and give some thought as to how it is going to be read. This is your shop window and you want to present an upbeat confident demeanour that emphasises your positive points and makes you sound an attractive personality. Words such as 'shy', 'retiring', 'getting over my divorce/husband's death' may be true but are too much information for the opening gambit. Don't use clichés, such as 'good sense of humour' or 'bubbly', either. Add some meat to your character description, show your humour and that you are a cheery sort in the way you tell it.

Internet dating is a great medium because writing and emailing is a way to get properly intimate, to share your thoughts and *really* expose yourself in those wee small hours.

Speed dating involves taking part in three minute 'dates' with around 20 other people at a pre-organised venue. If you meet someone you would like to see again you tick their name on a score card and if that person ticks your name, too, you're a match. The organisers will then pass on contact details to you both. If you are intrigued, put 'speed dating' into your search engine with your area, for an event near you.

Finally, however you find them, if you think you've met your match, make sure you send out the right signals, and the first of these is focussed interest in what they do and say.

Friends of Jane often wondered how she always managed to get her man when she really wasn't obviously attractive and didn't seem to flirt overtly. 'It's quite simple and almost always foolproof. Flattering someone by being (or even pretending to be) really interested in them and everything they say makes most men feel "interested" back.'

These days it's perfectly normal for both men and women to ask each other out on the **first date**. In fact maybe 'date' is the wrong word. Take the pressure off by viewing it simply as a first 'social engagement' which should be a 'getting to know you' exercise rather than the guaranteed first throes of a passionate romantic affair. It shouldn't be pregnant with expectation because at this stage you might just find you have fun together and that's as far as it goes. (But, if that's the case, who knows what friends he/she might have!) Whoever does the asking should expect to pay, if splitting the bill isn't easy. A way around this which encourages another meeting is to suggest you take turns and that it's theirs next time.

Try not to get too keen, or too heavy, too quickly, especially if you've been hoping to find someone special for some time. While you are theorising and scrutinising the ins and outs of every nuance in someone's words and actions they may well be either being put off by your analytical neediness or getting off on all the attention they are getting. Either way it doesn't make for a healthy relationship and you are laying yourself wide open to being abused or having your heart broken. Because while you are turning a brave blind eye to their neglect to call or care and seeing it as a deep-seated commitment problem they have from past bad relationships, it may, just may be selfish bad behaviour that you are giving licence to continue – and they know it. You need to protect yourself and keep some dignity. So, until they look as though they are going to commit equally, best keep things light, loving and cheerful. When all else fails in **the delicate early stages** of a relationship, don't reach for Freud or angst with your man or woman about *why* . . . seek safety in numbers – only see said troublesome lover in others' jolly company and go for walks and lunch out in country pubs or cook a fabulous casserole instead and talk about the weather, footie, their orchid collection – anything but '*lurve*'. Here is the best casserole recipe in the world. Foolproof for harmony and also a great fix for when there is nothing to be said to make things better. Serves six.

Pre-heat the oven to 150C/300F/Gas Mark 2 and melt **50 g of butter** and a **tablespoon of olive oil** in a large casserole dish, **brown 1.5 kg of beef** (chuck, braising or shin) cut into large bite-sized chunks and then add **two chopped onions** and **three large crushed garlic cloves** and fry for a couple of minutes to soften. Next, add **six peeled carrots**, cut into large chunks. Stir in **75 g of plain flour** and slowly pour on a whole **bottle of red wine**. Add **75 g of tomato puree, bouquet garni** and **salt and pepper**. Stir well and bring to the bubble before covering tightly and transferring to the oven for two hours or until the meat is really tender. (Make sure your casserole is well sealed, adding a layer of foil under the lid if not.) Separately fry **250 g of chopped streaky bacon, 12 baby onions** and **12 mushrooms** in **25 g of butter**. Add these to the casserole at the end of the 2 hours for a further 15 minutes. Serve with mashed potato, pasta or rice.

How do you know it's love?

Whether you ask yourself this question within minutes of locking eyes with someone across a crowded room, while you are breathing garlic fumes over each other after that casserole, or some way down the line in a relationship, I'm afraid only you can know the answer and, in my opinion, if you need to ask someone else then it just isn't so. I think that '**being in love**' is not as complicated an emotion as is made out. I think it is quite simply a deeply solid, secure and mutual feeling of becoming whole and just knowing that you are made for each other as soul mates. Mutual is important. It is possible to love someone deeply and for that feeling not to be reciprocated; it's also possible, of course, to be in *lust* with someone. Lust is a fiercely strong base instinct, like hunger, fantastically natural, and it can develop into love simply because it is an early part of attraction. It's nature's way of helping you select a partner and there are and will be incongruities about your attraction to unlikely people. You may be surprised by your own reactions at times – did your loins really just stir when that balding bank clerk smiled at you? Lust initially promises the blood rush of a sexual partner, and those heady first feelings inevitably change. Being *in* love is something additional between two people that brings with it deep contentment and certainty.

When love isn't reciprocated

If you love someone and they don't care for you in the same way, despite your best efforts, you *have* to deal with it and accept that there is an imbalance in that relationship. No matter how much you long for their love or physically ache for their arms around you, you can't *make* someone feel differently and it would feel a sham if they pretended. You would know anyway and so you need to be realistic about your own expectations. If you are going to continue to see them, can you enjoy the one-sided feeling of caring and loving someone, and do you think the relationship could ever lose some of its heat on your part and possibly develop into a deep and warm friendship? Or do you need to be loved back by this person in the same way and does it constantly pain you that they don't? If it's the latter, you must move on. It isn't happening and time won't make any difference. (See page 22.)

Commitment

This can be the moment of truth! Just as with trying to *make* someone love you, it's virtually impossible to make someone commit to you if they don't really want to, or to persuade someone not to need commitment. Commitment can be formal and public, such as marriage, or it can simply mean moving in together or just being faithful to each other. You can use various methods of coercion and emotional bribery but should ask yourself why, if something really matters to you, it doesn't matter to your partner. At the same time you need to work out why you need the reassurance at a time when your mate is reluctant. Set the day of reckoning by putting a time limit, which you can live with, on the decision and then forget about it until then. Get on with life and enjoy every minute of the relationship without letting the commitment issue get in the way, but know that ultimately it does matter to you and so it will have to be dealt with by your partner for these happy times to continue. For commitment to work it has to be mutual.

If the commitment you are seeking or considering is to **marry or co-habit**, religious or social preferences apart, choosing your route does come down to the business of making it legal. Either course needs this to be a consideration, to protect your personal and partnership issues. The law is constantly changing about the rights of couples, so explain your circumstances and get the answers to these questions from either a lawyer or Citizen's Advice.

- Are you legally recognised as a couple?
- What are your rights relating to your home and property?
- Should you have a contract concerning what will happen to the above, and to any monies, if you should separate or one of you dies? (You should make a will in any event.)
- How does co-habiting affect your rights, as a couple, to adopt or share parental responsibility?
- Are there legal agreements that can alter these rights?
- And if it should all go wrong, how long after being married can you be legally divorced?
- What are valid reasons (e.g. unreasonable behaviour, desertion, period of separation, adultery)?
- What proof do you need to provide for any of the above?
- If you are both in agreement about finishing the marriage and about the terms can you obtain a 'quickie' divorce?

- Can you do it yourself?
- Are there mediation services that can help?
- If you need to sort out finances or access to children are there specialist lawyers?
- Are there any financial assistance schemes available for legal fees?

Making it work: the big issues

Sex

Is there anything left to say about sex? For something so natural there's a daunting amount of theory attached to love-making it seems, so let's just be pragmatic here. There's Making Love and there's Great Sex. Nirvana is if both happen at the same time but, realistically, they happen separately and severally for most people too.

If you love someone and feel lusty, then you should find the physical act of making love the most natural thing in the world. Given that Life Auditors and the readership of this book range from twenty-year-olds to eighty-year-olds and beyond there will be many different interpretations and definitions of what constitutes natural good sex and how to resolve sexual difficulties.

You can **improve your sexual technique** at any age and at any stage of your sexual life. If you are reading this as a virgin, just remember, it may take some time and practice to understand what works for you and how to give a partner pleasure too. Don't be dismayed if it's not as you imagined. Just like everything else in life, experience and technique really enhance the act, so give it time. If sex was any other aspect of life people wouldn't be sniffy about working on it to make it better. You can raise your game in sport, at work or entertaining so why not in the sack too?

Of course people are coy about admitting they need to brush up their sexual tactics because they'd really rather just claim to be perceived as *naturally* skilled sexual creatures. But, for most people, the starburst quality of the sex you have when you fall in love wears off and even if you are only into sex for *self-*

gratification *you* will benefit from knowing how better to plea-sure your partner. That doesn't mean you need to take lessons or even tell another soul!

I know it's much vaunted by sexperts but most people find **talking about sex**, spelling out what they do and don't like, difficult, unromantic and un-sexy. I know I've just said there's a strong case for sorting sex out, as you would a game of bad-minton or golf, but at the same time, it's delicate. It depends on what sort of people you are but when the end goal is to lose your-self, too much analysis can inhibit the process and keep you in your head rather than your body! Sex is a basic instinct and a bit of Neanderthal grunting and moaning when the right moves are made will speak volumes!

It helps to know and understand the sexual working parts of your body and that of the opposite sex. Contraception should be an automatic consideration if you aren't baby-making. If you aren't grown-up and responsible about that, you aren't mature enough to have sex.

As great sex is something that involves *all* your senses, get back to basics with them too. Certain scents and smells, sounds and music all add to the sexual scenario along with the right touching and feeling, and you should consider the mix that turns you on most, this to include your own body, of course.

It hadn't even occurred to Alexis that boyfriend Joe objected to her winter legs. 'I only shave them in the summer and the first thing I knew about him hating them was two years into our rela-tionship when, just as we were getting cosy together in October, he groaned and rolled away. Then he blurted out that he found them a complete turn-off and preferred me silky smooth.'

Declutter your bedroom of unsensual objects, such as your computer of car-maintenance manuals and remove inhibiting photos of your parents or children. The atmosphere needs to be conducive to making love and a bit of deliberate scene-setting can't hurt. Keep all those senses in mind and even if satin sheets are too much of a good thing, a couple of silk-covered bed pillows could be just the right touch – literally.

Heady scents such as musk, ylang-ylang, sandalwood, narcissi and jasmine are sexy smells so use either a few drops of the essential oils on a lamp ring or choose a commercial perfume which uses notes of the natural extracts.

Mentally too you need to tune into what turns you on. Sweeping generatlisations coming up now, with apologies to sexually sensitive men . . . but men and women have a completely different approach to sex. Men are much more down-to-earth about their basic physical and earthy need for it while women tend to want their brains made love to as well as their bodies. Great sex tends to happen when a woman acts a bit more like a man to get what she wants and her man gives his feminine side a bit of a stroke. However, a bit of selfish self-pursuit of pleasure during the act is no bad thing either. Being overly considerate to each other can sometimes de-sex the passion.

If the earth doesn't ever move for you, indulge in a little **self-pleasuring** – it might be the quickest way to find the hot spots that lead to orgasm. The more you do it, the closer tuned into your body and what turns you on you'll become and the better you'll get at achieving orgasm either alone or with someone else. You may find a trigger thought process or fantasy that you can then use with your partner. View it as a sort of essential sensual message and allow it to be one part of the sexual side of your life which will increase your levels of desire generally. One proficient lady golfer cheerfully told me she viewed it as the same as working on her swing at the driving range and said it had helped her through a couple of sex-free patches both during and between her two marriages.

There are many books, such as *The Joy of Sex* by Alex Comfort or umpteen versions of the Kama Sutra, with elaborate illustrations of 101-plus **sexual positions** that have been tried and tested and may work for you. If you enjoy playing Twister or your sex life needs revving up but you feel shy about initiating the chandelier/wardrobe manoeuvre, suggest you work your way through one of these publications. Sara bought her partner, Joe, a copy of the Kama Sutra as a joke for his birthday. 'We'd had a bit to drink one night and as a laugh we decided to each choose a position to try. Well, far from moaning with pleasure, within minutes we were just in stitches with laughter, trying to do the contortions. Actually, though, the sex was great that night. Laughter is a great turn-on, I suppose, and also some of the manoeuvres produced some, shall we say, interesting results.'

One simple manoeuvre involves using some straightforward **pillow-positioning**. One under your bum may tilt you and her/him into the realms of ecstasy, giving a better angle for the mechanics. In fact, perfecting pillow-placing may be the only new bedtime skill you need to cultivate if you want to make love well into your dotage, so reports one octogenarian who tells me he still enjoys weekly rumpy pumpy, despite arthritic hips and hands which are propped up and cushioned in strategic places by the finest feathers.

Give free rein to the **fantasies** that press the right buttons for you. Apparently four out of five of us fantasise up to six times a day. In case you are the one that doesn't and wonder what you are missing, these are the favoured secret turn-on thoughts, although feel free to add your own: being tied up or tying up your partner, having sex with a stranger, threesomes, sex with a work colleague, sex in public!

If you are lacking in ideas, pornography is probably better than sex manuals, which can be rather terrifyingly academic and intimidating, especially if they are trendily written in street-speak. Although there may be some female tutting about this (I seem to keep meeting tutters), it's a physical fact (as in heart rate, perspiration, breathing, brain activity, etc.) that women are as turned on and titillated by raunchy photography or graphic literature as men.

Sadly, or maybe not if you're a bloke (although many agree with me), most easily accessible porn is pretty basic, in-your-face stuff aimed at men. But you don't need to limit yourself to Busty Belinda from Basingstoke's centre spread because there is much more subtle erotic material available if you know where to look.

Asian and oriental art is fantastically beautiful and very naughty. You could also feed your fantasies by a trip to some public institutions. Museums and art galleries have loads of erotica if you look for it. Rodin, Klimt, Boucher all rather excel at the genre and most artists have their moments – even Manet, whose famous *Picnic on the Grass* hung on a decorous aunt's wall during my childhood and puzzled me no end. Or you could join the Erotic Print Society, which sells erotic art, photography and literature – all in the best possible taste, of course. However, if you just want to get down and dirty, then busty Belinda can probably be found on a top shelf near you.

Don't feel embarrassed if you've **lost the urge** or don't wholeheartedly enjoy sex. Or, for that matter, don't panic if your partner has. Most people go off it for a period at some stage in their life. If the rest of your relationship is pretty solid, your emotional engagement should compensate for the lack of fireworks in bed, and your desire is more than likely to return. Meanwhile, if it hits the doldrums and if you have a loving partner, it's best to be honest about your lack of enthusiasm, without overplaying it, and let them continue to take their pleasure, if you can bear it, until your libido bounces back into action. Honesty is far better than faking or cheating, which somehow devalues the whole affair for both of you. Try not to completely get out of the habit of having sex because that will make it much harder to re-start. Don't underestimate or dismiss your partner's need for the physical act, just because you are off it.

There are many triggers that can flick your off-switch: tiredness, stress about work or money, or having children, which actually brings on all the former, of course, so are a primary cause in themselves. Relationship problems nearly always manifest themselves in sex problems, as sex has enormous potential to be used for leverage. Problems that may cause unhappy sex lives include drifting apart, apathy, taking each other for granted and discord about domestic, family or financial issues.

Don't be bamboozled by the many **sexual myths** that accompany successful love-making because they will only add to the pressure on you to perform well. Bear in mind that everyone lies about their sex lives and there is absolutely no right average of anything to do with it, from the number of times a night to how often you orgasm. Sex stories make great newspaper headlines and solving the elusiveness of the G-spot would win hands down over the discovery of Lord Lucan's whereabouts. As a result of how sex and sexiness are portrayed in the media and in films and music videos, lots of people have unrealistic sexual expectations. While it's good news that the inhibitions of social conditioning are easier to shrug off now, the downside is that the sheer weight of discussion about what does and doesn't constitute a good sex life is intimidating enough to send the most seasoned Lothario back under the duvet for fear of comparison.

The main fact is that making love and having great sex are good things about being alive and deserve all the attention and enhancement you can give them. Face up to any shortfall in your sex life, but keep real about it. Try to remember, if you are experiencing a dip in interest, that if you can nurture your libido back to form, it's an important part of keeping an aspect of your emotional connection with your partner happy and healthy. You owe it to yourself and them and there are things you can do.

'Making love' is an expression that has been used, throughout time, to mean so much more than just the sex act. If things are a little tense between you and your mate, agree to abstain from sex altogether for at least a week and instead indulge each day in naked **sensual massage** with some baby oil (or something more pungent). You don't need to be an expert masseur although, as with everything, there are books available that give specific instructions. Massage is a loving gentle thing to do to each other and, as long as both parties buy into the no-sex rule, which includes no touching of the key parts, should work to eventually heighten desire in anyone lagging behind.

There are also loads of **sex aids** out there, ranging from the tacky and tatty to elaborately designed works of art that cost a bomb. There are even experiments going on to implant an orgasm device into the body, and you can spend over £1,000 on a vibrator! In between those and the pneumatic life-size dolls with bizarre lips are some less extreme gadgets that may help boost a flagging libido.

Sex shops aren't all seedy affairs and there are some classier ones open now where you can even get a decent cup of coffee. Some are specifically run by women for women, removing themselves far from the stereotypical back-room and dirty-raincoat brigade. Most have a wide selection of sexual accessories and sell everything from underwear to vibrators, erotic films to condoms, hold events and exhibitions and run courses.

Vibrators come in all shapes and sizes, from discreet with subtle pulsing action to others, rather terrifyingly energetic, named after animals, some even with eyes painted on them! (I have to say I feel a bit faint just typing that.) Vibrators were invented in the 1870s as a cure for 'female hysteria'. My, haven't times changed – or maybe not. There is also a huge variety of condoms to choose from, including ones with anaesthetic lubrication to prolong the action! The selection of other toys and aids is very comprehensive and offers something to suit all tastes. I know that sounds suspiciously like sales talk – sorry – I think it's called 'distancing'!

If you are a bit shy about perusing such wares in public, most offer online shopping so you can browse in the seclusion of your home and avoid the embarrassment of bumping into your neighbour or old history teacher.

There are trained **sex therapists** who can help you solve your sexual problems. These are usually called psychosexual therapists. Your doctor may be able to refer you.

A therapist will first talk to you to try to identify the root cause of your problem and whether it is physical, psychological or medical. They will recommend counselling, if appropriate, for example to resolve relationship issues, then will address your sexual problems separately, with personalised exercises for you to do privately to stimulate the sensual and sexual side of you. Sessions can be attended by both you and your partner or alone, and report a good success rate of helping people overcome their sexual problems.

There can be physical or medical reasons too why you go off sex, such as illness or a side effect of medication, painful intercourse, problems with achieving erection, dryness, controlling ejaculation, etc. **Medical problems** are less likely if you are a woman, but it's worth being checked out by your doctor who might recommend a hormone-level check and medication, such as Viagra for men, which can help. Viagra is a treatment for men who suffer from serious erectile problems. It works by boosting the erection-making chemicals and blocking the ones that cause the opposite effect. It's mainly prescribed for older men for whom age or diabetes is affecting their performance. Some users report side effects and although it is available over the internet should never be used without consulting your doctor.

Children

Starting a family is one of the most natural things in the world for a couple to do but many people spend ages trying to decide when is the right time to have children, and making the decision has an enormous impact on their life as a couple. All I can say is that I have never met a single parent who regretted having a baby after deliberating about the right or wrong time, and all their practical, financial and career concerns have paled into insignificance. One friend who angsted for England about timing said when she had her baby, 'Of course . . .' which, I have to say, perfectly sums it up for me.

We are all, to a greater or less degree, subject to the **biological clock**, and it ticks more noticeably in the mid-thirties. The older a woman gets the harder it may be to conceive and carry a healthy baby to full term, while the quality and quantity of men's semen, sperm, testosterone and erection can also be affected by their age and lifestyle. If you are a couple, seek medical advice after six months of unsuccessfully trying for a baby. If you are single, and worrying that time is running out, the chances are that scientific developments will offer you more options in the future, such as extending your fertility or letting you easily harvest eggs. Currently both of those are possible, but complicated and difficult to access. Easier is anonymous sperm donation, fostering or adoption, all of them serious options that need lots of research and careful consideration.

Becoming **pregnant** marks the transition from one stage of your life to the next – both as an individual and as a couple. It shouldn't be surprising then to have mixed emotions, such as a sense of loss, almost a sort of bereavement, for the person you were and the life you led, mixed with delight and excitement about the coming baby.

Physical and psychological anxieties during pregnancy can affect all different aspects of your relationships, from your own self-image of the person you are within the couple to your sex life. Keep in mind the fact that your partner's hormones or yours are raging, that times of change are always unsettling and that it's the bigger picture of the family you are about to become for the future that matters, not the niggles and grizzles of today. When baby is born, be sensitive to how the other person is feeling and talk about that and not just about your new bundle of joy. Treat yourself and each other with loads of TLC, and remember, you are both likely to be tired like you've never been before!

Eddie and Miriam had been together for eight years before deciding to have their first child in their mid-thirties. 'We were totally unprepared for the change in our lives. I actually don't think anything *could* have prepared us. You just have no idea how all the things you set store by, before the baby, go out the window,' said Miriam. 'Everything has had to slow down and we just feel we have to really pace ourselves, getting baby sorted, and some shopping done and then catching up on sleep. Life has suddenly turned into a series of dealing with basic needs, and become very simple. How were we ever so busy!'

Of course for some couples it isn't such plain sailing. Joanne experienced shocking post-natal depression and Peter found her mood swings and apathy hard to deal with until he was brought up short by finding her in tears and still in bed when he got home from work. 'I'd felt cross because she just hadn't seemed able to pull herself together when the baby needed her and just seemed to be prepared to let everything fall apart. But finding her in such a state that night made me realise she really wasn't well, and we went to the doctor the next day to get some help. She needed support over the next four months and I made sure she had it. We're in this together with baby Holly. All's well now.'

Couples who *choose* **not to have children** tell me how fed up they get with being labelled selfish or cold-hearted and their lifestyles criticised as lacking in some way.

These are the advantages they list:

- As a childless person you have opportunities to really go for it career-wise while also having freedom to decide to maybe work less or downshift because you don't need as much money as married contemporaries.
- You can devote more attention to older members of the family and be supportive to them with resources and time that might otherwise have gone to children.
- You can live your own dreams rather than living through your hopes and plans for your children.
- You can enjoy just the 'fun' bits of company with other people's children and then hand them back.
- You can do the things you absolutely couldn't do with children – you can live on a houseboat, wear an outrageous mini-skirt without any censure or up sticks and go travelling in a two-man camper van.
- And you can nurture a group of close hand-picked friends and travel towards old age together, being inter-supportive.

What if you are in a relationship **when only one of you wants a child**? This is very hard on the broody one and miserable for the partner who will be anticipating the bereavement about what will be lost from life as a couple with the arrival of a small person. You need to talk and talk about it until all the needs and desires, fears and trepidation are articulated and spread out on the table to be properly examined. Wanting a baby is a basic instinct and this situation will force a deeply testing time for a relationship. Choices will have to be made that will reflect and measure the love and commitment you have for each other. If you are the one yearning for a child, only you will know if you can suppress that longing and whether its denial will kill a part of you or some part of the relationship you are being asked to make the choice for. If you are the one who doesn't want a child, are you sure those reasons are important enough to you to cause that pain to your partner and possibly to destroy your relationship? Both of you need to face up to the facts of the sacrifices you are being asked to make and weigh them against the strength of your love and whether you will be able to continue to be truly yourself in the aftermath of making the decision.

But what if you long for children and it is definite that you can't conceive – what about **adoption or fostering**? You don't have to be young, married or a homeowner. You can be gay, disabled and any race or religion. Adoption is where all the parental responsibility is transferred and the child becomes a full member of the new family, losing all legal ties with their birth parents. Fostering, on the other hand, is where the responsibility for the child is shared with a local authority and the child's parents. It is usually a temporary arrangement.

Although there are many parents for newborn babies, there are some older toddlers and children who badly need a loving home, and adoptive parents are desperately needed for children with medical or developmental problems, school-age children or for groups of brothers and sisters.

There are adoption agencies run either as voluntary societies or by local authorities. There are specialist bodies who help organise the adoption of children from abroad, which is obviously more complicated.

Another impact children have on your relationship with your significant other is when they leave home and leave you both in your **empty nest**. You have them, you love them and then you have to let them go . . . and *then* what do you do? An empty fridge, no mountains of washing, a tidy house, the use of your own car all the time – and just you and your partner alone again, and with probably just as many mixed emotions as when you had the little darlings in the first place. It's another big time of adjustment in a relationship, and it's no accident that a substantial number of marriages finish at this point after more than twenty or even thirty years together. The glue of family responsibilities and children's clamour vanishes, revealing the sparse fragments of marriages that then just fall apart. Allow yourselves time to adjust to this new set of circumstances and build on the positives. However much you miss the noisy Saturday mornings and the kids' friends calling around, relish the freedom and plan outings or activities together. Just enjoy the quietness, and reading the weekend papers undisturbed for as long as you like. You shouldn't need to work too hard at it to recapture the pleasure in some of the things you did before you had children. Doing some shopping together, having lunch out, being companionable and, of course, making plans. Decide on some longer-term things to do and maybe even take a good look around at other aspects of your life. The Empty Nest is not so much a time of bereavement as a time of opportunity to reinvent your life. A good time to conduct a Life Audit, maybe? Perhaps you will consider moving, downshifting or going travelling, taking up a new interest or hobby, even changing jobs now you don't have the financial outlay of the kids.

When Janey and Dick's last child left home, they had already organised a plan they were really looking forward to implementing. They both negotiated unpaid sabbaticals from their jobs and joined a voluntary organisation working abroad. 'Neither of us had had a gap year when we were kids and thirty years on we wanted to travel but didn't want it just to be a jolly! Dick is a project manager and I work with small businesses so we approached a couple of charities to see if we could be any use on any of their projects. We are spending four months helping build a school and get other community projects off the ground in Romania. I feel as though we are looking forward not back.'

After many years' marriage, though, some couples decide to reinvent their marriage completely and create different circumstances that will help keep the relationship refreshed. Both partners need to agree to this enthusiastically but, **living apart together** even if it's just for a short time, can remove domestic routine and let the relationship be centred on just nice things. Sometimes too it's a practical solution, driven by financial necessity where pension provision for the widowed is dependent on them not remarrying or co-habiting. Or maybe even where a divorce settlement's maintenance arrangement would alter if their single status changed.

Naomi and John decided to reinvent their marriage when their adult children finally left home. 'We had started getting on each other's nerves and were snapping at each other. The consideration was going out of our marriage and we didn't seem able to live up to the expectation of doing more things together once we had more time alone. In particular, I felt the need for space like a physical ache. We could actually have separated but before that happened, luckily, we had one of those really frank talks and agreed that instead of seeing the next ten, twenty, whatever years as a time for joint activities, perhaps we should free each other up and go our own ways in various aspects of our lives while keeping our marriage going and our relationship the loving supportive partnership it has always been. We turned two rooms into separate studies and one of the bedrooms into a large dressing room with a bed in it. We made a pact not to take umbrage if one partner slept there or in fact stayed up all night reading, emailing whatever. We have had separate holidays but we kept basic things the same and joint, such as bank accounts and household accounts. It was a risk and could have gone wrong but the truth is we do love each other and I think are closer now and much more loving. There is a sense too of excitement about the life ahead, not a sleepy sort of dotage looming.'

Money

If you are in a relationship you need to agree clear rules about money management. (See page 190.) The getting, spending and managing of it is a major, major source of discord in marriages and families. Are you a one-pocket family, in which case who holds the purse-strings, or are you separate account holders, in which case do you need a joint account or other system for paying communal bills? The best and easiest way to achieve this is by being strict about how and where the pennies come and go, and getting stuck into some of the checks-and-controls paper-work that will give you peace of mind. You may need to have several heated debates to get to a reckoning about how your money management is going to work, but persevere until every-one is agreed, clear on how it should work and all cheerily singing from the same hymn sheet. Don't give up on this or the money monster will rise bigger and beastlier for another round of rows another day.

Work

Work is somewhere else you are likely to invest a lot of time and attention. If you are fortunate, you will also love your work but it's then that it may cause strife with your loved one. If things aren't going well at home, work is an easier place to retreat to with its finite and clear demands and colleagues who don't require a big emotional investment. Getting the work/life balance right is important for lots of different reasons but prob-ably the main one is to make sure you have enough of the 'life' bit in the equation to spend quality time with your mate. (See page 117.)

> • Keep work in its place and make sure you don't invest it with greater importance than your home life.
> • Look to your working practices if you find yourself bringing it home, and look to your lifestyle if you find yourself only thinking and talking about work.

- Address any jealousies about the other's work or career opportunities. Flush them out and say straight up – I'm really envious, lucky you. Then address your own work challenges.
- If you value each other you will never forget that the most important reason you go out to work is to provide for your joint unit, and that while jobs come and go, careers end and long-service medals grow dusty, you have your loved ones to care for, for ever.

When things go wrong

People change, they do; but then so do relationships over time, and it's unreasonable not to expect to have to adapt to those changes. Many of us fall at these hurdles, but these changes don't have to be threatening, they can be exciting and stimulating. Keeping interested in, excited by and in touch with each other's development should see off any overwhelming shifts that could threaten the relationship's foundations. If life gets really busy, consciously make time for each other and timetable it into your agenda to find time to be alone. Talk all the time and share the minutiae of your lives and encounters. Don't let yourself slip into the habit of silently eating your meals in front of the box every evening you have free together.

And if you feel you have actually **fallen out of love**, you need to work out whether it is a temporary blip or catastrophic. Of course you can go right off someone even if you were once so in love. When the rose tint fades you'll start seeing how they eat with their mouth open, have selfish instincts, snore or have a mean side. Don't underestimate how disastrously **simple irritations** can erode a relationship. My family mythology has it that a distant relation came home one day to find a note left by his wife who had taken off to Australia with their two children because of his table manners – or presumably lack of them.

Annoying habits such as teeth sucking, noisy eating, toe rubbing (I know bizarre! – but several Auditors reported this as divorce-inducing!) often irritate in spurts and what you find intolerable one minute you might view benignly the next. So, if something is driving you insane and your partner really won't or can't address it, try to mitigate it by turning the radio up, leaving the room or organising your routine so that your paths don't cross when it happens.

All relationships, those with your parents, colleagues and friends, have ups and downs, and your closest one is no different; in fact it is more vulnerable because it is or was once so intense. Also, you may be a couple, but you are still individuals, and people have crises that change them, develop habits or dependencies that alter their behaviour and may be provoked by stresses and events outside your partnership. Suddenly you can find yourself not part of a team love-match any more, more the carer, the whipping boy, and more alone in this pairing than you could ever have thought. So what do you do?

Well, there are wonderful relationship counselling services such as Relate, if you want to talk to someone unbiased and wise for advice, but assuming this sad state is not due to one specific event, such as infidelity or violence (see page 50), I think you need to give the situation time. As much time as you can. It rather warrants it given how good it once was, doesn't it?

Time tends to resolve most things, either by allowing you to gain some perspective on the situation or by events, rather than you, naturally forcing things to a head. Time will allow you both to address some of the contributory factors to your current irritation or lack of interest. You may feel pretty belligerent about it not being your fault but for your own peace of mind and sense of honour, put some hard work in to identify the root cause of the problem. Trace the rows or unhappiness back to where they started and what sparked the first flare-up. Look for practical problems, remove those triggers and see if that eases the tension. The main thing is not to be too quick to give up on this important relationship, giving due deference to how it once was. If your partner is being a pig and resisting all attempts to get the two of you back on an even keel, get your head down for a while and take comfort from all the other bits of your life that are fulfilling or joyous. Getting some independent control over your own happiness level, even if it's only in parts of your life, will make you feel less trapped. And there is always the possibility you'll fall back in love–it happens! – not overnight, but the chance is real.

There may be other people involved too – as in children rather than lovers (see page 45) – and giving time to your falling-out-of-love crisis will make sure you properly assess the duty of care you have to provide for their needs emotionally and practically. However unhappy you feel, you may have to be unselfish about putting the majority needs first and making the best of the situation with as good a heart as you can muster. I know that's a hard truth, but facing up to that is what being a grown-up is all about! Be wise to the fact that although you may be sure there could be no one worse out there, there is no guarantee that there's anyone better, either. You need to choose what course of action is going to cause the least amount of pain all around to everyone involved, and that includes you, of course, but does not make you the only person to be considered.

Martin had resigned himself to having to put up with the bitterness of his wife over the failure of their business four years previously. 'She never gave up reminding me of mistakes I'd made. Because of the children, and frankly because of our financial state, I could hardly walk away although I certainly felt like it. It was as though she was determined to drag me down even further. Then one day when she was going on, I realised that I wasn't really hearing her any more and actually really, really didn't care. I was going to do my duty by the kids but find ways to enjoy the rest of my life. I took up learning Spanish at night school and began building a boat with my son in the garage. Within days she'd stopped going on and I'd catch her looking at me oddly, wondering what had changed. I needed to reach that point where my priorities were clear and feeding her anger with my lack of confidence was no longer one of them. I think she needed to see me acting confidently although she was so much a part of eroding it. We are much calmer together now and there is some tenderness coming back. We both dealt with our disasters badly. But I'm glad I didn't leave and I feel we might just make a recovery from our mistakes.'

Depending on circumstances it may be possible to give yourself and your partner some real space. A bit of separation, without a 'Separation', can help both parties see each other more clearly and without the accumulating day-in day-out tensions that have dragged the relationship down. Maybe just a short holiday alone or a spell working away – it's a high-risk strategy to recapture love but it's worked for some and may be worth considering if other options get you nowhere, having been given a really decent shot timewise. If it doesn't bring you back together it may force the end, so be aware of that! It's the action for when there is nowhere else to turn.

Sometimes no amount of time will heal a poorly relationship. You've had **enough**! One or both of you have decided you aren't prepared to carry limping on into a miserable future. You may feel emotionally spent when it reaches this stage which, grim as that is, will at least help you concentrate on the practicalities of **leaving and separating**. To reach this point you presumably feel you have tried everything, including counselling, and either you, he/she or the pair of you can't make it work. Your partnership has irretrievably broken down and now you have to look to your own future. 'I just didn't want to be there for even one more night,' said Ann. 'It was over, had been for ages, but we had a really big row about money one night and that was that. I just wanted to leave and get on with the rest of my life. We'd tried to make a go of it, Dave wouldn't go to counselling so I'd gone on my own but, to be honest, I knew it was over. I didn't want any more rows or tears. I wanted to be out of it. I wanted my own place, with none of the chaos. I wanted to start again.'

If you decide to leave you should consider the following:

- Face up to it. Essentially, you are about to be on your own. That means looking out for yourself. Keep in mind that there is absolutely no guarantee you will meet someone else who will be the soulmate you want.
- Be realistic about the unravelling of your joint domestic and financial affairs and about what there will be left for you to rebuild your life as a single person.
- Get advice and understand the legal protocol and what you need to do to protect your rights.
- When the moment of truth comes, if you are the one who is going to finish it, allow time and privacy for the conversation and know what you are going to do after it's been said.
- However disenchanted or angry you are with them be calm, compassionate and honest with the person you are leaving.
- Anticipate their reaction and if you are concerned about it, consider how you are going to deal with that and how responsible you will continue to feel.
- Do you need to contact someone else to help support them?
- Have a plan for drawing the conversation to a close and what will happen next. Are you expecting them to do the physical leaving? Or how will you effect *your* departure? What will you take? Where will you go?
- Be clear in your own mind about how further contact is going to happen between the two of you.
- Whether you are the one leaving or the one being left, prepare yourself for a period of extreme adjustment.
- You will need to look after yourself, and however much you may have been looking forward to being along you are likely to feel lonely at times as well.
- You should welcome any support you get from family or friends.

- Even if the separation is what you sought, you will almost inevitably feel some sense of bereavement about what has gone, which is why, if you are reading this before making your move, make sure you are very clear it is what you want because, if it is, that is the only thing that will make it worth the pain and ensure your future is a better place.

Most important of all if you do go through with it and decide to have a fresh start is to keep in mind that it is just that – a new beginning, full of promise and opportunity. As long as you know you did what you could to make the failed relationship work, accept that it didn't. Grieve a little, store away the lessons learnt to help you in the future but don't waste too much time regretting what wasn't meant to be. (See page 90.)

If you are the one who **has been left** you need to rally all your reserves to deal with the shock and trauma. While you may well be in emotional freefall you do also need to consider practical aspects of your life without your partner. Take things very gently though, and above all, look after yourself – you will be experiencing a form of bereavement and, as advised on page 343, you need to take care of your basic needs and stay as strong and healthy as you can to help you cope. See your doctor, call in the cavalry of friends and family, and nurture yourself through this painful time. As the affected party there is not a lot you can do, especially once they are gone, to control your ex-partner's behaviour and although you may rail at their retreating, eventually you have to find a way to come to terms with what they have done and what your life is going to be like without them and the routines you had built up together. Try to pay more attention to rebuilding your happiness than dwelling on their betrayal or deceit.

Being unfaithful or **having an affair** is a painful betrayal of a relationship and is likely to rock it to its core. Affairs happen most often because there is something going wrong in a relationship that has not been addressed and resolved by a couple. This 'something' does not necessarily mean it's an issue that is affecting both parties or indeed that both are even aware of it. Just one partner could be affected and not communicating it, and maybe until the forbidden fruit was presented to them *they* weren't even aware they were dissatisfied. The most likely triggers for affairs are boredom either in, life as a couple or in the person's individual life, loss of desire for sex or absence of romance. (See page 26.) Individually too the attentions of some-body outside your partnership may bolster low self-esteem and make you feel attractive.

If you are in the throes of an affair and seeking some reassur-ance, I sort of apologise for not giving affairs any good press. Oh well, OK then, I admit there's not a lot bad about being made to feel desirable or feeling desire, but in terms of everything else it's almost impossible not to sound 'po' about infidelity on the page. The short-term sugar rush of great sex and the intimacy that affairs offer may be scarily intoxicating and irresistible at the time but are pretty indefensible and hardly compensatory for the destruction they can cause. But they happen to loads of people. Fact of life, love, lust!

Affairs usually have all the heady characteristics of falling in lust/love along with the added titillation of being illicit and secretive. Affairs often serve to bring relationship issues to a head although some can continue for years. A one-night fling or indis-cretion is different to an affair, although potentially just as dam-aging. Lasting affairs are often about more than sex, and the affair and the person concerned may fill voids in a main rela-tionship that otherwise might have been resolved.

Although there are serial adulterers, most people involved in affairs don't go out looking to be unfaithful. This, though, is cold comfort to the cuckolded partner who will find it hard to believe something so devastating could happen in a split second of attraction to someone else – which is as long as it takes to step over the line.

I haven't ever heard of anyone having an affair who honestly felt they were in a mutually strong and loving relationship at the time, so the way to avoid affairs is to work on having a good relationship in the first place. If your relationship is going through a tough time, you are vulnerable, so if you are on the verge of being unfaithful, know what you are risking. Don't be blinkered about the fallout. Think through to being discovered, to the guilt you will inevitably feel, to the moment of confession and be aware of the pain that is going to be caused to all concerned. Remember that you are seriously threatening a relationship that has or has had strengths on lots of *different* levels and may just be going through a bad patch which needs more of your attention rather than less of it. If the desire for sex with the other person is the driving force, can you really say that it is worth possibly losing your family, your home, and all you have built up with someone else? Intellectualise it and walk away.

People who've had affairs have told me that they wish they'd been stronger and sterner with themselves. Even if they had still gone ahead with the affair they wished they hadn't been so self-deceiving about what they were doing. The consensus about the strategy for **how to stop an attraction turning into an affair** seems to be to take whatever measures you can to avoid seeing the other person, especially alone, or putting yourself in a tempting situation. Give yourself time for the madness and desire to fade. It will. Create distance from the person and the situation in every way you can. Put more effort into your home life. If your relationship does eventually founder then at least you really genuinely did give it your best shot, without external interference and you can then consider other liaisons honourably. Worth noting too that the affairs that break up relationships are often not the ones that replace them.

If you have had an affair, have ended it and then, full of genuine remorse and regret, decide to confess, do think very carefully. First of all, decide whether it is remotely possible that your partner will discover the affair. Sometimes staying schtum is the best policy: why cause unnecessary pain if realistically, you don't need to? Expurgating your own guilt to make *you* feel better might be the most destructive thing you could do for the ongoing well-being of the relationship. I struggle with writing this because I am a great advocate of honesty in relationships – however I know of too many cases where infidelity has passed undetected by the innocent partner but *has* done something to shock the misbehaving person into realising and nurturing what they have jeopardised. Your playing away and the fact of keeping it secret has to be a one-off activity if your questionable discretion is to have any integrity, though – this is not a long term policy of deception I'm advocating here!

If you decide to confess, you obviously need to be very sensitive to the shock your partner is going to feel. Make sure you have time and privacy for the conversation. Don't beat about the bush. Tell them you have something difficult to say but that you want to be honest. Then *be* honest and brief, reassure them quickly that it is over and that you are not going to see the person again. Say this again and again. Take the blame for your actions but at some point say you want to talk about the problems you have as a couple, which you think went some way to making the affair tempting. Be prepared for their distress, be *very* sorry and know that you will have to spend time and pay a great deal of attention in rebuilding their trust. Talk and talk and be patient but if the conversations are always destructive and 'about' the affair, point this out and try to make your discussions focus on your issues as a couple or plans for your future together.

If you suspect your partner is having an affair, analyse why you think that is. You will almost certainly be feeling sick to your stomach but stay calm. You may be over-reacting and feeling suspicious without reason and there is nothing like having a jealous partner to drive someone into the arms of someone else. However, the green-eyed monster is unlikely to get back in its box, so I think you'll probably feel the need to do something to prove or disprove your fears. You can either try to confront them – but then what happens if they deny it? People having affairs lie – it's the nature of the beast. So although this makes some people in relationship counselling wince, I think some judicious espionage is needed. I suggest you keep a diary of the instances that are making you question their fidelity and discreetly check out their stories. If their routines change and they seem to have regular evening or out-of-town meetings, suggest at the last minute you meet them afterwards at the venue. Watch their reaction closely. Mobile phone bills are a good source of evidence. So is their smell, not necessarily of someone else's perfume, more of being freshly showered. If you think you are right, confront them at a time when you have privacy. Think through what you are going to do if they confess. Be as calm as you can and try to talk about what caused the affair rather than the actual actions and meetings of the individuals involved. Be aware that this will be the first of many talking sessions you are likely to have about their infidelity and keep at the forefront of your mind and the discussions how important it is to you for the relationship to survive – if it is, of course. I personally think it is nigh on impossible for a couple to stay in the same home while one is conducting a liaison with someone else, when the truth comes out. If this is the case, or indeed if you feel the need to be apart for a while and you can keep calm enough to organise it, arrange some separate accommodation for the unfaithful partner, at least for sleeping. Big tip this – try not to discuss your problems with many people in the early days. While you may want to rally the support of friends, the oxygen of their outrage or sympathy may ignite more emotional fire-works that could get in the way of you and your partner finding a way through this crisis as a couple.

The relationship can survive and you can learn to **forgive, trust and love again** if you both want to and if the reason you want to is for the sake of the relationship and not to recover hurt pride. Recognise what went wrong and any part you played and bear in mind that just about every one of us is at least emotionally or mentally unfaithful at some time. If the guilty party is genuine about wanting to repair the damage, consider the guilt they have about the hurt they have caused to you and possibly the other person too. Make the mission to save your relationship a real goal and give it time, time and more time, being realistic about the obstacles, the need for reassurance and each other's insecurity. Don't be naive about the hard work of having and maintaining a good partnership. It can't be full flush like the first flush of love all the time. But new lovely things in your partnership may and will arise. Savour the calm ordinariness of togetherness without the chaos of infidelity. Talk until your ears bleed about putting the wrongs right, about your love and plans – *not* about the affair. Take delight in real little things that enhance life for the pair of you. Eventually your relationship will be more honest and stronger than before, which is something to aim for.

Domestic violence

The term domestic violence covers a wide range of situations and you don't necessarily need to be living with the perpetrator . . . it can include physical, emotional, psychological or sexual abuse in the home, as well as what you may feel is more nebulous harassment, such as nuisance phone calls or being pestered in a malicious way, by someone with whom you have had a relationship. The most important thing to do if you find yourself a victim is to take action as early as possible. One attack is one too many. Putting up with bad behaviour allows it to continue and violent behaviour can be cyclical, inherited and resistant to reform. If you have children, it is even more important, even if it's a lot harder, I know, to remove yourself and them from the threat of violence.

Don't allow yourself, as so often happens, to get ground down by your partner, to the point where you start feeling you must be responsible for the ill treatment. And don't opt for the course of least resistance, putting up with their bad behaviour because retaliation or resistance from you might exacerbate matters.

Relationship dynamics are complicated but ultimately have to be founded on love and respect, and although everyone has rows, you shouldn't expect to be hit, humiliated or bullied. If you find yourself on the receiving end of domestic violence, leave your home if necessary, make yourself safe, tell someone and take legal action.

Family

Oh, goodness – where to start. Families, huh! SO important! The bits that work are SO fantastic and the bits that don't – well, they have the potential to blow your world apart. So no pressure, then, and before you start dishing out the blame chips – parents, children, grandparents, brothers, sisters, aunts and uncles, it's a collective thing – OK!

I presented a TV show about family life for the BBC called *'Everyone's Got One'*, which of course we all do, whatever their make-up. The show was called that because it determinedly didn't want to convey any 'conventional' image of what constitutes a family.

Seeking inspiration for how to start this section I went and sat in a local hotel in Devon during the holiday season to have some lunch and watch typical families being at play together. Well, it went like this – the first person I bumped into was an old friend, with her partner, who had in the last month adopted a one-year-old baby and who was meeting her brother who was over from New York who in turn was meeting his wife who lives with their two children in Holland. Have you got that? All very happy family they seemed too.

Then I watched two different family spats, both actually over children's table manners, with all members at hammer and tongs; then a lovely sight of a really old man, a grandpa I assume, with two under-fives, all sharing a fabulous ice-cream confection and having the greatest of chats about dinosaurs. And then we were all drowned out by a table of disapproving older folk talking VERY LOUDLY and comparing notes about their daughters' and sons' unsuitable matches and how the grandchildren were all allowed to run wild and eat junk food. Then there was,

I think, a single dad, with his young son on the first day of what I assumed was an access holiday, searching for common currency to 'chat' about, and finally there was an older woman with her mother, talking non-stop together about something and nothing and everything.

So let's start there, shall we, with the indisputable truth that there is no such thing as a typical family. Today's family make-up comes in all sizes and shapes with single parents, extended families and step-parents and stepchildren. While there are, of course, family blood ties so too many people manage to get their mothering and fathering, and indeed carry out their family nurturing, elsewhere, with people who are no blood relation at all.

Whatever components make them up, *good* **families** are evident by the following:

- They provide love and stability for their members.
- This supportive structure then allows each individual to grow and blossom in their own right and as their own character, secure and confident with a firm base. Enjoying this level of happy independence and self-sufficiency, the individuals never feel possessive or jealous.
- Enjoying this level of happy independence and self-sufficiency, the individuals don't feel possessive or jealous.
- The dynamics of a good family life allow individuals to play different roles within the unit.
- There is no desire for a payback and they don't get hung up about their level of contribution, either physically and practically or emotionally.
- Conversely this freedom is never abused by a family member as a destructive force against the others and in fact they feel uniquely part of a very special and rather fantastic interdependent unit.

Lordy, the easiest thing about writing this book is trotting out all these best-practice examples. Yeah right, so that's how to play happy families. And it all makes common sense, doesn't it – why, then, is it so difficult to achieve for so many of us? Same old, same old, actually. It's easy to hurt the ones you love and who love you, and then to 'expect' automatic forgiveness. You know most of what there is to know about them, especially the bits that will hurt the most. Plus there is that big theoretical '*have* to love', unconditional thing going on. Parents love children, children love parents, and brothers and sisters love each other. Got to, birthright stuff. Now throw into the mix all the basic instincts of competitiveness and territory, making sure each of us gets the right share of each other's affections, the expectations and pride involved in wanting the best for people, all of the same mould, never mind that they are individuals, and you can see how easily combustible it all is.

The thing is, I think, that with the way we live now, we have to be flexible about the rules and attitudes we adopt to those we love and whom we want to love us back. There are enormous changes to social and domestic arrangements and our mobile social geography is moving most of us way away from having family in the next street. The only thing that will survive the various traumas that could come our way and the potential for getting things wrong as we reinvent what we mean by family, is simply 'love' and a desire for these our closest relationships to continue with contact and communication.

Parents

As everything that goes wrong is all going to be their fault, let's start with **parents**. (I can say that, as I am one). Whether it's a mother or a father, stay at home or out to work, a parent's job is to love a child and nurture them to adulthood in a safe and healthy environment and then to continue to offer love and support. I think 'job' is the right word. A book I've got from the thirties, about home-making, has a magnificent chapter on training children. It's got not one single mention of the word love. That is a given, no need to explain further. These days we're much better at expressing our 'love', but that poses its own problems because parenting can at times feel a million miles removed from being loving; it can be jolly hard work, especially if they are handfuls, wilfully character-ful or constructively naughty. But you just have to do it. It is your job! Of course you would do anything for them but one day they will be adults and they need to be equipped by you to deal with failure or rejection themselves with maturity and realism, not least, so that maybe they can pass these strengths on to their own children one day. Parents are in charge of setting the boundaries for children's behaviour and these will most likely be based on their own instincts and background. More than all the toys in the world and being told they are fabulous, children need to develop self-control and respect for others, especially their olders and betters, and learn how to conduct themselves in company, in order to be able to survive and function as happy adults.

There are loads of support groups and helplines for mums and dads but most of us simply learn to parent on the job, with, if we are lucky, help from our parents, other family members and friends. A combination of love, instinct and common sense sees us through, which is comforting because I don't think there is any textbook 'right way' to do it. It can feel like a hard slog, a breeze, heartbreaking and joyous, stimulating and boring, unrewarding and the best thing that has ever happened to you. That's parenting.

Here are some best-advice guidelines:

- Make it so that children find it easy to do as you do, not only as you say. Be conscious of the example you are setting them. It matters. Children are great spotters of hypocrisy and need to trust you, to respect and follow your lead.
- Explain the rationale behind your rules (once) but don't negotiate. They will always win or wear you down.
- Be consistent and make sure that all adults involved in the child's care, your partner, grandparents, childminder,

understand the rules. (You may feel you are training the grown-ups too if they don't automatically buy into your methods or ethos.)

- Notice good behaviour as much as you pick up on bad behaviour.
- Let them overhear you say lovely things about them to someone when they have been delightful.
- When you get it wrong, say so. Let them know you are human too!
- Never allow yourself to be intimidated by them. You are older and more experienced in life, if less cool.
- Have clear penalties and never give in on them so they know you mean business – earlier to bed, docking pocket money, limiting screen time (computers, TV).
- Establish three line whips for attendance at key events, at an early age. Make it clear that you all sit down together for Sunday lunch, for example.
- Make spontaneous hugging and 'I love you's' part of your daily family exchanges might from the outset. I know some people hate public displays of affection but I couldn't do without them myself – set the habit early.

In most families, **both parents work** and that brings added pressures, with the business of parenting becoming something that happens along the way, its needs often getting squeezed out. I know the extra money is useful, indeed essential, but if this is happening to you, make a conscious effort to redress the balance and make sure that what spare time you do all have is given over to family togetherness first. Lower your standards about the housework, give up that weekend game of golf or shopping trip – put the family at the top of your list of priorities if time is tight, and make sure that just one of you isn't taking on the lion's share of good guy/bad guy parenting. It is important to build family habits and routines into your diary. Children respond to routine and love 'family rituals' such as the Sunday night board game, the Saturday afternoon walk, the Wednesday fish and chip supper. Any and all family activities, however small, may become memories they'll recall fondly as adults. And it doesn't have to be 'quality' time, jam-packed with activities, but there does need to be enough time in the right environment for chat and fun and the incidentals of conversation and news-exchanging. Doing the washing-up together after Sunday lunch was a point of contact I remember with my parents.

One of the scary things about parenting is that most of us won't know if we've done a good job until the kids are adults, and it's often too late then to put wrongs right. Ask most parents, and certainly me, how they have handled the highs and lows of bringing up their child to be a decent person and they will tell you it was as much down to luck as judgment. I had may first son at the age of 23 and looking back I know I was such a child myself then. How on earth did I know what to do? Well the truth is, I didn't. Most of us stumble through and miraculously most of us seem to get it right in the end, which is a comfort. Try not to panic and to trust your instincts.

Toddlers turn into teenagers almost overnight, and it's so much harder when they are older and flexing their independence, to try to coral them back into the fold to instil your family values into them. Those lines of communication haven't been set in stone. However hard it is and however grumbling and ungrateful the little wretches are, never give up on making the family sit down for meals together, share the chores, go for walks and outings together, talk about each other's days and friends and work and school and, well – just everything. Every minute counts. As my elder son once grumbled sarcastically, aged 12, when I started to make an analogy about something while getting his breakfast, 'I know, don't tell me; life is just like a tin of baked beans.' Hey ho – so much to learn, so little time.

If you are a **single parent**, it's tougher, of course. You can't share the responsibility of making all those right decisions and you have to go it alone being all things to your child. Lots of people are in the same boat as you and can be part of the trusted support network you need to cultivate that will also include family members and friends, to help you and bolster you through difficult times. Be careful not to become overly emotionally reliant on your child by sharing your worries and stress with them. You're the grown-up remember. It's important for your child's sake that you look after yourself, and if you ever feel overwhelmed by the challenges of being a lone parent you must get professional help too. Ask for advice or help from your doctor, health visitor or the school. (See page 76.) There are plenty of good parenting services that operate helplines, and parenting websites that have message boards and forums for single parents. When faced with those tough decisions you really don't need to feel totally alone.

If you are **sharing parenting** with an ex try to keep all your adult disputes separate from the issues involved in raising your child. This may be particularly difficult as it will need the pair of you to work together, something you have obviously been unable to do in the past. Agree on clear principles of behaviour in front of and about the children. Agree to work hard at being considerate to each other, on maintaining a child's routine without dramas, and on keeping arrangements, for example regarding access, civilised. Cooperate on making sure the child is aware he or she has the mature love and support of both parents who together want to share the responsibility for getting the best for him or her.

Frances felt very guilty when she found her six-year-old crying in bed and trying to hide a soggy crumpled picture of her dad. 'I'd taken down all the photographs of Nick when he left and just hadn't thought that Gemma needed him still to have that presence in our home. She was worried about upsetting me if I saw her looking at it. I've put some back out now in the sitting room, ones of Gemma with her dad and a couple of the three of us in happier days. It still pains me to look at them but I know it's important for her.'

If you are taking on a **step-family**, you are probably going to have to develop superior people skills overnight. However sweet-natured a person you are, there are likely to be those in the family dynamic ready to cast you as villain and, for their own part, longing to play victim. You, in the meantime, will be trying to be understanding while looking for understanding, and trying to be supportive while looking for support. You'll naturally want to know what your job and place in the pecking order is meant to be in this new set-up. Do you reprimand bad table manners or rudeness? Are you meant to stand on the touchline every week to watch little-un play mini-rugby, even though his real dad doesn't bother and you'd prefer to play squash with the chaps? Do you turn the other cheek to personal slights? How do you carve yourself a place in the 'family' affections that can become a happy extension of your life and love with your partner? And what about all the other people involved in the step-family – the children themselves, the grandparents and the ex? How do all these people with their emotional and family needs make a step-family work?

Here's what's worked for some:

- Be sensible about how you are not going to turn into the Waltons overnight and that the time of adjustment is going to be *enormously* testing on all elements of the family. Don't underestimate it!
- The step-parent has to acknowledge the fierce parent/child bond. The child is highly likely to act as though they have first call. They were there first, sort of thing. The step-parent has to take it as read that they can't compete in this relationship and it needs its own space.
- The parent has to understand how very difficult it is for the step-parent to put a foot right and that often their 'trying hard' will backfire. They have to be supportive and stand solid with their new partner about believing their actions, even if they go wrong, were well-intentioned.
- The parent needs to make it clear to the child that the step-parent is a permanent fixture and that nothing will

change that. And point out that they are hurting *them* by their ungraciousness as much as the step-parent.

- That said, the birth parent has to complete this balancing act by reassuring his or her children that they are uniquely special. This is especially important when the step-parent comes with children of their own. It's crucial that children don't feel abandoned.
- All the grown-ups have to be 'grown-up' and rise above being badly behaved in front of children, however tense and miserable they feel. Acknowledging that the stepchildren are the source of discord is very empowering for children's bad behaviour to continue.
- Watch out for double standards, spoiling and over-compensating. Adults need to talk through how something could have been better dealt with if an 'incident' occurs.
- Keep reinforcing the things you have in common – your love and the fact you are a family, which are both lovely and special things. Happy families make compromises and adjust to situations. These take time. In changing times that could threaten important relationships, people need loads of reassurances of their security and place in the affections of others.

Stepmum or stepdad in fact can be a bit of a misnomer, and step-mentor or even step-older brother or sister-type person, I think, would make a more suitable moniker. Yes, you are an adult in their life, yes, you will attempt to lead by example and look out for them, even maybe love them one day, but they've already got a mum and dad, and it's ultimately *their* job to be responsible for making the child a decent loving adult, unless, of course, a parent has died. So maybe, instead of taking on the weighty mantle of 'step-parenting', just becoming a caring adult friend with a vested interest in their welfare will be as good as it gets – and that's OK.

There are positives in the situation – the children end up with an extended family which brings new people and relationships into their life. They see that their mum/dad has found love again after an unhappy time and they learn from that. And when you all get through it and the children are older, hopefully they'll understand and appreciate how much effort you put into creating a happy environment for them, and really respect you for that too.

Grandparents

Becoming a **grandparent** brings with it mixed blessings, from what I hear. Some people have told me how wonderful it is to have a baby in the family again and discover a whole new type of love, while others feel anxious and burdened or resentful of the part they are expected to play. The truth for the majority, I suspect, is a mixture of both. As with parenting, it's a relationship that begins at birth and goes on to adulthood.

It's hard at the best of times to watch your own children make mistakes, even harder when they are making them with a baby of their own – your grandchild. Remember how you felt at their stage and what support you welcomed or wished for from your own parents. Offering it, not taking umbrage if it's rejected, not banging on about how things were in your day, and 'being' there for when they *do* want someone to turn to seems to me what it's all about. And then, of course, being the most FANTASTIC grandparent to the child. Textbooks may say one thing, but all the fairy stories say you'll always have sweets in your pocket and a shiny £2 coin every time you meet. (Or crisp folding stuff when they're older!) You'll always be jolly, play silly games and tell funny stories and NEVER get cross like Mum and Dad.

Seriously though, here are some good grandparenting tips I'm pleased to pass on:

- When a new grandchild is born, give your son or daughter and their new child space. They need to become their own kind of family. Especially if you sense things are tense, don't keep calling them or popping around. They need to work things through without you interfering unless they ask for your advice.

- Don't make them or their partner feel inadequate by criticising their way of doing things. Offer ideas if asked, otherwise be sympathetic and loving.
- By the same token don't wait to be asked about practical help. From the outset make it clear what practical support you are prepared to give, including occasional weekends or overnights for the grandchildren. Reiterate the offer often, so they feel free to ask when they want.
- Remember too the mundane chores that can get young families down; offer to do the shopping, cook a meal for the freezer, do the ironing, mow the lawn, sew on name tapes.
- Bite your tongue if your child's partner imposes different family customs and procedures. It's up to *your* child to introduce your way of doing things if he or she wants to. Parents of sons find this particularly difficult, apparently. Oh dear!
- If your child's relationship irretrievably breaks down keep any venom you feel about their ex to yourself for the sake of continuing your relationship with the grandchildren. The logistics and circumstances may have changed but you are still their grandparent and nothing can change that.
- If you are going to play a part in the formal childcare and childminding arrangements, be clear about what you are prepared to do and when. Don't be coerced into doing more than you want to do. Also be aware that you won't have as much energy as you did when you were a young mum or dad and that little ones are exhausting. Be cautious and suggest a trial period of a few months. Insist too they have a back-up Plan B. Your martyrdom will

surface above any of your good intentions at the outset and could lead to a rift.

- That said, having Granny or Grandpa involved in the childminding is fantastic for all concerned if it can be made to work. A tremendous bond between the children and their grandparent is forged, collective family values can be reinforced and the absent parent has a level of peace of mind they could never enjoy with a non-family childminder.
- And when a grandchild is older, savour and maintain a different sort of love and engagement, as friends and confidantes. Grandparents are that wonderful thing: supportive family who know your own parents' faults and shortcomings, while still loving them, and who remember and have survived family history and histrionics to become an ally for all.

When Margaret retired she was pleased that her daughter, Tania, and son-in-law asked her if she would look after her eighteen-month-old granddaughter, Isabel. 'It was for two days a week and to be honest I consider it a real treat, if exhausting. I'm very conscious how quickly this age passes and I worked all through Tania's childhood so it is lovely to be able to spend time at home now with Issy. I didn't want any money for it, even though they offered and they have treated me to a holiday. I know how Tania likes Issy's routine to be and our only disagreement so far is about the amount of TV Issy likes to watch. We talked about it and have agreed a compromise amount.'

If parenting and being a grandparent has its stresses so does being a child. This book is not aimed at giving advice to children. It's for adult problem-solving. And being an **adult child** can sometimes bring its own challenges. In your parents' eyes you will probably always be little Johnny who holds his knife the wrong way, and there will be times when you look at your parents and wonder how they can behave so badly at their great age – but you just have to accept that that's how things are. If they weren't family you'd probably shake your head and let them get on with it. You're all adults now so be your own person and take their well-meant criticism with good heart, and try to bite your tongue.

Denise's story mirrored that of many Life Auditors. 'I think that as I got older I found it harder to maintain a good relationship with my parents. As my own children have grown up I realise the ways my parents didn't pull out all the stops for me when I was young. I feel less tolerant of them now and less forgiving. I feel rather disappointed in them to be honest. Sometimes, too, I catch my mother watching me and I can tell she totally disapproves of the things I do and the way I live my life. I feel less inclined to put up with it than I did.'

If Denise's mum was disapproving, then she wasn't alone because it was a recurring theme among older Life Auditors to feel let down by their adult children and many reported a sense of loss of contact points in conversation and lifestyle. What a shame, we should all share the responsibility for keeping common interests and concerns alive once we are adults.

The fact is, you will continue to be expected to live up to their expectations, however old you get, and you will probably come up with an unspoken set of criteria you'd quite like them to observe too, as in helping you more with the grandchildren, the DIY or money.

Money seems to be a flashpoint issue between adult children and parents. While you may be looking forward to a bit of (£) help, handouts or an inheritance, the wrinklies may be set on having a good time and booking cruises. It may be disconcerting to find yourself an adult child with 'expectations' of a parent who triumphs in being part of the Ski generation (Spending the Kids' Inheritance). It's equally sad for parents to see their currency on the family love balance sheet seem to dwindle if they don't put money the way of their children. I heard one desperately sad case of a father leaving his children a video tape of himself telling them that he was leaving his estate to charity and how betrayed he'd felt by their obsession with his money.

It seems to be common too for people to get depressed about their elderly parents or in-laws getting increasingly mean as they get older. It's another case of 'expectations' in family matters, I'm afraid. It's *their* money and it's their prerogative to be mean, generous, spend it all on costume jewellery if they want. People are funny about money and place different priorities on how to spend it. It's a subject best avoided in most relationships, especially family, unless, of course, you are worrying about an older person's mental capacity or if you suspect there is fraud involved. And no, learning to sky dive at seventy-five doesn't constitute insanity.

And what about when elderly parents or grandparents are the vulnerable ones and look to the family expectantly to provide **elderly care** for them. It's an enormous subject and will require lots of research and consideration to find the best solution.

Here are some things to think about:

- Thoroughly assess the care need and the prognosis for future provision needs. It may save having to make new arrangements at a later date. Get advice from doctors and social workers and contact your local benefits office to find out about any state benefit entitlement. This can be a complicated and lengthy procedure so start the process as soon as you consider there may be a need.
- Consider in-own-home care, for instance is there an alarm system that could be used? Or has your relation a spare room that could house a mature au pair or companion for a small rent in return for keeping an eye on them?
- Might a sheltered housing scheme suit? Think carefully about moving an elderly person from a familiar locality unless you and they want to be closer to family.
- If you are considering a residential care home, make sure you visit as many as you can because there are great variations in levels of care and cost. Ask to see the latest inspection report. Check the staff are qualified and watch how they talk to the residents. See if

your relation can have a trial stay, and finally look at the quality of the T-bags and instant coffee. I can't remember who told me this but it made perfect sense when they said it was an indication of how miserly the management would be in budgeting the home.

Finally, of course, there is the rest of the family. **Brothers and sisters, aunts, uncles and cousins**. Geography will play a large part in how connected and close the extended family are and it will be down to individual members to stay in touch. Usually one or two family members make it their business to relay the clan news. An annual or bi-annual family gathering can be a good way too to keep family ties strong, especially for younger members who otherwise may never get to know each other.

If you can afford to, choose a neutral venue such as a family hotel. This will serve to both make the event a bit special and save one part of the family doing all the work. Plan far ahead so everyone can make sure they'll be able to attend. If it is for more than just a meal and you would like to make more of the event, build in some different activities, such as sport or a walk. Don't have too high expectations of everyone getting on brilliantly for the whole time – remember this is family!

Friends

Nobody wants to admit to being a Betty or Billy No-Mates but for all of us there are times in life when you just might call into question the number of friends you can count on and what those friendships *really* mean. And then, if you find either aspect a bit lacking, you may want to think about making some new friends.

For some people, their friends are more important than their families. Families, after all, come with all that baggage that is impossible to shove under the sideboard and ignore because Gran will always drag it out at some point, usually at Christmas, to remind everybody *it* did happen. But friends are chosen, *specially* chosen, because of spontaneous 'liking' that happens one moment and then again and again until the friendship becomes ripely enriching and warm. Good friends are people with whom conversation will never be stilted or reserved, with whom every laugh is likely to be a belly laugh, every tear and trouble shared and every triumph a cause for collective celebration.

For others, friendships are sidelined and less important because of a consuming intimacy shared with a partner, children or a passion. And for passion ready fly-fishing, career, food, etc. People become less important than the solitary pleasure gained from the focussed pursuit of the one that got away, the promotion, the perfect Yorkshire pudding!

And then there are those who truly are lonesome souls, who may just prefer their own company, who, for whatever reason, say they don't really need the company of others. Others may be reluctantly lonesome and long to have a mate or, even better, a couple of mates.

How to make friends

Unless you are a very lucky, lovable and naturally likeable, easy-going person, making the right friends is not, necessarily, simple. Hooking up with a lover is often a darn sight easier with all that subconscious attraction stuff going on, and parenting or being a child has its automatic givens of birth and connection. No, making and keeping true good friends, in most instances, involves making choices and effort. The onus is back on you, chum! You want new friends – you've got to make them and keep them.

Dale Carnegie in his 1936 classic best-seller *How to Win Friends and Influence People* turned 'making people like you' into a six-point plan. *Winning* friends might seem mighty calculating and a bit too competitive for our caring, sharing noughties, but he has a point. We might not want to call it a strategy now, but there are some simple common sense things we can, could and probably should do to be more likeable to others . . . and actually, let's be honest – that's *really* what it's all about. Being friends with people who *really* want to be friends with us!

First of all you need to consider what you want new friends for. For example do you need friends or companions? Think for a minute about the friends you have and the friends you'd like to have. If your life is compartmentalised into different areas where worlds don't converge, then allow for the different categories, such as work, sport, social, etc. Ask yourself these questions:

Do you want to make friends because you feel lonely?

Is that loneliness because you have no one to talk to and share views or news with or because you have no one to go out clubbing, shopping or playing golf with?

Do you want to feel that somebody cares about you?

Does your phone just never ring or does it ring but not with the right kind of invitations?

Are you stuck in a rut and bored with the friends you've got because they and the social routines you share have become, metaphorically, habitual cardigans you shrug on because there is nothing else to wear?

Does time spent with them enhance your life, or make it harder?

Are you scared to break out of your familiar territory and be a bit more the different sort of person that different sorts of friends might want to meet?

It's fair to say most of us have different friends for different reasons and happenings. Amongst your friends, do you have a confidante, a mentor, a good laugh, a voice of reason, a pick-you-up, a shoulder to cry on? They may all be rolled into one person, but is there someone missing? It's an opportune moment now to think about what sort of friend *you* are and who you want to be to your friends. What you put out, you are likely to get back. One of the great joys of friendship is knowing that someone else loves having you as their friend because you are honest and true and giving. It really is the most warming feeling in the world to be needed by someone you care about.

Types of friends

Well, first of all, without sounding too reminiscent of the playground, we should all cherish our **best friends**. These are the ones you count on one hand. Feel blessed if you have more than one or two and don't expect many friendships to reach this grade because it can take time, a lot of time, and it takes sharing, a lot of sharing. It's hard to be close to someone and care about them if you don't know much about them, their lives or their feelings. Any, reticence from them is likely to restrict you from being genuinely open with them so the relationship will never really drill down into deeper mutual support and affection. Sharing highs and lows, tears and tantrums and still feeling secure in someone's regard for you is what really close friendship is all about. But it does take time – sometimes a lifetime. When it happens and the life currency between you is so deep then such friends sort of transmogrify into family.

Cherish too the **mentors** and **strong shoulders** amongst your friends. Look for people you can provide the same sort of support to because you may not always be able to repay friendship in kind to the same people. Mentors need to be kept informed and appreciated, however modest they are. They will relish any of your successes or triumphs and by nature have assumed a type of responsibility for your achievements. Always keep them in the loop and be very thankful! Strong shoulders, on the other hand, are usually quite stoic about being the opposite to fair-weather friends. They know their place is in stormy weather when they have to be rock-like to help you get through sadnesses and upsets. They are ready with the tea and sympathy and know just the right things to say to put a smile back on your face.

Always have among your friends too some real **life enhancers**. You may have little in common with them, even despair at some of the things they do or say. But their ebullience and relentless good humour cheer along the days and enliven every encounter. And always try to have a **wise and honest friend**. This person may be different to all the above – they may not know you very well and they may never become very close but they can be trusted to tell you the truth, however painful, and to attach to it some advice tailored for you and given in friendship. Finally, and without wishing to sound frivolous about such important business – know your friends' areas of excellence. I have friends I can ask about what I should wear, what I should read, how I should cook something, where the best deals are, where I should go on holiday or even who I can exercise with (don't see much of the latter).

Get a strategy

First off – have an open mind because the least likely people may turn out to be very close friends. Awful old cliché, I know, but don't judge a book by its cover. You just don't know what lurks beneath the packaging and while on the surface someone may seem at complete odds to you, it may be that a chance remark or shared look will reveal a whole lot of common ground.

Julie met a friend, Vanessa, at an evening class and thought on first sight she looked very square. She had bad hair and Julie assumed she would be an uptight primary-school teacher. But she happened to look up and see Vanessa grimacing at something someone in the class was saying, just as she too was pulling a face. No one else seemed to have noticed what they were both grimacing about and Julie instantly liked her for being 'the same' and noticing this small and subtle comment. A short chat later revealed Vanessa was in fact very dry and funny and not a primary-school teacher at all but a pleasingly jaded psychologist with a wry take on life. They ended up firm friends.

Let's say you're **starting from scratch**. Perhaps you've moved to a new area. What do you do? The first step is to find some friendship glue. This is the common stuff that binds people together. It may be sport, a shared interest in the local area, a hobby, a craft, a campaign, children or pets. Think about what you are interested in and think about the people who inhabit that world, who they are and most importantly *where* they are. Mr or Ms No-Mates will stay exactly that if they stick at home – and no, sorry, internet buddies aren't enough of the real thing!

You need to get out there and meet people in the first instance and get into conversation with them, but that shouldn't be difficult if you find a common interest. At least you won't have to *pretend* for a minute to be interested in what they have to say. Being interested is crucial. Most people love talking about themselves and their activities, families and events, and with your knowledge of their chosen subject, that glue, it should be easy to turn pleasantries into conversation. A simple initial exchange commenting on or observing something is enough – a compliment is rarely ignored, so look for something nice to say about their performance, creation, kit or outfit. Don't allow yourself to be shy, however much it cripples you. I know you think everyone is looking at you and will make judgments, but take my word for it they are more interested in themselves and just about everyone else in the room first. Shyness really is a kind of selfishness that puts the onus on others to make the running and keep a conversation going. Make yourself talk – it won't kill you. The worst they can do is refuse to answer, and they won't. (See page 10.)

Be generous about exchanging common experiences although save any 'heavy' life-story stuff till way down the line. In general, keep the conversation light and be self-deprecating. Make a joke against yourself!

Look for ways you can take the contact further by offering to lend that book you mentioned, to pass on the useful address or to make a pair for sport. Sport is a great way to make friends because it requires you to make arrangements to get together but not in a pressurised, consciously 'making friends' context. There are so many different sports there will be one even the least athletic person could have a go at. Join up for classes if you are a complete beginner. Bear in mind that for most people, simply joining a gym is not enough because most gym-based activities, (unless you sign up for a class!) are pretty insular. (See page 166.)

Once past first base, it's more of the same. Only hopefully, in other encounters, different aspects of their life and yours will come into your conversations and be sufficiently interesting to engage the other. Be alert to the opportunities to cement your friendship in various ways and in different parts of your life. Yeah, yeah, I know it sounds a bit too formal to be a good way to find fun friends, but listen – you're the one reading this chapter so maybe you've by-passed these steps in the past. That said, if you aren't making any headway with someone, move on. There are only so many rejected invites a body can take and there will be someone else who will be pleased to have the chance to connect with someone new.

Staying in touch

Be involved in keeping friendship alive. That means quite simply making an effort to stay in touch and up to date and interested in events in their life. You need to let people know you want to keep in contact with them. Don't wait for them to make the call. Even the closest of friends will drift away eventually. Put a date in the diary to meet up and make a point of agreeing that it will be OK to cancel as long as a new date gets agreed. Don't be embarrassed or upset about a postponed meeting. Life gets busy and real friends should understand.

Also don't be vexed if, for a while, you are the one who seems to be doing all the fixing. For all you know, they may be going through a stage when they are under other pressures so *you* may have to be the one to keep the friendship fire burning and be sensitive to the fact they are snowed under. Most importantly, keep in touch when you know life is not being easy for them and keep on keeping in touch. Don't be a fair-weather friend.

Remember, friendship is a mutual thing and even if you seem to be involved only in the crisis management of your friend's love life you should be interested in their life at other levels too. It's hard to sustain a one-dimensional relationship. Likewise, remember those who've been kind and constant in your life, and if you move away and the common glue is no longer there and your friendship starts to come unstuck, make special efforts to keep in touch.

When friends let you down

Don't be dismayed by friends' shortcomings or faux pas that leave you gasping! Sometimes, I swear, we *all* go a bit mad and do or say the most extraordinary things – almost like an electricity surge which blows a normal behaviour fuse). But you can't be accountable for other people's behaviour and it's their overall humanity that should matter, with real friendships based on mutual affection and warmth. However, if they ask your advice give it freely – your honesty should be respected and may be needed. (The key words in the last sentence were 'if' and 'they')

Try not to be mean – we all are at times! Forgive and definitely forget. Perfect pals are as flawed as the rest of us and even the most saintly will commit acts of extraordinary selfishness or crassness directed at you. If they are true friends they'll feel worse than you after the event and, as long as it's not habitual, beastliness is best forgotten. The fact it's happened will allow you too to be a human being one day. And when you do, say sorry!

Avoid the money trap at all costs. People place very different values on money and the spending of it. *Never* borrow or lend money with friends – if they need it and you can, give it as a gift. Be delighted if ever they should give it back.

Friendships have peaks and troughs like other relationships. Ride them in the same way and wait for storms to pass, estrangements to end and your star in others' friendship rankings to ascend after any temporary spell at the bottom of the league. Be savvy about your friends. If one makes you laugh a lot but you know he will always forget your birthday, the names of your children or to say thank you for lunch, love him for the bits that are lovable and don't get hung up about the rest. Know him and others with limited life-enhancing attributes and be thankful they light up that bit of your life; don't try to change them or force your expectations and disappointments into the frame. You'll lose them completely if you do. A quick thought on compartmentalising friends: some people have expressed their disappointment that not all their friends get on. It seems to me a bit odd to expect them to. Not everyone will fit with every new circumstance.

Avoid those gratuitously 'nice' people who are friendly to everyone and care about no one *really*. They are often, as well, the sort who get really intimate and overly solicitous about the goings-on in your life. For instance they will remember your cat's birthday, as well as yours, and will always send a card. They are scary; you don't warrant and can't match (even if you wanted to or had half a mind to) their assiduous observance of what's expected of a friend, and their technique may be tremendous but I think they should stay in the acquaintanceship category until the sincerity of their friendship is tested and proven.

In general, good advice is to learn to really trust your instinct with friends. Look out for overt concern and support that is disguising envy or negativity and especially for the subtle put-downs masquerading as well meaning reprimands.

Geoff was looking forward to telling his friend Tom about his plans to go travelling. 'However, he was really unenthusiastic about the trip and kept asking me if I was sure it was a good idea or whether I felt I had the stamina it would need. He was completely negative about it and just about managed to kill my excitement that night. I can only think he was jealous and that his attitude has more to do with his own disappointments.'

Auditing people

Be clear about what the problem is with people you want to audit. Ask yourself these questions:

Do they take up too much time?
Do they make you feel miserable?
Do they bore you?
Or do you no longer have anything in common?
Is it a lazy friendship where you meet from habit?

Auditing people does not necessarily mean auditing out. It may mean that you simply want to modify the amount of time and energy an individual takes up in your life. You need to give your relationship with this person careful consideration and decide what has brought you to the conclusion that you don't want them to have the place and priority they have previously had. Is it complete severance you are after or just a reduction in the hours it takes up – you'd like the relationship to continue but not to be given the same amount of time and maybe have a different tone? If it's the latter, first look back at the notes on confrontation and decide if you need to explain why you are going to put the friendship on a different footing. (See page 13.) You don't have to be hurtful unless you are feeling particularly vengeful or there is a slight that you want to explain for your own satisfaction. If there is a friendship you'd like to keep but the person in question saps your soul with insidious swipes at your dress sense, choice of boyfriend or the way you bring up your kids, try the more in sadness than anger tack and say seriously, 'I wish you wouldn't say . . . (whatever it is). It makes me feel terrible. I'd never say that sort of thing to you.' See if that does the trick. If that doesn't feel right for you, look them straight in the eyes when they say something horrid and after a moment's pause, say, 'Really, is that what you think?' as you hold their gaze. Or even more killing, say, 'Interesting . . .' with a raised eyebrow and an ambivalent smile. Ouch! I learnt that from a very dear friend who uses it with enormous efficacy.

If you just want to reposition the relationship timewise, here's a radical idea – try the truth! Presumably there are other things or people you wish you could spend more time on or with. So what you is stopping you? Go ahead and make these alternative arrangements which will automatically otherwise engage you. Hand on heart, you can then say you are busy and offer whatever sort of modified time you have decided is more desirable. Of course you can dress it up in whatever cosseting words you want. Say, for example, you want to stop meeting them regularly once a week for a whole evening out, you can cushion the news by saying that you really love your regular catch-ups, but life is too hectic to do them weekly at the moment (true), so can you sort out a definite date for a couple of weeks' time. Brook any attempts to be bamboozled into compromising your decision. Stay resolute, and at that next meeting make the point that you have had a great time and have so much more news to catch up on. Don't fix a date there and then to meet next time. Keep your plans fluid and refuse to let them hijack your diary and force arrangements on you.

It's tougher if you want rid of them completely, but maybe *you* don't have to do *anything*! Are you quite sure that they will notice you've gone or that they will do anything much themselves about keeping in contact? If they do keep phoning, consider getting caller display on your phone and not picking it up when their number appears. And if they do get through, keep with the policy of doing nothing. Just be a bit unavailable, a bit distant and unenthusiastic and unable to commit to any firm social arrangements because – err, well, you're busy that night, and that one and can you get back to them – and then just don't. I know this might sound a bit messy but the other option is full frontal confrontation and do you really need that, or for that matter, do they?

What to do when you're the problem

Sometimes, however much you want to be somebody's friend, they just don't want to know you. You just don't fit in with their group and they'll make sure you and everyone else knows it; you'll see it in their eyes and feel the chill however much you try to be friendly. Yes, it is you. You are the problem, their problem! And no, there is absolutely no point in taking it personally. It's one of those things that just happens, from kindergarten to the rest home. People won't share their Smarties with you in the playground and then they ignore you at adult social gatherings, same difference. You're just not part of their gang. They feel threatened by you, they're envious of you or they think they are better than you. All pretty poor reasons to be rude, but there it is. If you're the one being audited out of someone's life, try to cultivate graciousness. I'm pretty sure I've been audited out of people's lives in the past and the above scenario has happened to me. They'd made their point and, to be honest, I've been glad they haven't compounded the rejection by telling me why. In life sometimes you just won't gel with some people and that's that. Give up and get over it. Stop trying and don't seek out that company. In fact, do everything you can to avoid being around them. Not being wanted, having your friendship rebuffed and unappreciated is killing and soul-sapping and nobody needs it.

Professionals and support services

By rights the relationships you conduct with the people who provide various support or professional services for you should be straightforward with no need for much emotional engagement. The reality is often quite the reverse – somehow paying someone to do something can become complicated and confrontational if they fail to deliver the goods or services you expected. So whose fault is that? Yours, of course! Either you have selected the wrong person, with the wrong level of ability for the job, or you haven't made your requirements clear, or you have failed to establish ongoing effective communication about how the contract between you is being delivered. Because that is what it is, whether it's your local dry-cleaners, your nanny, lawyer, accountant, builder or cleaner – you are entering into a contract by buying their services.

Here are some tips on how to have pragmatic low-maintenance relationships with the people who help your life run smoothly:

- Always make sure you have chosen the right person for the job by exploring who else is available and getting several quotes – in writing if you are contracting someone such as a builder. Bear in mind that cheapest is often definitely not the best option.

- Follow up personal recommendations verbally and if possible see their work. Remember, if they don't come up to scratch you've only yourself to blame. *They* may think they are fab at what they do or have lower standards than you.
- Look up whether there is a professional body and find out if they are members. Familiarise yourself with any codes of professional standards. This will take minutes on the web and will sanity-check your expectations.
- If there is a language issue, make sure communication is adequate and that they are up to date with legislation.
- Be very clear from the outset about what it is you want done. Remember that they are not 'you' and so are unlikely to do something *exactly* the same way as you.
- Be frank from the start, couching any early concerns as enquiries, so they understand you want to know what's what about *everything*. Pick up on any reserve in their relaying of information.
- Respect their professional status and show you expect them to rise to it, after all they have been hand-picked by you to do the job in hand.
- Remember you are the one paying but never forget either that they are human beings doing a job – just like you probably do a job for someone else. Think how you like to be treated by those for whom you provide a service.
- Finally, have a back-up plan up your sleeve in case the relationship reaches a terminal demise. You don't want to be held over a barrel, risking a job left undone because they are your only option. Remember *nobody* is indispensable.

Sophie was in a permanent state of angst about how good her childminder was. Eighteen-month-old Hannah seemed happy enough, but Sophie couldn't let go of her constant worries of what happened during the days she was at work. 'Eventually, I just had to say something. I told Marie that I needed more re-assurances and information and that it was not a reflection on her but something for *me*. I was going mad with worry and I didn't know what about. I asked Marie to keep a diary of what happened in the hours Hannah was with her and paid her an extra half-hour's money to do it. Seeing what she ate, when she played, when she slept and what made her laugh seemed to puncture my anxiety and Marie realised how important it was to me to have peace of mind and that it wasn't a personal criticism.'

There are organisations that represent most services and service providers, many of them regulatory bodies with members' codes of conduct which can be useful to quote if you need to.

How to complain

OK, despite your best efforts you have been let down. How do you go about complaining effectively? Well, hopefully you've kept a close record of all your dealings up to this point. Be very literal about this, with a recorded history of conversations pre-viously held about rectifying the problem, dates and times of phone calls and who was spoken to, photographs of shoddy workmanship or disappointing results.

Taking some of the basic points from the beginning of this Relationship section with regard to the general rules of communi-cation and confrontation, also bear in mind that you need to stay extra calm and considered, if a bit chillily so! Be very clear what you want to get out of this exchange – your money back, the job redone properly, them to leave immediately, an apology or a restart. Have your Plan B in place and be careful of putting your-self in an even more vulnerable position. For instance you don't necessarily want to antagonise your childminder if you then have to leave your baby in her care while you are finding another one. You will only feel more anxious.

You may find it helpful to have some notes of what you want to discuss and be mindful of who you are dealing with. If your lawyer or accountant is the problem, they could eat you for breakfast by wrong-footing you with complex details of your case and account, so staying calm, very serious and 'concerned' is likely to work better than shouting and screaming. Equally, avoid being hoity-toity with anyone doing a job you consider lowly. They quite rightly may put you in your place subtly and to their own satisfaction. There was once a customer in a pub I worked in, who was a terrible pompous and condescending snob, and I know the head barman delighted in peeing in his beer. I also know of unmentionable things that happen in restaurant kitchens to the food of rude customers (although in none Mark and I have owned, of course!).

If you are doing your complaining by phone, however hard it may seem, try to keep your voice 'light' and communicative by smiling as you speak. It's all too easy for the person on the other end to be obstructive and this makes everything harder. By the way, to get to talk to a real person if you are dealing with a call centre, either always opt for customer services or simply fail to choose any of the press-button options and eventually a human being will come on the line. This is a general call-centre provision meant to take care of little old ladies, and it's saved me hours of hanging on. Make sure to get the name of any real person you talk to and the number of their direct line.

There are some rules of engagement that you might find useful when complaining. They are organised around a hierarchy of complainees, the premise being that you will work your way up to the CEO until you get things resolved.

- Observing the above advice about being prepared, in the first instance talk directly to the person involved, the shop assistant who sold you the faulty goods, the individual hairdresser who gave you a Botham mullet.
- If you get no satisfactory response turn your attention to their superior, for instance the manager of the store, and repeat your complaint.

- However much they may seem unwilling at first to recompense you or make good, show them your determination by repeating your dissatisfaction and continuing to ask what they plan to do about it.
- The next step is to complain to the head office or the owner of the company. Most large companies will have a customer-service department and an online procedure you might want to try first.
- Read their website to make sure you are filling in online forms correctly.
- Here is where knowing their industry code of practice comes in useful. As will knowing the reporting procedure to the regulatory authority in question. A few comments showing your understanding of these things can work wonders.

If you fail to get satisfaction, do complain to said body and contact either Citizen's Advice or the Trading Standards Body. And if all else fails and you are still convinced you have a case and want satisfaction, consider legal action.

Pets

This chapter about relationships wouldn't be complete without mentioning pets. In the past thirty years I have only been catless and dogless for a couple of months and life felt very lacking without them. Having a pet is great on many different levels and very good for you. If they need exercise they can help keep you healthy; looking after them, being responsible for them and generally having them around is good for your soul; and their unique companionship offers uncomplicated comfort when humankind lets you down – they tend to (cupboard) love you unconditionally, and what's more they don't answer back!

The lessons of love

And so that brings us to the end of Relationships. Is there a general point to make about them all? Well, I suppose (and I admit it's a hard lesson to learn and to live by) to face up to their inadequacies and to temper expectations. We so depend on love in order to function as happy people and yet there are so many different ways of expressing warmth and affection – we're all human after all. Try not to let your need for relationships or your standards for their conduct dictate your appreciation of what's on offer. And remember that we all feel alone at times. If things are difficult, take comfort from the idea that even suffering sad times in a close relationship, whether with a parent, child or partner, aren't necessarily all bad. It may bring you closer to someone else, make you strong and resilient and better able to deal with other challenges in life, and certainly more appreciative of love and good times when you find them. Lots of conventionally nurtured people don't have that sensitivity. Nearly all the people I most admire, who are the wisest, most joyous or fulfilled, have survived tough times in one or more or many relationships.

All relationships matter, it's up to you to work out how much. Cherish the complement of people you have in your life, your partner, your family, your best friend, your mentor, your wise and honest chum and all the rest. They should be knitted into that jumper that helps you deal with life's hiccups and hell-holes. Do that because, like most things, maybe you won't appreciate them until they're gone. I regret not nurturing some friendships in the past that have fallen by the wayside now, and I regret not spending more time with my grandparents when they were alive. Someone once said fatalistically to me that the way to stay properly appreciative was to look upon every goodbye as possibly the last one. (I'm utterly hopeless and weepy now, waving farewell to anyone.) That's a desperately sad prospect but certainly one to make you cherish the moments with those you love and to make sure you have said all that ever needs to be said.

Soul

After Relationships, Soul is the aspect of Life Auditing that most people want to discuss. And I have to say, after 'true love' and, OK, possibly 'the perfect linen cupboard', I'm right there with them. Soul is a difficult but rewarding area to get right in your life and it's an area that I personally want to dwell on and feel is very important. I think there is an increasing appetite for spiritual nourishment, as the world and our lives seem to speed up. Mobiles and laptops and twenty-four-hour supermarkets and longer and longer working hours to buy more and more stuff, with TVs endlessly on and the family slack-jawed and silent, watching rubbish. Churches are empty, doctors' surgeries heaving, people binge-drink on a daily basis and rush from one day to another. It's really no surprise that many of us are feeling the need to stop and take stock and get off the bus before it careers off round another blind bend.

I know from those who have raised it with me that there are many different definitions of what constitutes a person's soul. But they have things in common. It seems to be a universal catch-all and holding place for someone's *raison d'être*, for their sense of spirituality, their fears and insecurities about who they are, why they are, where they've come from and where they're going. Considering one's 'Soul' seems to imply an element of *searching* and brings along with it loads of questions that many, many great minds from the classic scholars of ancient civilisations to today's contemporary theologians and philosophers have sought to answer. These are the sort of things people have wanted to talk about.

How do I try to find meaning to my life?
Is there a God or greater power than humanity?
Can religion help?
How can I cease to regret the past and stop fearing the future?
How can I be happy?
How can I be hopeful?
How can I stop being depressed about the reality of my life?

I'm certainly not saying this section of the handbook will offer any definitive answers to the above. What follows is a mixture of things I consider helpful that have been said by others and things I believe. Those others are a combination of religious believers and non-believers, philosophers and just happy souls I've met.

I think the minimum we could all strive for is a level of quietude and peace for whatever we define as our soul. I also think our souls and the spiritual side of us need as much nourishment as our health and relationships and that it is important to be active soulfully and mentally, i.e. to think and ponder and to do some literal soul-searching, about the health and state of one's inner world.

For what it's worth, and in case you were wondering, my personal view is that our souls are what really, truly make us individual, vulnerable and lovable. I think one's sense of soul matures and changes with age and life experience and that it lies at the bottom of our still waters and is defined by sublime and personal moments of joy, fear, revelation, despair or peace. I really do believe it is as important as our physical and relationship well-being. I think there is an intangible spiritual part of us that is separate to character, genes and upbringing that can be called a soul and I also believe there is a sporting chance that it is so separate from our physicality that it can exist separately and will do so after our physical demise. So I have 'faith', which many people might associate with religious observance, although they should not necessarily do so. My faith is basically an innate belief that something more than that which we can see and touch exists and can determine events. Martin Luther King said, 'Take the first step in faith, you don't have to see the whole staircase, just take the first step.' On the basis that no one can conclude decisively that there isn't something more powerful than mankind and that science keeps on confounding its own certainties by fresh and astounding discoveries, I see no good reason not to have faith. Faith, if you've got it, gives you a personal certainty that makes it OK not to have all the answers.

Religious beliefs and other soulful strategies

Organised religions offer answers and those answers may satisfy your questions or reinforce your faith and belief in one God or theology. Observance of a **religious faith** and attending its services at least ensures that space is allocated in your life for consideration of your soul and spirituality, with the rituals of a religion providing a structure for that contemplation. Shared worship provides a community to be part of whilst nourishing one's soul and replenishing faith and hope.

The R-word is heavy with implication, especially when it lies at the root of so much discord and war, but the world's religious faiths also provide comfort and succour to millions. While most of us are brought up in one faith with which we remain familiar, others, when they become adults, choose to do some spiritual shopping to find the right faith for them. If this describes you, I strongly suggest you ask yourself questions and do research.

People increasingly shape their own soul-nurturing experiences to find a **personal path**, using the components of religion. Worship and prayer are the key activities of religious observance. Worshipping with others who believe in the same God in a communion sense should be a reassuring and warming affirmation of your belief: being with others on the same journey towards the same destination with similar baggage, alone but together. And prayer too, with others, has the comfort of shared and familiar aspirations and words, even if they are unspoken.

Many of the world's religious faiths encourage their worshippers to go on **retreats** to nurture their souls and to do some studied worship and prayer. This sort of holiday for the soul can bring many different benefits to the non-believer as well, especially with today's hectic pace of life which offers so much to get away from. Sometimes you just need silence to allow room for peaceful thoughts to come in.

'I was really looking forward to giving some dedicated time to contemplation because I never seem to have enough time to think,' said Jacqui when she booked to attend a two-day Catholic retreat. 'The nuns were really kind and I was shown to a simple room with a bed and a view out over a lovely garden. It was so peaceful. But I started to feel very tearful and actually through the course of the retreat did quite a lot of crying. At first, I felt quite afraid of being alone with my thoughts, despite having looked forward to it. I slept a lot and joined the nuns for meals and their services, although I'm not Catholic. It was quite a salutary experience confronting my innermost emotions and felt very spiritual and cathartic.'

Different faiths and practices offer different sorts of retreats. There are ones of complete quietude and meditation, others specifically religious and others that employ psychotherapeutic methods. To find one that will give your soul nourishment and a break, consider what you want to get out of the experience. To decide what would suit you, ask yourself these questions:

- Do you want solitude and silence to allow you to think?
- Do you want some spiritual guidance?
- Is there a particular faith you would like to go on retreat with?
- Would you like some help meditating or praying?
- Do you want to do it for just one day or can you afford to spend more time away? If the latter do you want the time to include any other sort of therapy or exercise?

Or you could organise yourself some private and personal retreat time which will require a degree of self-discipline and a bit of planning. Organise some time which you can isolate totally for yourself. Less than one day is unrealistic. Remember, the point of this exercise is to 'just be' in an undemanding and quiet place. If you can, go somewhere away from your home or familiar surroundings. Try to find somewhere where there is natural beauty, a beautiful view or garden, or go to the countryside. Take basic supplies including food which needs no preparation, such as fruit and salad. Don't take books unless there is one that you want to concentrate on to help with some aspect of your retreat. Don't watch the TV or listen to the radio. Turn off your mobile phone.

Let your body dictate the flow of your time. If you want to sleep, sleep, if you want to walk – then walk. Listen to your thoughts. If at first the clatter of the busy life you've left behind crowds out calmer thoughts, try simple meditation and breathing exercises. In any case pray or meditate (see page 88) at least a little but don't force yourself to concentrate too hard if it feels at all stressful. If you find it difficult to be still, practise gentle stretching exercises, interspersed with relaxation exercises, along with steady breathing.

Some people find the idea of silence and solitude completely abhorrent and the principle of removing themselves from the everyday, real world and other people counterproductive. Some report being able to lose themselves or having a cathartic restart from throwing themselves into an exhausting and energetic physical challenge, which works the same way for them as a retreat; or by placing themselves into a full-on different experience, such as a street retreat where people spend a day down-and-out without any resources on a city's streets. There isn't a formal movement that organises them and they are usually the initiative of local churches or clerics.

For myself, as a cradle Catholic, **praying** was very much built into each and every day of my childhood. Reciting the rosary each morning, saying a prayer before *every* lesson, knowing the stations of the cross and my Catechism, let alone how many indulgences I could earn by the saying of certain prayers, which would reduce the time spent in Limbo, certainly left its mark. One of the positives being that praying is still something that I unconsciously do during each day and whether it's just habit, enforced or not, I am thankful for it, find it immensely restorative and can highly recommend it. As do many others.

Any time when you can't talk to *anyone* about something and your life feels a complete spiritual wasteland, praying can give your soul solace. If you are religious and you know who you are praying to that's particularly grand, but even without such certainties the conversation, expression of gratitude, off-loading, trouble-sharing, the private communion into the ether has an inexplicable way of providing comfort and support. Anyone with a specific faith might say that me saying something works *inexplicably* is a bit of a cop out. Lucky them to know who they are talking to, and I suppose, in advocating the power of prayer, I know I am speaking here to the probably *un*converted. But, by way of irresponsible encouragement, for me and lots of others I've met, prayers have a strange way of being answered. I'm not talking Father Christmas lists here . . . more of the give-me-guidance, what-should-I-do sort of prayers. Answers come . . . – they do, time and time again! Sometimes really spookily and in material form. Sorry – I know that if you are a non-believer this will seem, well – inexplicable.

I was wary of putting this into the handbook because I know when *I've* picked up seemingly ordinary books and they've been full of God-bothery stuff, it's been such a turn-off (even if you are quite open to that sort of thing), but the following are examples of real-life prayers being answered, told to me by very down-to-earth people.

Charlie had lost his job on the Friday and hadn't told his wife because they were going through a bad time. He determined to tell her on the Sunday morning but the previous night they had a terrible row. At ten o'clock on the Sunday morning he looked at his reflection in the bathroom mirror and asked, with no real conviction, for someone (God?) to bloody well tell him what on earth he was to do. He was convinced he was about to drive the final nail into the proverbial coffin of his marriage. Then the phone rang *at ten o'clock on a Sunday morning* with someone offering him a job starting the next day!

Sharon had to have tests for a strange lump that had suddenly appeared. As a young mother of two, she was desperately worried and prayed all would be well. She describes with some shyness the powerful sudden feeling that engulfed her. 'It was an overwhelming sense that everything would be all right. It was an extraordinary sense of complete reassurance. The relief was physical and I just knew with total certainty that I'd be all right.' She was.

If you haven't had the benefit (hmm) of a religious upbringing and wonder **how to go about praying**, it's quite simple. Start a dialogue each morning and keep it going. It's a bit like having wireless broadband access. You don't need to switch it on or off, it's live all the time and as you go through your day, instead of internalising observations, mental reactions, irritations and thankfulness, extend it outwards to be inclusive to a third party. Sometimes it helps to pray/talk to someone you loved who has died. You might be able to hear the answers they would give and their physical absence becomes almost irrelevant. After a while praying becomes second nature.

Meditation is where you manage to direct your attention to alter your state of consciousness and to 'still' your busy mind while achieving clear awareness. There are many different types and levels of meditation, some involving chanting and different body positions. It's something that gets better with practice and the more you make it a part of your life the more loath you will become to relinquish it. It is an effective tool to counteract feelings of stress, panic and overload. There are lots of different techniques and some specific ones are integral parts of religions such as Buddhism. At its simplest, meditation is the act of finding conscious relaxation, most commonly achieved through steady focus on breathing in and out while trying to empty the mind of 'chatter'.

How to meditate

- Sit comfortably and upright with your shoulders relaxed and your hands resting on your thighs or knees.
- Close your eyes.
- Breathe in and out calmly.
- Concentrate on being aware of your actual breathing. Your breathing in and your breathing out. Be aware of the air travelling through your nostrils and throat and the gentle rise and fall of your chest.
- Every time external thoughts push in to break up your concentration, settle yourself and start again from a new breath in.
- Sometimes it helps to visualise a scene of peace and beauty, such as a wide shoreline or rippling meadow, and to let your thoughts wander over the images, sensing the air, feeling the light or sunshine and smelling the scents.
- Place yourself in this scene, on a bench, maybe inside a shelter looking out on it, and relax. Use this as a mental retreat to come to as oasis moments in the day.

If I am failing miserably to successfully zone out meditatively, I opt first for a spell of busy daydreaming. I make myself sit still, away from my desk, have a notepad and pencil to hand and let my thinking go free range, writing down the headings of the resulting scattergun brain activity. The list, within minutes runs thus; buy yoghurt, why are we rowing, must lose weight, why isn't Mark home yet, look at the dust on that table, are James and Ben all right, wonder why I haven't heard from Elaine, oh, tomorrow is Wednesday, must remember to water the tomatoes . . . and so it goes on until my mind runs out of steam and the pencil hovers in vain for the next busy thought and then I feel I can put it down and try to meditate again, usually successfully this time.

 If meditation is something you would like to become adept at, seek out some more in-depth instruction to help you from books, classes or websites.

Meditation

Attitudes to cultivate for a healthy soul

Aside from the more active strategies for encouraging mindfulness and an awareness of your spiritual side, there are some general aspects of a mindset that I and many Auditors have found to be helpful. Since not everyone is deeply motivated by spirituality but almost everyone aspires to be happy and since happiness is crucially dependent on what I would call a healthy soul, here are some tips for finding your own inner peace.

Don't regret the past or fear the future

Easy to say when you are consumed by angst, but regrets and fears really are wasted and indulgent emotions – dwelling on things that either cannot be changed or may never happen. The negative energy you put into them will further sap your soul and make it even harder to reconcile your remorse or prepare for tomorrow. Sure, we can *learn* from experiences in our past but they don't define or determine what the future holds. The things that happen *today* are the nearest we can get to that and thinking too much about what might have been is destructive behaviour.

Life Auditors have found it really useful to adopt a pragmatic approach to seeking **closure** on past unhappinesses by working through from the time they happened to the present day and charting the progress of the regret and recriminations. This is a very helpful thing for anyone to do and I recommend it to you. Along the way, spot the conversations that were missed or went wrong and the actions not taken – see if any could be revisited. Calculate the collateral damage to you and others of trying to right a wrong or say sorry. Deal with your own pride if it's an obstacle and stopping you moving on. It's a costly luxury that you may be holding on to at the expense of your own peace of mind. Don't allow regrets for what might have been hijack time now or monopolise a future that could be lived hopefully and energetically. What's done is done – don't compound it by dwelling on it interminably.

Address your **future fears** by fronting them out and laying them bare before you in all their grimness. Isolate the biggest bogeyman – is it fear of failure, fear of rejection, fear of loneliness? Articulate the sequence of events that could lead to this fearful situation happening. Are they a random set of circumstances that could be chucked up by fate or are they the result of possible inadequacies on your part? Be honest about how real a danger they pose to your future happiness. Now come up with a couple of plans.

Plan A which sees you bravely heading for your future – eyes peeled and personally prepared but sailing through the anticipated choppy waters and hurdles of a course you are likely, or are planning, to take. At each of these identifiable challenges think now about how you will deal with them. Get those ducks in a row and be prepared for that frank conversation, to cut back on spending, find a new childminder, or rewrite your CV. (See page 106.)

Plan B is for a major hiccup in your plans. A 'what if' contingency that will steer you into calmer waters and buy you time if you need it because something stops Plan A in its tracks. Your end goal won't have changed but the route to it looks as though it might be very different. Plan B is for treading water while you reconsider your moves.

Then finally Plan C. Plan C is for when an about-turn is required. In other words you had a plan (A) and the plan has changed (C). Plan C is a different route altogether towards a different future goal and may need you to open some new thought routes and create some new options. Always have a Plan C and make it something you would like to do.

Don't have tunnel vision about where you are heading. Have you noticed how life has a way of deliberately thwarting blinkered focus? People who don't want to commute end up working hours away from home, those who plan on having dozens of kids end up with just one, etc. Your A/B/C plans should stop you feeling so scared about what lies ahead. They will guarantee no more success than you had before making them but they will prick the fear bubble and make it more like something you can deal with. For all the planning, what you are actually learning to do is to live within the moment and with the reality of your circumstances. Remember too, to take only one step at a time, one day at a time. Deal with today's problems and live today as best you can, with confidence that you'll be able to do the same tomorrow.

Be optimistic

Not fearing the future is all about being optimistic and I believe it is possible to cultivate an optimistic spirit which is a key part of having a healthy soul. I think happiness is a choice that can be made, and positives sought and found in most people and situations. All through this book I hope there are ways to make the best of different issues in life – here are some of the more nebulous ones, the ones that relate to the big soul stuff but also underpin the details.

If you are inclined to be a pessimist, bite your tongue to stop those negative comments coming out, because every time they hit your radar or anyone else's they'll kill a bit of enthusiasm for life. Sometimes it may be necessary to just pretend to be happy. So *think* of yourself as someone with a happy demeanour. Never mind that you feel doom-laden – put on a happy face and work really hard not to let your miseries show to others. Spot the negative waves and turn them on their head. So instead of 'looks like rain coming' it could be, 'it's lucky I'm having my walk now and not later, and the garden will appreciate a shower'. Or instead of thinking, 'I bet I won't get that job,' you could try – 'I must be in with a chance because they're seeing me. I'll be interested to see what they ask; it's a chance to meet those in charge and at the very least to be put through my interview paces.' Although it seems like hideously hard work to **consciously change the way you think**, you'll be amazed at how easy it is to retrain yourself, really quite quickly. Shanaz tried some physical aversion therapy by wearing a couple of elastic bands around her wrist. 'Every time I thought about how my last relationship had ended miserably I'd snap them against my wrist to stop the sad thoughts becoming bleaker and to make me consciously think about something else.'

Stand up straight and tall, which reinforces a sense of positivity. When you walk, lengthen your stride – sounds silly, I know, but somehow it helps. If something insurmountable gets in your way, instead of feeling defeated, be turned on by the challenge and come at it from different angles, becoming terrier-like in your determination. You can't say something is impossible until you have really proved it to be so.

An optimistic person feels their **life has a purpose** and if you can't think of one for yourself, find one that will help others. OK so you feel pessimistic about your lot; well, why not make the world a better place for others if you've nothing better to do? Certainly don't catastrophise or feed your unhappiness and go around bringing others down just because you feel that way. Keep your dignity and shore up the reserves and resources, people and activities that sustain you elsewhere in your life. Contact with other people somehow invariably helps to lift depression.

Make sure you have parts of your life and interests that are nothing to do with money. This might be doing something creative such as a craft or painting or writing for pleasure.

Be grown-up about the brickbats and the bouquets of life. I keep a folder of things that warm me when I look at them: lovely letters, tickets and menus from memorable nights out, articles in newspapers that made me laugh. I plan to do the same thing with music and put together all the tracks that are virtually guaranteed to lift my spirits, as well as the films that I know will make me laugh out loud. It's hard to stay miserable if you've managed to do that. Bizarre, I know, but a spritz of Charlie Original scent takes me back to my carefree student days because a flatmate used to wear it, while the comforting smell of beeswax furniture polish makes me think of my gran.

Have memories of wonderful times or moments that you can bring to the fore of your thoughts and remember with a glow. Treat them a bit like a gorgeous video or DVD you've recorded. One person I know just thinks of the birth of her children and it gives her an instant lift, for another it's the memory of fishing trips with his dad . . .

Conversely, when I started out as a freelance TV presenter I kept a file of all the rejections I got, determined not to take them personally and not to forget where and why I hadn't succeeded. In a cavalier moment when jobs were a-plenty I threw it away – something I've always regretted. They were career battle scars. And actually, many grim experiences can have a positive side by making you tougher, more determined, self-supporting and empathetic to others, although I have to say that the three word 'Yes er well . . . . . .' response to my showreel from Channel Four took a bit of getting over.

Don't underestimate the happiness order can bring. Bonkers, I know, but my car definitely goes better when it's cleared out and clean. I'm instantly happier when I've washed my hair, and somehow life itself always seems to be a cheerier affair if my bedroom is tidy.

Getting fresh air and exercise will kick-start sluggish spirits especially if it's a glorious day (although I am personally partial to walking in high winds and driving rain). Then come home, batten down the hatches and tuck into comfort food such as an enormous cooked English breakfast or roast lunch.

Get passionate about something that makes you want to do it whenever you can, so you'll always have a reason to get out of bed – or into it, I suppose. On the same theme allow yourself to give in to sublime moments of joy, bliss, ecstasy. And the company of friends is an obvious boost. If you ever feel blue because your phone never rings – make the effort yourself to get in touch with people. It's unlikely they are deliberately avoiding you (if you discover they are then at least you'll really have something to be fed up about), so make it your turn to make contact.

If it's you who is beating you up, stop it now and *make* yourself like you more. **Stop being critical** and dwelling on miserable thoughts. Think of your achievements and the situations in the past that you have handled well. Remind yourself of compliments you've been paid, of who loves you and what a good friend, daughter, mother you are, or could be, given half the chance.

Get over it! **Keep your miseries in context**. Deal with the here and now. Many things that make you unhappy don't warrant the attention you continue to give them. Just look at the front pages of newspapers to see big reasons for human misery. Forgive, forget, move on when people hurt you. Spot when it's your hormones, a grey day in February or the budget round that's bringing you down. Really treasure those relationships where you are honest and feel secure. Show your feelings. Make a nice cup of tea.

How to make the perfect cup of tea

George Orwell described the perfect cup of tea as 'one of the mainstays of civilisation' and certainly it's been at the centre of life for many generations of my Irish family who have a pot of tea continuously on the go from first thing in the morning to bedtime and who drink it hot, strong and sweet. From an early age I knew not to serve even slightly stewed tea and to warm the pot first. Much as I applaud the practicality of teabags, nothing beats a brew of loose leaves in a pot.

Builders', Everyday and Breakfast teas are blends which aim to and do produce a refreshing drink for the constant tea drinker. Other different tea leaves and processing practices produce more distinctive tastes. Your choice of tea will depend on when you like to drink it, what effect you want it to have and what accompaniments you wish to take with it.

- Assam – strong and rich
- Ceylon – bring amber with a delicate flavour
- Darjeeling – light golden with a muscatel flavour
- Lapsang Souchong – strong and smoky
- Earl Grey – pale in colour, scented with bergamot
- Chai – black, spiced with cardamon, cinnamon, cloves and ginger

- Green teas – lighter, delicate taste
- Decaffeinated teas – exactly that

Flavoured teas are also popular, with the flavouring added during the processing. It's easy to make your own flavoured teas naturally by infusing ingredients such as ginger, lemon, mint leaves or other herbs or fruits, in the pot for several minutes before straining and serving.

- Boil fresh water.
- Make the tea in a china pot, even if it's just for one cup, in which case use a tiny pot.
- Heat the pot by rinsing out with hot water before putting in loose tea. Use one teaspoon per person and one for the pot.
- Pour boiling water onto the tea leaves and give a stir before putting the lid on and covering with a tea-cosy.
- Leave to brew for two minutes then pour through a tea strainer into a cup or mug.
- Add milk, lemon or white sugar to taste. Many people say that the milk should go in last but there is no real reason for this; traditionally it was put in first to stop fine china cups cracking from the hot tea.

How to make a jug of iced tea
- Pour a litre of boiling water over two teaspoons of your favourite tea (or two teabags).
- Stir once and leave to infuse for a few minutes.
- Strain into a jug and leave to cool.
- Add the juice of three lemons or limes, one sliced fruit, and 2–3 tablespoons of sugar according to your taste.
- Add loads of ice, stir and serve in glasses.

When you just can't cheer up

If I just can't cheer myself up and get happy, I know I've got one or two other options that may help. If there is nothing I can do to lift the miseries and nothing constructive that will change an unhappy or uncertain situation, I just **get busy**. *Very* busy. I think that over-thinking about something that is making you unhappy can make you feel worse, and often you only do that it you have time on your hands. I drag myself kicking and screaming to the pile of paperwork, I clear out the kitchen cupboards, I invite people around for supper and I organise business meetings. Often, by the time I've emerged from twenty-four hours of wall-to-wall being busy, the glums have passed and I'm feeling happier. Loving what you do as your job is a great solace in unhappy times. (See page 100.)

If that fails then there's the final resort of taking to my bed or going on a long lonely walk and having **a really big cry**. Sometimes there is nothing for it but to sob for England for just one night, to get it out of your system. A big boo-hoo that makes the pillow wet, followed by wiping your face with a soothing flannel wrung out in cold water and then falling into an emotionally exhausted sleep somehow has a cathartic way of really making tomorrow another day – a better day.

Know when to get help

A doctor once told me that one of the main conditions presenting at his surgery was 'disappointment' masquerading as depression. He had patients saying they felt poorly, were not sleeping and feeling low, and who were in fact just bitter and unhappy at life not coming up their expectations. With my 'Put a jumper on . . .' mentality, you'll have guessed I have little patience with this but it *is* important to distinguish between temporary sadness, disappointment or feeling unhappy, and deeper medical depression or a serious breakdown. These are crippling psychological states and need to be taken seriously. Sometimes too an unhappiness is so deep-rooted and so intractable that it can feel as though your very soul is dying and no amount of comfort will help. **Clinical depression**, mild or serious, can be treated; and if your own best efforts founder, you should visit your doctor who may give you some medication. Also, the different sorts of therapy and how to find a therapist are covered in the Health section and the advice just as relevantly applies here. (See page 149.)

'Just being . . .'

Finally I think that the key to having a healthy soul for most of us is to learn 'to just be'. Most of us make 'just being' harder than it should be. It involves being content and happy with the 'here and now', with what you've got. Being either of those things in regard to any one part of life, such as a relationship or work or your image is difficult enough but all bundled up as 'being content and happy in toto' – well, I agree, it does seem like a deal to ask.

'Just being' means knowing yourself and your place in the bigger picture, which is why my take on 'soul' is a mixture of spirituality, faith and one's inner sense of contentment. Bound up in the latter is your sense of humanity and compassion, the level of happiness or sadness you feel and the strengths and frailties of your self-confidence. 'Just being' also means that you are in touch with your sexuality, sensuality and even any dark side you have. It means you don't deny these aspects of yourself, and accept them as part and parcel of your make-up, each with their own place in the person you are and the life you lead. Even your own demons, which shock and surprise you, are acknowledged by you in the scheme of things and so fail to overwhelm you. 'Just being' basically means that you are comfortable with yourself so if there is a part of your psyche that you are unsure of, try and explore it and understand it better. Be excruciatingly honest about the 'real' you, spotting where you allow yourself to be dishonest. Deal with the deception and either be more transparent or have it as a personal secret you are now aware you keep.

Ultimately there are only so many things you can control. For instance a friend's bad behaviour, public transport running on time or the rain chucking it down are all things you have no control over, whereas your own habits, routines and reactions you do. It's the things you think that make you unhappy and you *can* try to control your thoughts.

Work and Leisure

feel passionately about work. I love it. I've always loved it. I love the energy it needs, the people I meet through it, the bit of my brain it uses and the fact that it gives my down time a reason to be. It takes up so much of life and can dictate how we feel and function in so many other areas that I don't think any of us should settle for it being unfulfilling or unhappy for long. Your job description, of course, may be studying for a qualification or nurturing a family, both enormously important and dealt with elsewhere in the book, but this chapter deals with work in its most conventional sense – an active employment that earns you the means to live.

Life Auditors also felt passionately about work. It was an issue many wanted to talk about and consider with improvement or change in mind after looking at the balance of their life in the round. These are questions they wanted answers to:

What aspects of work are important to me?
How can I get the job of my dreams?
Am I earning as much as I can with my skills?
Apart from salary what other things motivate me to do this job?
Can I minimise the aspects of the job I dislike?
What are my prospects?
Should I consider changing career?
What transferable skills have I got?
How can I have a more flexible working life?
Could I set up in business on my own?

A working life has so many different parts that can make it good – day-to-day satisfaction, fulfilment of ambition, great colleagues, pleasing environment and, of course, the practical reason you do it in the first place – the pay cheque.

Of course being paid decent money can compensate for a deal of job dissatisfaction, although funnily enough it's not often to do with job *satisfaction*. Working with a team of pleasant people who enjoy their work and each other's company and take pride in doing it well, or working for bosses or customers who appreciate what you do is sometimes all it takes to keep you happy in your work. I know we all need to earn a crust and to do so, at some point, most of us end up doing jobs we loathe, which doesn't necessarily mean they are lowly or menial. I've been as fed up frying chips at the Golden Egg as I later was as a TV Controller: the former was grim in terms of working environment but I worked with lovely people; the latter's status and rewards were great but the corporate treacle made me want to kill myself. And I was a darn sight unhappier at times running my own TV or restaurant businesses with all the pressures than I ever was during a spell selling double glazing door to door when I had no overheads and success was mainly a numbers game of how many doors I could knock on in an evening.

Whenever I have found myself feeling persistently grim about the day ahead at work I have moved on as quickly as possible, when necessary taking a lower salary, moving to the other end of the country, or learning a different skill. I feel so sad when I hear people moaning about feeling trapped or miserable in their working life. That doesn't need to be the case. So if you are frightened to make changes – let that fear motivate you and get prepared for an adrenalin rush. The only time I've had to do a job I hated has been because at that moment it was the only offer on the table to earn money, learn something, or because I had a wrong perception of what was involved. None of those meant they were a life sentence and I've been eager to put plans in place to change my lot.

Getting the job you want

The following section is to help you make your 'lot' what you want it to be. I make no apologies for the fact that it addresses the very basics of job-seeking, job-finding and career-building. In my experience people in their sixties have as much to gain from brushing up on these basics as those forty years younger. You may be starting out job-seeking, fresh out of university, you may be bored witless or frustrated in your current job and seeking to change career, you may be facing redundancy or toying with setting up in business on your own, you may even be retired but looking to continue working in some way. Each situation has its own set of circumstances but the basic tenets of being realistic, organised and getting the most out of your career apply to all. You should feel motivated every morning to go into work. You should have the right skills to do the job you are employed to do and the right attitude. Bear in mind, there is a difference between doing a job and having a career. If you are *just* doing a job your primary concerns will be to have a level of job satisfaction and to be paid what you consider to be a fair wage that will allow you to enjoy the other bits of your life. A career is something that you expect to develop and that you can put some strategy and planning into, towards a goal, advancement or reward.

Working out what you want to do may not be as obvious or easy as you would think and it's something that can have school-leavers, redundos and people unhappy in their work equally perplexed. It may be easier to start deciding what you definitely *don't* want to do, such as not do a job that involves travelling or sitting at a desk all day. What are your interests? What do you *really* love doing? The best job in the world is one where you never feel it's work at all because you love it so much. Don't dismiss anything. For instance say you love football but can't kick a ball to save your life. Well, look harder at that world. As well as footballers and their coaches, there are hundreds of different associated jobs. Merchandisers, kit designers, management bods, nutritionists, physiotherapists, masseurs, sports therapists, journalists, advertising and marketing people – the list is endless.

Be constantly alert to the jobs people do around you, in newspapers, on TV. Do any appeal? If so, do research and find out how people got that job. Contact companies and organisations and ask for information and advice. See if it would be possible to shadow someone for a day. Work experience is not just for sixteen-year-olds.

You then have to make a match between your ambitions, your abilities and skill-set and, of course, what you need to earn and how flexible you can be in your working life. In all ten aspects of life *The Life Audit* suggests you adopt dreams as projects and have a strategic approach to making them come true. Nowhere will this be more effective than with your work so, having identified a goal, the next thing you need to do is be very clear about the overall set of skills you will need to have. Being informed about choices and decisions is empowering and confidence-boosting and confidence is a key ingredient in successful job seeking.

- Work out what route or routes you could take to reach your goal, get that job, pursue that career change or start that business.
- Research it thoroughly and check what training or qualifications you might need.
- Get in touch with relevant companies as above, read the trade newspapers. Establish the entry point for you.
- Are there short courses, private courses, distance-learning courses?
- Are there grants available? Might future employers pay for your training?
- Might you need to cut your cloth, take in a lodger or take on another part-time job to help with funding?
- Will the resulting change to the pattern of your life have other knock-on consequences involving, for example, childcare arrangements or the need to move somewhere else?
- Most importantly how much do you need to earn? Can you sustain your income during any training?

- Are you maybe in a category that is eligible for extra help, with a disability, single parent, carer?

Write down anything you need to do to add to your skill-set, including experiences, and prioritise them into a sequence of steps. Work out how long it will take you to accomplish them and set a realistic time limit to reach your goal. Be very clear of the benefits that lengthy training for qualifications will give you. Don't retreat into a comfort zone of getting more and more qualified to do something and actually never getting to do it.

Right, you have decided on the *sort* of job you want so where do you **find the vacancy** that has got your name on it? The obvious places are newspaper adverts, the Careers Service, Job Centres and recruitment agencies. Look into each of these and see what they offer. For instance the job adverts may only appear on one day in your newspaper, or there may be issues dedicated to one particular type of work. Visit their websites or ring up their advertising departments to find out. Do the same with specialist periodicals and find out about specialist internet newsgroups too.

The Careers Service and Job Centres have much more to offer than just noticeboards with vacancies pinned to them. There will be trained advisors on hand, databases, facilities you can use and loads of information about training and grants. Become familiar with what you can access and don't be dismissive of the support and help you can find here. Research too the recruitment agencies in your locality or that specialise in your area of work. If you register with them, be cautious about any charges and be clear what they are for; check out their procedure in regard to how much of your personal details they disclose to prospective employers and whether they notify you if they put you forward for a position.

You can also be even more proactive and contact companies you would like to work for to see if there are any existing opportunities or likely to be in the future.

Work and Leisure

- First of all research the company well. Your aim is to understand how their appointment system works and what the entry level would be for someone like you.
- You need to get a contact on the inside, so from your research make a stab at finding the name of someone who seems appropriate.
- Find out if it would be possible to call in to see them for five minutes to ask their advice about opportunities within their business. People love being asked their advice and by putting it this way, you are making it less difficult and taking the pressure off them because they know there is no expectation on your part to be presented with a job then and there. They may also applaud your initiative and their interest be gingered up enough to want to see you, for future openings.
- Either write (as in type – never hand write) or email them a note of introduction and enquiry. Whichever method you use, make it formal and brief. 'Dear' at the beginning, 'Yours sincerely' at the end and absolutely no smilies.
- Mention that you will be in their area a couple of times in the next month and include your telephone and postal contact details and attach your CV.

If you email and haven't had a reply for seven days, then send a hard copy letter, saying the same thing. Hopefully you will hear back from them within the week. If it's a straight nothing doing, reply promptly thanking them for getting back to you, saying you hope they don't mind but you may contact them again in the future to see if the situation has changed, and in the meantime could they suggest anyone else you could talk to, because you really would appreciate some guidance. Do not get downcast. The fact they got back to you is good – trust me – these days, it is. Sad but true. You now have an embryonic contact in the business you want to work in, and although they haven't delivered this time it is vital you keep that door open to revisit in the future.

If you don't hear back from them at all, either with a rejection or inviting a meeting, call their office after another week, cheerfully remind them who you are and that you have been in touch, and say that you find you are going to be actually in their street/building the following week at another appointment and were wondering if you could possibly pop in – just for five minutes, as you'd asked in your email. The message they should be getting from all this is that you are focussed and determined and that you are not likely to just go away, so at the very least they might as well just see you or pass you on to someone else.

When you **apply for a job** formally, remember to make it easy for the person who is going to be reading your application. Use their online form if that is what they want you do. All the obvious advice – neat and tidy presentation, not crumpled and answering all the questions concisely. If you have researched the requirements for the post properly you should know what sort of skills they are looking for, but think too about the personality or life skills they might want in the person they appoint and flag these up under any other information or personal information. Keep to the parameters set by the form but try not to be bland. Try to find a distinguishing characteristic somewhere that makes you stand out from the crowd.

There is loads of advice out there on **how to write a good CV**, some free and some to pay lots for! My personal experience, however, is that all too often CVs are too wordy and made up of lists of information that are not relevant to the job, deadly dull to read, so nobody does, and all look the same. Having waded through thousands in my time this is my advice, which I know flies in the face of what other 'expert' CV advisors say. Veteran job seekers or anyone over the age of thirty-five would do well to revisit the tone of their CV. Times have changed.

How to write a good CV
- Consider the CV as a back-up document to the covering letter that should accompany it or the application form you have filled in. It is a parking place for detail that is not necessarily relevant to your current pitch but which a

prospective employer might want on file or to look at out of curiosity. For example, you may still be pink with pride that you got an A star in biology, but what does that have to do with the price of spuds in your bid to become a fashion buyer?

- Your CV needs to headline relevant experience so don't make it chronological. It may only get a cursory glance as one of hundreds, so the first few lines, headed 'relevant experience', should really shout out why they should see you for interview.

- If an advertised job doesn't have a job description included, contact the company and ask for one. Study it and make sure your skills and experience match the qualities they are looking for. Be realistic about this; don't waste their time and yours if you are not a likely candidate.

- Use bullet points rather than sentences to explain previous jobs or experience. As an employer I hated candidates telling me that the fact they worked in a department of thirty people showed they were a 'team player'. Or the fact that they project managed meant they had 'leadership skills'. I could have worked that out for myself.

- You should include your education history with your qualifications and don't forget any extra-curricular achievements, such as sports, adventuring, citizenship, travelling. Don't go into more than cursory information unless they are unusual and need explanation. There is something embarrassing about someone older than twenty-five being expansive about the success of a university-time experience – and trust me plenty do.

- Don't exaggerate, never lie and don't leave gaps on your CV because they can make an employer suspicious. For example, if you took a year off to go travelling or were ill, make brief reference to the dates and what you were doing or what happened.

How to write a good CV

- Unless asked I don't think you *need* to put in whether you are married or have children, current salary or expectation, or reasons why you left previous posts. Know the verbal answer you would give if asked.
- Do be savvy about what you put in your personal information. Reading or watching television are 'so what . . .' activities that everyone does, whereas playing a sport or a musical instrument or having an absorbing hobby are interesting and not so passive.
- Include any good references or details of work experience, and pay attention to the people you offer as referees. Relevant to the field of work rather than tutors or the family doctor makes sense.
- If you take a good picture, staple or scan in a head and shoulders black-and-white picture into a top corner. This is not a vanity gesture. This is to make the letter less passive as a document. A pic of you with a friendly smile will engage the recipient and make your bit of paper more memorable than the many others. Put below it your contact details including mobile phone number and email address.
- Use good quality paper, only print on one side in a straightforward font. I personally like Arial as I find Times New Roman *too* staid. Whatever you do, though, don't use a handwriting style or coloured ink and do make a copy of the form to refer to for when you get called for interview.
- Double-check for spelling errors and send off within the closing deadline with your covering letter, which should be no more than three or four paragraphs typed on one side of paper. Make it clear which vacancy you are applying for, succinctly describe your key skills and explain why you are enthusiastic about the post and consider it the job for you.

The job interview

Hooray – the call or letter comes asking you to come for an interview. You've made it to the next step and have got through the door.

You have to assume now that what they read on the application form, in your covering letter and on your CV has illustrated that you have, on paper, the skills they need. Now – are you a person they would like to work with? This is all about you as a person – this is people meeting people and working out whether they want to stand next to you in the queue at the canteen, let alone sit next to you in board meetings.

So it's about personality and projecting the very personal brand that is your character. These thoughts might help you do that:

- Take up the challenge and view any interview you get as an exercise in making these people like you and want to work with you.
- Ring to confirm that you will be attending and check out the form the interview will take. Will it be a panel, a one on one and who will you be meeting?
- Will they also include aptitude, psychometric or personality tests in your visit?
- Will you have to do any sort of presentation?
- Prepare – go back to your research and remind yourself about the company's focus and aims. See if you can search the people you may be meeting to find out more about them and their background.
- While you are on their website confirm directions to get there, and on the day give yourself plenty of time, allowing at least half an hour contingency travel time, knowing public transport stops or where you will park.
- Revisit your application paperwork and start working out what questions you may get asked. Practise answering in front of a mirror, with a friend, get someone to film you and be uber-critical about your performance.

- Decide what you are going to wear. Unless you are going for a particularly artistic job where they may be looking for creativity in your outfit – something well-fitting that you feel comfortable in and can imaging wearing to work there is the best bet. 'Smart' can mean so many things now. (See page 298.) For instance ties are unnecessary unless it's a job in an environment where ties are worn and I don't think jeans are 'out' if it's a business where everyone wears jeans. (However – I know it's safe, predictable and boring, but black is good. You can't go wrong with black whether it's jeans, a dress, or a suit.)

On the day of the interview stay focussed on what you are doing. Do not take a friend with you who is going to wait outside. You need to keep single-minded and undistracted; and anyway, your future employer may be watching you arrive and seeing you having a fag in the car park while you wait with your friend sends out all the wrong signals. When you go into the interview remember all the good communication advice. (See page 10.)

- Shake hands firmly, wear a friendly smile, keep eye contact and watch your body language.
- Listen intelligently, answer whoever asks the question (if it's a panel) with a sensible response.
- Don't um or err and don't be negative about anything! Don't slag off former employers, don't dwell on difficult times in the past, don't overstate difficulties the sector is experiencing. This interview is about you being upbeat, positive, enthused by the new challenges this job might offer.
- Know why you want the job – a change, a new challenge, advancement, the next step.
- Have off-pat answers to side-swipe questions – know where you see yourself in five years' time.
- Know your strengths and weaknesses.
- Be prepared to answer questions about yourself outside work – the last book you read, what newspaper you buy, what TV you enjoy.

- Have a couple of intelligent questions ready and not ones you could have found out from their website! What training do they offer employees? Is the company likely to have much growth and might there be opportunities for advancement down the line?
- And if they do ask you to sit any tests, stay calm. If they are psychometric ones where it is almost impossible to know what is the right answer don't even bother to try to second guess them. Just be honest and get it done.
- Finally, at the end of the interview ask when you are likely to know the outcome. Then another firm handshake and warm smile and off – back you go out of that door to await the verdict.

And then it arrives – fantastic if you get the job but what if you don't? Well, first of all be honest with yourself; if you know you got one bit wrong, determine not to let that happen next time. Don't beat yourself up if you were wrong-footed and made a mistake you couldn't help – these things happen. Ring the company if you want feedback, but personally speaking, I doubt if it will be useful – why should they go through the pain and awkwardness of blunt honesty with someone they are not going to employ? They will probably say it was the strength of the other candidates and not you at all. Most of all, don't dwell on it. Get on to the next goal and move on. These things happen for a reason and the next opportunity is just around the corner. You may have been banking on getting that job but you just have to comfort yourself that it wasn't meant to be. All you can do is all you can do and you did it, and all right you had a plan but the plan has just changed and needs your attention.

Career planning

Moving on now to when you have that job which has got *career* potential. You need to come up with a personal plan with some targets. Some of the following is aimed at people starting out on the career ladder for the first time. But even if you are an old hand, remember that many of us will have two or more careers in our lifetime.

- Spot the level within your chosen career that you aspire to.
- Look around at others who have got where you want to be and find out how and how long it took them to get there.
- Work out the experience and training your role models had got by the time they were promoted, and begin trying to get similar things on your CV to put you in pole position for when a vacancy arises.
- Take all and any training opportunities and, if the company doesn't offer them, look into going on some short courses or ones you can fit in around your working life.
- Work out who the king maker is for your plans in your organisation. For instance it might be a boss a couple of steps up the ladder because your direct superior might block your promotion – they may feel a bit threatened by you or they may be lazy and it would mean they'd have to replace you and retrain someone else.
- Don't talk about your ambitions to colleagues and don't be 'scary' eager to get on or blatantly impatient about moving up the ladder. An easy, friendly, interested and enthusiastic person is more likely to succeed than someone intense and obsessive about seizing opportunities.
- That said, set yourself a realistic timetable for advancement and quietly make sure your boss/the king maker knows it.
- Be prepared to move on out of the company, maybe sideways, if the powers that be aren't taking your ambition seriously. Often people have to leave and work elsewhere then come back re-invented into an organisation in a more senior role.
- Be emotionally intelligent as well as professionally smart. Understand the dynamics of your colleagues. See the role you play in the bigger picture of your company's operation and understand where it fits into their profit and success. Be someone that others would like on their team as a person, as well as someone who could do the job.
- If you are looking to be promoted it's often not enough just to do

your job well. You need to be *seen* to do it well and to be willing to go the extra mile. if you are starting out you are likely to be the lowest of the low along with other beginners, and without turning into a complete creep you need to become visible to the powers that be. That can mean either coming up with some ideas, volunteering for any new projects or simply smiling and saying good morning to the boss in the corridor (this last has creepy potential but is effective).

- Another way to get yourself noticed is to take on any of your superior's tasks that he or she would be pleased to offload. You will get experience, brownie points and be able to add more things to your CV.
- Be super-organised and manage your time effectively. Little things like setting up your speed dial and having a clear desk at the end and beginning of each day all send out positive vibes about being someone going places, without bellowing that you want their job.
- I am not a fan of personalising your work station, especially if you are ambitious to be perceived as a good corporate prospect. Everything says something about you and the cutesy, laddish or family pics give intelligence about the non-work you.
- Don't hang around in the office just to be seen putting in extra hours – that might send out the opposite signal, saying that you are inefficient in not getting done what needs to be done in the time expected. Also it's good to be seen to have your work/life balance sorted and a fulfilling life happening outside the office.
- Don't be a workaholic. Binge-working is just like binge-drinking. It will rob hours from other parts of your life and cause you stress. Either you are not doing your job properly or your boss or company have miscalculated what is achievable. Don't ever be a jobsworth; take on extra responsibilities cheerfully if you want to be considered for promotion.
- Also get involved in extra-curricular corporate activities, such as charity campaigns or sports, where you will have chances to show different sides of your personality or abilities and get to know different people within the organisation.

- Be wary of being constantly ambitious for ambition's sake. People hungry for success, the next move, the bigger challenge, never settle and savour what they have got, and in never ever being satisfied are rarely ever happy in their work. If you are constantly hankering for more, maybe look around at the rest of your life to see if there is something lacking there instead that's driving you ever onward.

In the same way, if your escape clock is ticking and you want to **change career**, ask yourself if you are sure you really want to change tack completely. Is there no way that your current career can offer you the fresh challenges or benefits you are seeking with something completely new? After all you have invested a deal of time and energy already which you won't see a return on to the same level you would if you stayed. If you are still determined all the above applies. IT expert, forty-two-year-old Stephen felt bored rigid by his job and was on the verge of handing in his notice. He didn't have any other career ambitions but was keen to pursue his passion of sailing and spent much of his spare time at home and work talking about making a long sea trip. Understandably his wife, Millie, was anxious. 'The sailing thing went from being a bit of pie in the sky to suddenly becoming quite real and I could see him chucking everything in and sailing off. I made him sit down and tell me what it was he thought he was going to get out of it, and it was excitement, adventure and the challenge of doing something different. He said he knew that deep down it was an impractical proposal right now because we have young children. What is really clear, though, is that he has got to look around and see what other jobs there are that might fulfil him more or be associated with sailing. After all there must be computers involved somewhere in the sport!'

Working mothers are one particular group who may want to consider changing careers or looking for more flexible working hours. Priorities often change when you have children and are juggling home and a job. You need to give yourself time to work out exactly what sort of working life will be best for you and once you've decided that, you need to spend some time coming up with a plan to achieve it, following the guidelines in this chapter.

Professional relationships

Having great colleagues can keep you in a bad job longer than you should be, while working with awful people can make you quit a decent position with prospects – that's how important your working relationships are and, in my opinion, 'networking' is a cold word for actually a rather joyous part of the working world.

Someone who understands **networking** completely, who has written bestselling books on the subject and who is one of the most joyous 'people' people I have ever met is Carole Stone, a broadcast producer turned professional collector and connector of people, in the UK and the States. Carole's enthusiasm and delight in meeting different people is tangible. She constantly has a little notebook at hand to take down names and contact details of her encounters and makes every single person feel special and interesting. Her contacts database has more than 25,000 names and addresses on it. Carole has no hang-ups or ever feels embarrassed by being upfront about networking and thinks it should be part of daily life for business and pleasure. She has been described by the British press as a 'phenomenon – probably on friendly terms with more powerful people from all sides and professions than any other single person'. But she is not only interested in 'players', her regular salons and lunches are attended by people from all walks of life, from prime ministers to struggling musicians.

Carole says, 'To me, networking is making the most of the people you meet to your mutual advantage and the great secret of successful networking is taking an interest in other people.'

Whether you are the boss or the office junior it's vital you employ best practice in regard to networking and your working relationships.

- See every day, every meeting, every project as an opportunity to meet people and learn.
- Keep a comprehensive contacts book and make note of everyone you meet, even if they aren't in your department or your company. Remember everyone's name and especially remember their PA's name – they are the gatekeepers.
- Don't be drawn into office politics. They are totally destructive and (note to managers) a sign of poor communication from top to bottom and an underemployed and unhappy workforce.
- Although the priority at work should be to get a job done, the relationships you have with colleagues should be friendly and well-mannered.
- Develop emotional intuition and learn to trust your instincts about the people you work with.
- Address problems head-on and deal with them or put in motion plans to sort. Have high expectations that people can and will deliver and, if they let you down, examine the reasons why.
- Welcome mentoring and training sessions and, even if budgets don't allow, encourage and welcome informal sessions between junior and more senior staff. If you are in a position to delegate let people get on with the task; people should feel they are being trusted rather than exploited.
- Ask for or establish clear, routine reporting sessions to ensure everything and everyone is working well.
- Win the eternal gratitude of colleagues, if you are in charge, by *never* letting a meeting go on for more than two hours and always have a written agenda – even if it's just an email that's been winged around those attending.
- If there is a lot of business that needs to be waded through, suggest sub-groups do the grunt work of the matters and succinctly present their headline options to whole group or departmental meetings.

If a working relationship goes wrong, from bullying to bitchiness to simply falling out especially with a superior, you may need to tread carefully to resolve it to avoid any lasting damage to your career. Most companies have formal personnel dispute procedures but I think it is worth trying clear up any discord yourself first. Examine the situation from all angles, including the other person's, and make sure you understand how it came about and why. Be honest with yourself about any culpability. Seek a private and quiet opportunity to talk to the person in question, placing the emphasis of the conversation on your hope to resolve the dispute, clear up any misunderstanding and find a way to continue working together productively and harmoniously. Don't talk to other workmates about the situation. If your personal approach doesn't work, then seek advice from a senior member of staff or the personnel department. If it is a superior who is the problem, be aware that personnel's loyalties may be primarily with the company and the bosses, so keep 'asking advice' not 'seeking retribution' as your official motivation in the first instance.

Flexible working

If flexible working would make a difference to the way you feel about your job, or it would allow you to pursue another interest or activity, it is an option worth pursuing. More and more companies are seeing advantages in accommodating different working patterns and indeed in some circumstances are legally required to consider them. For instance if the alternative might be that you would leave the firm, which would mean them having to recruit and retrain another person, they may find it a more attractive and cost-effective proposition to make the workload fit your hours because you have invaluable knowledge of the way the company works.

- You need to work out what are the hours you want to work and where the 'flexible' bit comes in.

117

- Do you, for example, want to fit five working days into four longer ones to save on a day commuting?
- Or do you want to finish each evening in time to pick the children up from school?
- Think about how your changed hours will impact on the company's business. For instance it's going to be very hard if you man some phones or are involved in sales and there is no cover available.
- If the boss agrees to you working flexible hours, will he/she have to do the same for others?
- Will the system be abused?
- Can you guarantee that you and others are organised enough to change your working patterns?
- Think beyond just having flexible working hours.
- What about going part-time, job-sharing, having an annualised hours requirement where they are calculated over a year rather than a week, working from home, or even taking a sabbatical?

Going part-time will obviously mean a cut in salary and could have the biggest impact on a business's operation as they will most likely need to take on another part-time employee. Job-sharing works best when there is an existing colleague you have worked with, who knows the ropes and whom you and the employer both trust. Annualised hours can be a helpful arrangement especially if the business is seasonal, such as tourism, and you can agree to put in extra hours at the peak time. This, however, may not suit your plans. Working from home has many advantages and is easy now with today's connectivity. As long as you are getting the job done, the employer might be pleased as you are effectively reducing the overhead. You may also find you work smarter and quicker – but be careful you don't end up with an extended working day. There is no formal clocking-off with working at home, I say, typing this at 10 p.m. And then the big one – talking a sabbatical of several months or a year. You need to have worked yourself into an extremely valued position, I think, to ask for a block period of time off work.

Putting aside the personal organisation you will have to undertake as it will be unpaid leave, and your need to seek an assurance of the job being kept open for you, your employer will have the hassle of arranging temporary cover and will want convincing that you will return. They might also appreciate any arguments you can give about why it might be a good thing for the company if you go hiking in the Andes or novel-writing in Devon. (Developing leadership skills, character building, etc.)

Once you've decided you want to change the way you work, this is how you should broach it:

- Ask for a meeting with your boss.
- Have your thoughts set out briefly in a written proposal and leave it with them.
- Show that you have considered the possible downside and anticipated problems.
- Show how you see these being resolved.
- Don't be naive about your salary and, if appropriate, let the boss know you understand there may be a reduction in pay involved.
- Don't pressurise your employer to agree to the scheme starting immediately.
- Expect to wait a couple of months to allow them to consider all aspects of how it will work.
- Suggest a trial period of three months with a review meeting agreed before the scheme is adopted fully.
- Suggest a buddy system is established where colleagues pair up and therefore give more personal cover.
- Be prepared to take calls at home.

Redundancy

Once you have got over any feelings of outrage, resentment and sheer bloody fury that your services have been dispensed with in the cause of the corporate good, sit down and assess your position.

I know the last thing you will probably want to hear is that this time is one of opportunity – but indeed that is exactly what it is. There will be very few times in your working life, and none at all in some people's, where you will get a bung of money and be told to go away and find another job. Determine that the next job is going to be a better one. If you feel that really is pushing the powers of positivity to their limit, believe me when I say that in my experience, for 99 per cent of those colleagues and friends of mine who have been through redundancy, and indeed myself, it has ultimately proved to be a good thing, leading to opportunities and career experiences and advancements that just wouldn't have happened if we'd stayed put.

Brush up on your skills – especially IT, use any retraining offers from your soon-to-be late employer to take courses or get work attachments. Ask, nay, insist that you have career and redundancy counselling with a professional advisor who will be objective about your skill-set and its compatibility with the current work marketplace. This really does make sense because, while your friends and family may say all the things you long to hear about how the firm have made the wrong decision and how you'll be snapped up, what you really need right now is to get real and be non-emotional or backward-looking. You need to look to the future and suss out what it holds.

Seize this opportune moment. Before heading single-mindedly back to the career path of widget-manufacturing on which you have spent the last ten years, consider for a moment whether there is something you have long been keen to try. Or is there a money-making scheme you've wanted to explore, a lucrative hobby you are interested in – a partnership with someone in a similar boat you are being invited to join? **Consider reinventing your working self**. Take into account the sort of working day you want to put in; do you want to get several jobs, be self-employed or a freelance operator? Might a more flexible working life mean that another aspect, such as leisure or family, would benefit? Think too about the working environment and what type of colleagues you want to be enthused by, and of course, fundamentally, the level of income you need to achieve.

Think laterally about your **financial requirements**. Maybe even *rethink* them too. Broaden the spectrum of this opportunity and decide whether this apparent crisis is the cue to move house or change your domestic set-up. Don't be too hung up about plans that you may have held dear, such as early retirement or second homes, having to be put on hold. Dealing with the reality of here and now really does require all your attention.

Use the buffer of the redundancy cash to buy you time to research your options thoroughly, and don't feel over-faced by the fear of the unknown. It's likely you are at an age when you've gathered plenty of workplace experience and know what is good and what is bad. Don't, though, drag your feet; there will be plenty of time for that holiday in the sun when you've secured some sort of work or at least come up with a concrete plan.

Starting a business

There are many, many considerations if this is what you want to do. Much of the advice on redundancy, about how to research and reality-check your dream working life also applies in this situation, but setting up your own business is a big deal with its own set of issues. Think first of all why you are keen to be your own boss. Trust me, having been there and done it several times, unless you have a copper-bottom proposition and don't need to borrow any money to cover your start-up costs, the freedom and excitement of running your own show may well not compensate for the stress and wear and tear on other aspects of your life.

So, take apart your motivation – freedom, flexibility, money, fulfilment – and then, as you begin to explore your business proposition and plans, hold them up to each of these factors and see how they match up.

These are the things you need to think about. Firstly, gather around yourself a clutch of good advisors. There is lots of free friendly support available for small business start-ups, with people who will help you draw up business plans, apply for grants, understand regulations, develop your business and seize opportunities.

You will need to cultivate a healthy relationship with your bank and find an accountant and lawyer. Join trade and business organisations and check out the free support they offer members. Be careful about being too quick to take on partners or to offer friends or family work. Often those relationships don't work in a different context and turn sour despite everyone's initial best intentions.

Next, stripping out the excitement of enterprise, be cold-headed and cold-hearted about your proposition. Find out about the field you are interested in, the competitors, the customers and the current trading climate. Mystery shop a typical business and try to see it in a different light, and spot new opportunities. At all times, however, look out for the challenges, the difficult bits and make sure you are in touch with the gut feeling that this might not be the opportunity you first thought it was. Learn to listen to those warning murmurs and move on quickly to looking for something else. When you find something, test it against the following questions:

- The idea – why do you think it's a go-er?
- How are you equipped to make it happen?
- How do you know that?
- What other personnel will be involved – designers, manufacturer, sales personnel?
- What will you do if you are wrong – are there variations on the product/service you could offer?
- The market – what is the competition?
- How do they market and sell their products?
- Have you got the catalogues and mystery shopped all of them?
- Why will your product or service be better?
- What will it cost to make/do?
- What price will you sell it for?

- What is a typical customer profile?
- Where will they find you?
- Can you sell online or will you need premises?
- How much money do you need to borrow?
- How much will that borrowing cost you? How much do you expect to make?
- Will you take a salary?
- If things go wrong, how long will you be able to trade/survive on available funds? Have you a contingency sum you can draw on?
- How will you cope with the lack of financial security?
- How do you see your working days?
- Will you get lonely?
- Is your partner or family going to be fully supportive?
- How does your personality deal with set-backs, long hours, difficult customers?
- What are your Plan B and Plan C?

Picture yourself in the situation of running your business. Are you sat in a shop all day? Are you driving around the country? Are you packing orders in a store room to send out? Sit down with a pessimistic friend, give them free rein to tell you all the things that could go wrong and address now how you will deal with them. And finally in this big reality check decide now on what you are going to do if it all goes wrong or if you fail! Do not let the fear of failure paralyse you but face up to it as a possibility and have your Plans B and C at the ready.

Working in retirement

Depending on your pension provision, maintaining some level of working life may be essential. You may be pretty fed up about that and there's probably not a lot that will make you feel better. I will pass on, though, that when I made a TV series about British dynasties involved in traditional ways of life, the happiest and the healthiest elderly members were the ones still working, and they didn't necessarily have cosy little numbers, either. One was an eighty-six-year old oyster dredgerman who set off fishing every day at 5 a.m.

If money isn't the main consideration and it's the fear of giving up the company and stimulation that work gives you, consider looking into part-time or voluntary jobs either within your current profession or industry or elsewhere. (See page 234.) Schools, for instance, can make use of plenty of available, competent people to get involved with remedial classes, fund-raising and extra-curricular activities or even joining the board of governors, as my father has in his mid-seventies.

Finally, whatever your working situation, don't ever settle for doing something that makes you abjectly miserable. Work is just one part of life, sure, but it is a big part and will colour many other aspects. You may be giving over many hours of each day to your bosses and colleagues but those hours are still your life and it's down to you too to crank as much enjoyment or fulfilment out of them as you can.

Leisure

Why put this in the Work section? Well, leisure should be something that happens in work's down time and in fact plays an enormous part in the way you function *at* work. Indeed it could well be the reason that motivates you go to work in the first place, or just the thought of how you are going to spend your leisure time that evening or weekend may be the thing that makes a horrid job bearable. Several people have said to me that one sadness of retirement was that it made their weekends and other leisure time seem less precious and pleasurable. What you get out of your leisure time is very much to do with your work.

But how to define 'leisure' – there's a thing. One man's leisure is another's anathema. Apparently one of our biggest leisure pursuits these days is shopping – *shopping*! I know, I can tell *you* are probably not surprised. But I was horrified. Shopping! Leisure?

Shopping is serious graft for me, not leisure – certainly not leisure! No, *my* idea of leisure is being at home, in my kitchen and cooking for lots of people. I know *that* will make me sound like a freak to some.

Leisure is really hard to define and impossible to categorise. Basically, it is **whatever is utterly delicious** in your life. Whatever allows you to completely chill. The thought of doing it is like a secret hug, anticipating it gets you through life's grunt work of washing socks, caring for Gran, or smiling at the boss you hate, and it's the only bit of your life that it is really all right to be selfish about. You could find information about leisure pursuits in any one of the sections in the book. Think of sport in Health, fashion and beauty in Image, doing up your house in Home. What allows you to feel leisured is most definitely 'me time'. Even if all you do is keep the remote control company of a night, that's OK – your leisure of choice is your call.

The only problem with leisure time, though, is that it can easily be hijacked by others and many Life Auditors reported that they actually had nothing leisurely in their lives at all. There was no 'me time'. It was all his time, or her time or their time! So you may find you have to take a very unrelaxed approach to securing your leisure periods by defining them clearly and giving them real importance. Because important they most certainly are. The total mental and physical relaxation they give is as important for refuelling your energies and spirits as eating and sleeping well. All work and no play makes Jack not only a dull boy but probably a prematurely dead one as well. Ask yourself these questions:

What periods in your life can you ring-fence as leisure time?
Are you sure that what you do in this time truly is leisurely and something you love to do?
Does your busy life squeeze out some leisure activities you enjoyed in the past?
Could a bit of planning further enhance what you get out of your down time?

Absolutely only *you* can answer questions about your leisure, why it is leisurely, what it requires you to do, where you do it and when. Be very aware that it is often the part of life we attach least importance to. As an exercise it's worth thinking of something you love to do and being real about how much you *really* commit to doing it in terms of time and resources. You'll probably spot the people, things and events that get in the way and, rather than just allowing it to be sidelined, it might be worth looking a bit closer at ways you can make your chosen leisure an easier fit with your other obligations.

For instance – let's take a leisure activity. Goodness which to choose? It is so much whatever floats your boat. All right, that'll do – boat-floating. So Boat Floating is what you love to do but . . . there's never enough time, the kids hate going to the park, you can't afford it. Now – think again. More than four and a half million entries came up when I typed 'boat floating' into my internet search engine. There was every sort of suggestion for boat-floating nuts all over the world ranging from floating origami boats to clubs for boat floaters, from making mini balsa boats to crewing holidays afloat on big boats. What do you mean, you can't float your boat? Get out there and get on with it in some shape or form if you want to.

Leisure is important and while it's also vital that we don't build in unnecessary stress or expectations into what we do to relax, a bit of thought to make sure we are making the most of it is time well spent – in my opinion. Now if you don't mind I have people coming for supper . . .

Health

The best bit of good health advice I can give you is to say be *very* careful using the internet to check out any health concerns you might have. I became a complete cyberchondriac after researching this chapter. The information available is breathtaking. In particular be very steeled if you go near any search engine images for visuals of health problems! I am very much in favour of confronting your demons but looking up mouth ulcers, fibroids, geographic tongue and very briefly (!) haemorrhoids (for other people, of course) left me needing a lie-down in a darkened room.

The World Health Organisation's (WHO) definition of someone in good health is that they will be in 'a state of complete physical, mental and social well-being and not with merely the absence of disease or infirmity'.

Easily said, eh? Most of us manage to get the 'state' bit right and the rest is a lottery, with our health receiving nowhere near the attention our relationships, careers or finances get. Which is, of course, foolish. Health really should be right up there, a top priority, because if you aren't well, every *other* aspect of your life will be affected. As the WHO say, your good health should include your physical well-being and your level of fitness, which is in turn influenced by your weight and body mass index, so your approach to your health has to include your diet. Being healthy is also about being mentally and psychologically well and being able to deal with daily emotional pressures and stress.

I know, I know, best practice healthwise is all such common sense and stupid not to, etc., except we don't pay it due attention, do we? Life Auditors spend a period of time monitoring their health and it really does pay dividends to try to get a true picture that will include any related problems or trigger circumstances, which is why I'll be asking you to carry out a mini-health audit.

The rest of the chapter gives you a summary of the check-ups you should or could have and what expectation you can have of the various health professionals and alternative practitioners available. There is guidance on DIY health checks and first-aid provision and advice on diet and exercise. It's important to manage ongoing problems effectively and take advantage of any support available. This is one area of life where personal responsibility really is crucial.

Your health and your age

Before we get to the personal assessment stage, though, it's worth acknowledging that age and circumstances of course play their part in how healthy you can expect to be.

During childhood most of us fall prey to the usual infections and diseases, for example chickenpox, and we may also show early tendencies to conditions such as asthma or eczema or allergic reactions to foodstuffs or environmental conditions. Adolescence means raging hormones and changing bodies, with acne, migraines and growing pains possibly making appearances. Some conditions, such as asthma, can also suddenly appear and then disappear during the teen years. Early adult life is likely to reflect how an individual's attention to their health is either paying dividends or not. As they assume responsibility for their own lifestyle and dietary habits, the effects of positives such as good diet and plentiful exercise and negatives such as smoking, drinking or drug abuse will start to become evident. Being sexually active will also bring with it health responsibilities.

In late twenties and early thirties, maturity, career and relationships put health issues under the spotlight and physical changes start to appear as the ageing process begins to kick in. Movement and activities taken for granted may suddenly start to cause problems. Suppleness will begin to decrease as the connective tissues around joints begins to harden and deteriorate. Strength decreases too and every year you can lose up to one per cent of your aerobic capacity. From your mid-thirties onwards the way you live your life really will be taking its toll. There may be occupational, lifestyle or environmental circumstances which will have had health consequences on some aspect of your body or mind. All this is happening at what is probably one of the busiest times in your life. The pressures of building a career and raising a family can be a drain on physical and health reserves and these pressures can be manifest in any number of ways. Adult stress reactions show up as physical problems, such as stomach and digestion discomfort, insomnia, breathlessness or obtuse aches and pains. Women may also start to go through the menopause towards the end of this time.

Post-fifty you really will begin to reap what you have sown, although that is by no means as terminal as it sounds because there are still plenty of good health habits you can cultivate at this stage, such as regular exercise, that will pay dividends. The bad news healthwise, though, is that post-fifty there's no avoiding those inescapable signs of the passage of time. Coordination and reaction times begin to diminish, and less obvious changes happen in physical make-up which it makes sense to be aware of so that you can take action. For instance a woman's coronary arteries and heart muscles are protected and strengthened by her hormones prior to the menopause. Ten years after the menopause she has the same likelihood of cardiological problems as a man, so if she hasn't been following a heart-friendly diet and exercised previously, she should start now. It's very likely, too, if you haven't been looking after yourself, that you'll be at least one stone heavier than you should be at this age, putting even more strain on joints and muscles.

Obviously old age, past seventy, brings with it vulnerability to poor health with the body being less efficient, less immune to disease and less supple. The cardiovascular system continues to weaken and bone density can start to reduce. Along with sight and hearing deterioration there are many other conditions, such as osteoporosis and senility, that may start to be evident.

There's not a lot good to be said about ageing with regard to health and fitness, although by the same token it's encouraging that so many of the negatives can be combated by being aware of them and taking positive action to counteract them with informed health-monitoring, exercise and diet.

Your mini health audit

Right, generalities aside, whatever age you are, you are the best-placed person to spot any problems so take some time to be aware of what constitutes for you a 'control' level of good health. Really think about every part of your body, bit by bit, notice any twinges or aches and pains you experience. Identify your personal weak spots. These might be susceptibility to catching colds, getting chilblains, suffering from hayfever or indigestion. Most of us have an aspect of our physical make-up vulnerable to illness or under-performance. Consider too how your body reacts physically to stress or anxiety.

For me, a sore throat is often the first indication I get that something is subconsciously worrying me and it can be a couple of days and several packets of throat pastilles before I realise the cause of my stress. Even more curious is that once I became aware of this I was actually able to pinpoint anxiety about my children to one set of glands and other worries to the other side of my throat. The body works in mysterious ways!

Being a bit under the weather and not being in peak condition can become something you find yourself getting used to and accepting. Also it's very easy to take good health for granted but, serious illness aside, it is an area of life for which you have ultimate responsibility and can do something about. If you look after yourself and deal with problems or seek help as soon as they arise, you will get gratifying payback in your body functioning better.

Many men in particular are very backward in coming forward to get help. They'd rather let a health problem adversely affect their lifestyle and careers and avoid relationships where it might be exposed than go and see a doctor – especially if it's about anything *down there* or that might be serious! If that's you, for goodness sake think of your body as a car – you wouldn't ignore a persistent rattling coming from the engine, would you? It might be your Big End and you know what damage that can do to the rest of the engine! Early medical attention makes successful treatment more likely. Your doctor is a professional, your condition will not be unique, the consultation will be confidential. Go in clutching a holiday brochure to an exotic destination and talk about the risk of yellow fever as a decoy for waiting-room nosy parkers, if that is what's worrying you.

Whoever you are and whatever your age and general state of health, the key thing is to ask yourself if your body easily meets the demands made on it by the life you lead, and whether, if you would like to have a different sort of life, you might need to raise your game to improve your health. Remember too, although you should be in for the long haul, having a healthier life is something you do one day at a time and, just like everything else, will power gets stronger with every day that passes. So here are the things to ask yourself along with some suggestions that will help if you find that your answers are a bit negative.

Do you sleep well?

Most people need between seven to eight hours sleep a night and it's not easy to make up a sleep debt strung out over several days. Sleep is needed by your body and brain to recharge and stay healthy. Too little and your immunity can decrease and your concentration suffer. Too much and you may feel lethargic and even depressed. Tips for a good night's sleep:

- Don't eat or drink too late, especially not spicy foods, caffeine or alcohol.
- However, a warm milky drink does help as milk contains brain-calming tryptophan.
- Don't carry out strenuous exercise close to bedtime. Allow your body several hours to relax and cool down.
- Establish a regular pre-sleep bedtime routine, building in rituals such as baths or make-up removal.
- Make your bedroom a restful environment. Remove the computer or gym treadmill and make it more relaxing with soft lighting.
- Use soothing aromatherapy vaporisers, such as lavender, neroli or camomile.
- Make sure the room is well ventilated and the temperature around 16°C–18°C.
- Get really good black-out curtains.

Most of us will experience some period of sleeplessness on the odd night and this shouldn't be a cause for concern unless it is persistent and your waking hours suffer as a result. The amount of sleep you need and when you get it also changes with age. Teenagers' body clocks chemically make it hard for them to fall asleep at night and wake up in the morning – true! Elderly people's clocks, on the other hand, determine that they are likely to fall asleep early and wake early. If you have difficulty sleeping:

- Try relaxation exercises such as lying still on your back with your arms by your side and your legs relaxed. Starting at your toes and working your way up your body, tense each joint and muscle in turn, holding for six seconds and then relaxing.
- Or you could try breathing exercises, such as lying in the same position and slowly breathing in to the count of three and then exhaling slowly over six seconds. Or if you sleep with someone and they are sound asleep, try mimicking their breathing in and out – always works for me.
- If it's stress or worry that is keeping you awake, try writing down your anxieties in a notebook kept by the bed. They will still be

there in the morning but in the meantime you've symbolically offloaded them for the night.

- If it's the actual still of the night that allows all those wakeful thoughts to flood in, consider playing some 'white noise' to fill the silence. You can buy different versions of this, some more pastel than white, with distinctive sounds such as the sea or grasses blowing in the wind.
- If all else fails and you are having an *occasional* bad night, I think it's best to give in to your wakefulness and just get up and do something monotonous, such as ironing or the VAT return. If the problem is a recurring one, go and see your doctor – you won't be the only insomniac in the waiting room.

If you have sleep problems such as chronic snoring, sleep apnoea or narcolepsy, seek help. Sleep disrupted in this way will cause problems in other areas of your life and will certainly be debilitating, and sometimes seriously so, even if you aren't aware of it. Jim suffered from a degenerative condition causing vertigo and tinnitus attacks. Each of the recurring incidents left his hearing a bit more damaged and he was becoming increasingly concerned about how he could continue his job, which involved considerable driving. It wasn't linked at all to this chronic snoring until he started using a special breathing machine at night to stop it and the attacks immediately stopped. There are special Sleep clinics which can assess your problem and prescribe you medication or help you choose an anti-snoring aid.

Do you feel stiff or have creaky joints when you wake up?

This is probably a reflection of your level of fitness. Have you recently taken up a new exercise, or do you not exercise at all? If you are worried about it, of course see your doctor, because it can be an indication of medical problems, but first try stretching out and gently flexing the offending creaking parts while lying in bed and before negotiating the route to the bathroom. And, of course, look to your lifestyle to see if it does include anything to actually improve mobility, flexibility and suppleness. Even gentle exercise, such as swimming, can help if it's carried out regularly. (See page 167.)

Does your tongue look less than rosy pink?

Tongues really aren't at their best in the morning, but serious badger's bum furring is most likely to indicate that you are dehydrated and so drinking the recommended eight glasses of water a day and not overdoing coffee and booze should help.

What colour is your urine and does it smell?

You urine will tell you things about your health. It should be pretty colourless and odourless. Smelly pee means you might have a urinary tract infection and the darker yellow it is the more likely you are to be dehydrated. Drinking a lot of alcohol can dehydrate your body so your urine may be dark after a night on the toot. Rehydrate to see if the problem persists and if it does, see your doctor.

Also go and see your doctor if you have any of the symptoms of bladder or prostate problems that might first make themselves evident with your wee-ing habits. Frequently visits to the loo, especially at night, being caught short, being unable to go or experiencing pain are all possible indications of conditions such as urge incontinence and unstable bladder, stress incontinence or prostate problems, all of which are treatable. (See page 146.)

Is your waist size over 94 cm (man), 80 cm (women)?

If so you should make sure you don't put on any more weight. Look at your body fat percentage, your blood pressure, resting heart rate and cholesterol levels to get an overall picture. Your doctor can advise on getting measurements for all of these. (See page 143.)

Have you got your stress levels under control?

Stress is a killer, which is ironic given that it was once a lifesaver as the body's front-line defence mechanism. Primitive man needed that surge of adrenalin when faced with a wild animal and the body was preparing for either a fight or flight. With his heart racing and his breathing speeding up, blood would have been diverting from his skin and stomach to power his muscles and it would have also increased its clotting characteristics to reduce the amount of blood lost if there was an injury. All those same physical things happen to us today although, of course, now they're more likely to be caused by a jammed photocopier or the computer crashing, and the only thing stress is good for is increasing the risk of heart disease.

You are probably stressed:

- If you feel guilty when you relax.
- If you like awake at night fretting and your body feels tense, especially around your neck.
- If you get impatient or irritable at little things.
- If you feel tired all the time and have difficulty getting up in the morning despite getting plenty of sleep.
- If you have difficulty concentrating on more than one thing at a time.
- If you can't make decisions.
- If you have butterflies in your tummy, heart palpitations or sweaty palms.

You can have stress in your life in the most unexpected places, even in your favourite leisure pursuits. There is such a thing as *Match of the Day* angina – and heart-attack figures rose during the Rugby World Cup. Obviously it's going to be difficult to curb the tension felt during that sort of excitement but be aware when stress might add to the strain on a heart with any underlying weaknesses. Stress very easily can become DIS-stress, so do take it seriously. It can be managed. First of all work out what the stress triggers are in your life by monitoring at what points in the day, in the company of which people and doing what, you feel any of the signs mentioned previously. Then try some of these techniques:

- The quick and shallow breaths associated with feeling stressed can actually add to the feeling of stress, so close your eyes and take a few minutes out to breath deeply and calmly by exhaling to the count of six and inhaling to the count of three.
- Can you mitigate the stress – for example, if the traffic of the daily commute does your head in, is there a better way or time you could make the journey?
- If you feel overloaded with commitments can you shed some, delegate some, put off some?
- Do 'stuff' on a need's must basis and be realistic about how long you need timewise.
- Learn to say no.
- Also learn what things de-stress you and fit them into your timetable, such as that twenty-minute soak in the bath after work.
- Be careful not to drink or smoke *more*, in fact cut down. Both habits will exacerbate feeling stressed.
- Cultivate better habits to help instead. Take up some gently *rhythmic* exercise, such as swimming, cycling or jogging.
- Prioritise the chores in your daily routine and do them one at a time, allowing more time for them than they may need.
- If you have an ongoing source of stress – try to plan something fabulous for in the future and every time the unhappy or unpleasant event or person starts to needle you, try a visualisation trick by picturing in your mind's eye being at or enjoying whatever light it is you have put at the end of your particular tunnel.
- Write down your thoughts – maybe even as a letter to the person causing you grief – don't send it, though.

- Get the stress in perspective. In the scheme of things does whatever it is *really* matters – to whom and why? Count your blessings and accentuate the positive in your life. Try to stay optimistic! It's an established fact, borne out during medical tests, that optimists respond better to medical treatment so being positive is a good preventative measure against bad health! (See page 93.)
- Try visualisation to calm down. Jane, a senior television executive, used to 'zone out' to help her deal with work stress. 'I'd imagine I was in a helicopter and would mentally take off and fly up and look down at the office. Then in my mind I'd fly off somewhere. It's a trick that has helped me in lots of situations and the great thing is no one knows you are doing it.'
- Don't forget the bottom line option: consider whether it is possible to remove yourself from the stressful situation.

Do you eat at least five portions of fruit and vegetables a day?

A typical portion size is one banana, a tablespoon of vegetables or a glass of fruit juice and five portions is the amount recommended to provide the body with a good supply of essential vitamins and minerals, such as vitamins C and E. They are excellent sources of antioxidants which can reduce the risk of heart disease and cancer and will also aid efficient digestion. A simple way to make sure you get your quota is to chuck a handful each of five different sorts of raw fruit and vegetables such as cherry tomatoes, green beans, grapes, broccoli florets etc, into a bowl and pick at them throughout the day. (See page 171.)

Do you take some form of exercise for at least half an hour five days a week?

This helps keep your heart healthy, your joints supple and your weight in check. It also encourages the release of chemicals in the body called endorphins, which will make you feel good. (See page 161.)

Healthy eating

Do you eat a sensible diet with restricted fatty or sugary foods?

The effects of eating too much food with high fat or high sugar content are well documented. A high-fat, high-sugar diet can lead to many health problems including obesity, heart disease and diabetes. (See page 146.)

Do you keep your salt intake low – to less than 6 g a day?

This is approximately the same amount as one level teaspoon. Too much salt is a main risk factor for increasing blood pressure which can lead to heart attacks. Because so many processed foods and bread and cereals contain salt it is important to keep track of your intake elsewhere in your diet.

Do you drink enough water?

Eight or more glasses of water a day help digestion and keep the immune system healthy. Other benefits include healthier-looking skin and eyes. This healthy habit can help weight loss too.

Do you have any Bad Habits?

If you acknowledge that you have a problem with alcohol or other drugs, then you are already halfway to kicking the bad habit. Start a personal diary of your habit so you are completely eyes wide open about how it affects and dictates your day-to-day existence. If you are determined to break the habit, contact the support organisation allied to whatever vice is yours because it's proven that you stand a better chance of success if you follow a programme of withdrawal created from others' experiences and with the support of their understanding. If you are strongly addicted, talk to your doctor too before you try to go cold turkey, as not only can it be dangerous to stop suddenly but you may be offered some medication to get you through the toughest withdrawal stages.

Alcohol

There are clearly defined safe limits for drinking and in fact 2 units a day has been shown to actually lessen the risk of heart disease in some men over forty and in some post-menopause women, by influencing the amount of cholesterol carried in the bloodstream and making it less likely that blood clots will form.

One unit of alcohol is the equivalent of half a pint of ordinary-strength beer or lager, a 125 ml glass of wine, or a pub measure of 25 ml spirit. The upper recommended daily limit of alcohol is 3 to 4 units for men and 2 to 3 units for women. A drinking binge means you will have had more than six units in one sitting if you are a woman, eight if you are a man. Health problems such as increased blood pressure, which can lead to heart attacks or strokes and damage to the liver and brain, can result from overdoing booze. Other problems include depression, anxiety, poor concentration and memory loss. Also consider the effects your booze intake has on your life, socially as well as medically. Resist social pressure to over drink by sticking to lower-strength drinks, alternating alcohol with non-alcoholic drinks, drinking smaller measures and eating a meal to slow down the effects. Have at least two non-drinking days a week. Of course there is a difference between heavy drinking and alcoholism. If you suspect you are addicted to alcohol, seek help. Approach your doctor, look for a local AA meeting, do everything to address the problem. (See page 140.)

Smoking

The statistics say it all. Every cigarette you smoke is said to shorten your life by fourteen minutes. One in two smokers will die of a smoke-related disease and there are at least twenty of these. Half of these deaths will be in middle age. There are more than fifty different health-related problems attributable to smoking and those little white sticks can also cause impotence, reduce fertility and age the skin prematurely. There is plenty of support for those who want to give up smoking, from nicotine-replacement therapies and patches, tablets and nasal sprays to smoking clinics and private counsellors. There is a network of Stop Smoking services and these can range from one-to-one support from your GP or your surgery's practice nurse or health visitor, to a phone helpline or Smoking Cessation Support at Walk-in Centres. Smoking is such a known killer – don't be defeated and never give up giving up. Keep trying and trying until some system, routine or method works for you.

Drug abuse

Drugs, from painkillers to cocaine, all cause damage to the body and brain and are addictive to varying degrees. This in turn produces mental health problems and can have serious consequences, from accidents, negative impact on relationships, involvement in crime to death. Whether you are abusing cannabis, tranquillisers or heroin, recovering is a complex business that requires commitment to change and willingness to confront the underlying causes of your drug abuse. It absolutely must be carried out with the support of professionals. The good news, though, is that people do recover, of course. It can be done.

Do you have any mental health problems such as eating disorders or depression?

Men and women, boys and girls, regardless of background or ethnicity, can suffer from mental health problems. Excessive tiredness, feeling constantly weepy, or developing eating disorders are different ways unhappiness and depression can manifest themselves. You must seek help and get the support you need to cope with both the underlying problems and their consequences. They are common problems that your doctor will be very familiar with and there are specialist clinics and treatments you can be referred to. Don't be ashamed or feel stigmatised by feeling the way you do. Minds are complex parts of human beings and just as prone to faltering as any other part. (See page 149.)

Bring in the professionals

Remember that you're not in this on your own. There's an army of health professionals who can supplement your own health-monitoring with routine check-ups. For most of us the basic set will include a doctor, dentist and optician. However, there are many other specialists, such as chiropractors, chiropodists and complementary or alternative practitioners.

To make the most of an appointment or consultation with any of these experts make sure you are prepared. Write down what you want to discuss about any symptoms, triggers, treatments or medical history. Make notes while you are with them in case you forget anything afterwards.

The following information includes how often you should have which check-ups, how long an appointment you can expect, questions you should ask and possible costs involved.

Making the most of your GP

Your Health Service number and accompanying medical notes are kept from birth by whichever doctor you are registered with at a particular time. You should be entitled to see your **medical records** unless it's thought information may harm someone else. There may be some form-filling and a fee to pay. When you become a new patient at a practice it is usual to have a **new patient check-up** when basic things will be tested, such as your blood pressure and peak-flow breathing strength. This is a good time to find out about specialist treatments, personnel and clinics they have which might be helpful or relevant to an existing condition. For instance there may be an asthma or diabetes nurse and there may be Well Woman, Weight Loss and Stop

Health professionals

Smoking clinics. Usually too, surgeries will have health visitors, midwives, physiotherapists and occupational therapists as part of the practice. On average, doctors divide their surgeries into ten-minute blocks. Book a double appointment if you have a complicated issue to discuss.

If your doctor wants to make a **referral to a consultant** or specialist, you should check out their credentials. Ask how often they carry out the treatment or procedure in question. Check who will perform any surgery. You may find that someone other than the actual consultant is more experienced in a particular technique. Ask them about the success rate of the procedure against that of other hospitals. What are the risks and what will happen if anything goes wrong?

If you are taking long-term medication, book an annual review of your medication with your doctor to discuss your condition and discuss any medical developments or whether tests should be carried out in case your prescription needs revising. If you have a chronic condition you may be able to join an Expert Patient Programme, which is a course which aims to help people stay as healthy, pain-free and positive as they can.

Provision of all drugs and treatments can be patchy and if you feel you are not **getting the drugs or treatments you want** and that should be available, contact your local primary care management (your doctor will tell you how) to ask why. Also patient groups and voluntary organisations can be supportive in applying pressure.

Seeking medical attention and receiving diagnosis and treatment can be a challenging and uncertain time when you are both a patient and a layperson. There may be times when you feel unhappy about some aspect of the care you receive and want a **second opinion**.

Inevitably you may feel anxious about this and your practitioner may feel affronted, so the best way to handle it is to really make sure you understand the information you have been given and have asked exhaustive questions about the advice or treatment being recommended.

Health

Carry out some personal research by either contacting an organisation that supporters sufferers of your condition or going online where there is loads of information available about every medical problem. If you still feel that you want a second opinion, first try to see another doctor within the same practice or talk to the practice nurse to discuss your concerns, but if you still feel uncertain about the diagnosis and treatment you are getting, ask to be referred to a hospital specialist or find out about your local private options.

The relationships you have with any of your health professionals is an important one and needs its own health check that shouldn't wait until a crisis finds it wanting. Think about your expectations of this relationship. It is one where you may have to discuss the most intimate matters; these conversations may happen at critical moments in your life and, without being too dramatic, may concern matters of great consequence about your own health or that of your loved ones.

Ask yourself how confident and comfortable you are with them and if you really aren't happy, then consider finding someone with whom you will have a better relationship. It's a straightforward procedure to **change your doctor**, simply involving registering with a new practice with your medical details. It is a matter of courtesy, although not essential, to inform your current practitioner of the change.

You can, of course, take out **private medical insurance** and there are well-known companies who have various different plans to fit different pockets. It is highly unlikely you will be able to get cover for any existing problems. You can also take out bank loans and opt for some private treatment, such as hip replacements or varicose vein repair, and there are also cash-back plans which pay directly to patients up to certain limits.

Surgery check-ups

There are some crucial tests and check-ups that it makes sense for everyone to have at least once you hit a certain age! All these services are available at your GP's surgery. Unless you have a history of problems, you probably won't get reminders about them, so it's worth noting what you need and how frequently.

Blood Pressure

This is literally the pressure of blood in the main arteries of our bodies and is made up of two readings systolic and diastolic. The first is when the heart beats, pumping as it pushes blood into the veins and the other is the pressure when the heart is resting between beats. The pressure ensures the flow through our vital organs making sure the blood carries oxygen and nutrients to them.

Your blood pressure varies from day to day and is highest when you are excited and lowest during sleep. If it stays high for any period of time, damage can be caused to the blood vessels, including a hardening. High blood pressure, also called hypertension, increases the risk of kidney failure, stroke and heart disease. One in four middle-aged people is reckoned to have high blood pressure and black people are more susceptible. Woman, post-menopause, can see their blood pressure suddenly start rising faster than previously. Smoking, excessive drinking, stress, high salt intake, lack of exercise and poor diet are all contributory factors. There are no distinct symptoms, although sometimes sufferers with very high levels report a throbbing headache at the back of their head when they first wake up.

It makes sense to have your blood pressure checked every three to five years. The levels vary between individuals and at different times of the day. A blood pressure of below 120/80 is optimal.

Cholesterol

Cholesterol is a type of fat we all have which is made in the liver or brought into our system by certain foods such as eggs, some shellfish and offal. There is good and bad cholesterol, confusingly; the former helps remove excess cholesterol from our bodies and the latter clogs them up. High levels of cholesterol can cause narrowing of the arteries which can lead to heart attacks and heart disease. There are no clear symptoms of high cholesterol and you don't have to be fat to suffer from it. Thin people can also have high cholesterol. The important measurement that needs monitoring is the proportion of the two types in blood. Your cholesterol level should be checked at least once before the age of forty and much earlier if high cholesterol is a familial problem, and from then on every three to five years. You will normally need to fast for several hours before the test. The level is measured from a blood sample and an ideal level is less than 5 mmol/l, mildly high is 5 mmol/l to 6.4 mmol/l and moderately high is 6.5 mmol/l to 7.8 mmol/l. Very high is above 7.8 mmol/l. (In case you were wondering, mmol/l is the term used to describe how much glucose there is in an amount of blood.) Family history and your other health indicators combine with your cholesterol level to make up your overall risk of heart disease.

Smear tests and Mammograms
Women should have smear tests every three to five years between the ages of twenty and sixty-four. You shouldn't have it done during your period and in fact the ideal time is two weeks after the first day of your period. Women should self-examine their breasts monthly and have a mammogram every three years after the age of fifty. (See page 156.)

Osteoporosis
Bone density is also something to be concerned about, particularly for women although men can be affected too. From your late forties onwards there are several instances that should prompt you to ask your doctor for a bone scan.

- If your mother had a hip fracture or there is a family history of osteoporosis.
- If you have a history of anorexia nervosa or experienced a spell of missed periods.

- If you are prescribed oral steroid treatment and are under sixty-five. (Get this as early as possible as bone is lost from the beginning of the treatment.)
- If you have experienced an early menopause or had a hysterectomy before the age of forty-five.
- Had liver or thyroid problems, coeliac disease, Crohn's disease, Cushing's syndrome or gastric surgery.
- Long term immobility.
- Are a heavy drinker or smoker.

Diabetes

It's reckoned that almost one and a half million people in the UK have undiagnosed diabetes. The condition can go undetected for many years. Common symptoms are increased thirst, frequent urination, especially at night, tiredness, weight loss, genital itching. There are two types of diabetes. In Type One, where the body is unable to produce any insulin, there are additional symptoms of cramps and constipation, blurred vision and possible recurring skin infections. It can lead to heart disease and strokes and cause serious damage to your eyes, kidneys and nervous system. You are more vulnerable if you are female, between the ages of forty and seventy-five, if there is a family history of the condition, if you are of Asian or Afro-Caribbean origin or if you are overweight. A healthy diet and regular physical exercise reduces the risk. Type Two diabetes is when the body becomes resistant to insulin and is more common and likely to occur later in life. Diet, medication and occasionally insulin are used to get the condition under control.

Prostate Specific Antigen (PSA)

This test for men, from middle age onwards, assesses their risk of prostate disease by measuring the levels of protein in the bloodstream. Although it is not foolproof, prostate cancer is the commonest cause of death in men over seventy-five, so is certainly worth having, and the test might indicate whether you need further prostatic examination.

Immunisations

From childhood onwards it's down to you to have whatever jabs are necessary and if you have had all your immunisations, you should be protected from diptheria and tetanus for at least ten years, whooping cough for at least three years and will have long-term protection from cerebrospinal meningitis and polio. Other long-term protection does also appear to be offered by the measles, mumps and rubella and meningitis C jabs.

But you are advised to have a booster dose of tetanus every ten years, and an annual flu injection in the autumn if you are over the age of 65, have heart, kidney or lung disease at any age, have diabetes, low immunity levels or live in a residential or nursing home.

Plus, of course, the relevant jabs or pills if you're off to exotic destinations.

Places, other than your GP, to get medical advice

There is twenty-four-hour telephone support available from **NHS Direct** or you can go online to get immediate and practical advice from trained nursing staff who will also direct you for further personal attention if they think it appropriate.

There are also **Walk-in Centres**, open from early in the morning until late at night, seven days a week, where you can get a wide range of medical advice and support without prior appointment or registration. This includes advice on local doctors and chemists, emergency contraception and other contraceptive advice, advice on coughs, colds and flu-like symptoms, stomach upsets, vomiting, diarrhoea, hayfever, bites and stings, muscle strains and sprains, rashes or sunburn and women's health problems such as thrush and menstrual advice. Most centres will also carry out blood-pressure checks and offer suturing and care for dressings of minor cuts and wounds. As back-up health care provision it's worth finding out the location of your nearest Walk-in Centre.

Health advice

If you are having **sexual problems**, because it is difficult or painful, or if you are worried you may have a sexually transmitted disease, you can also go to your local **genito-urinary clinic** for which you will not need an appointment or a referral from your doctor. Or you could contact the **contraceptive education service** (CES) who will give free confidential advice on all aspects of sexual health and contraception and point you in the direction of your local clinic.

Dentist

Most people should see their dentist every six months for a general check-up and maybe to have a session with the hygienist. This should take no longer than twenty minutes. If you are terrified of going to the dentist or need some specialist dental work you should contact the national dental association for details of local sympathetic experts. There are also emergency dentists at Dental Access centres, who work outside normal hours.

Daily tooth care

Teeth brushing is such a habit that it's easy to do it the wrong way, for example brushing *too* hard is a problem that can damage gums. Your dentist will be able to spot any problems and may refer you to a dental hygienist to show you how to keep your chompers healthy, with particular attention to any vulnerable areas.

How to brush your teeth

- A smaller, softer-headed toothbrush is generally better than a large harder-bristled one as it can reach more places. The angle of the head and the choice of handle design is down to personal choice and comfort.
- Toothbrushes should be changed every three months and you should spend at least two minutes at the job at least twice a day. The aim is for the brush's bristles to make contact with and dislodge any dirt or food debris on and

> between the teeth, so brushing to and fro won't work efficiently.
> - Gently roll the brush head at an angle down from the gums to the bottom of the teeth for your top teeth and then up from the gums for your bottom jaw.
> - Do this on the outside and inside of your teeth.
> - Make it a slower and more considered action than you are used to.
> - Brush the chewing surfaces of your teeth with a circular motion or to and fro or straight across.

A dentist once told me that the best way to teach children to brush their teeth properly was to get them to do it looking in a mirror, with the challenge to flick as much oral effluence as they could using the roll and flick technique. The more splattered the mirror, the better job they were doing *and* learning the lesson of seeing what actually does lurk in the crevices. (I appreciate the houseproud amongst you may struggle with this.)

Optician

An appointment lasting twenty to thirty minutes once every two years should suffice if your eyesight is good, more frequently if you have sight deterioration, or wear contact lenses. Don't miss eye tests as these can be early indicators of other health problems, such as diabetes. A child's eyesight is fully developed by the age of eight and their first check-up should be before starting school so that problems can be identified early.

Mental Health

Lots of different conditions come under mental illness, ranging from stress and eating disorders to depression and Alzheimer's. So the symptoms can range from feeling anxious and panicky through to being out of control, vulnerable and suicidal. It's reckoned that at least a quarter of us will suffer from a mental health problem at some time in our lives. Mental illness is not an easy thing to self-treat and if you feel at all desperate you should always seek professional help and talk to someone who will understand how you feel. There are therapies and medication that can help.

Your doctor should be able to refer you to someone who specialises in the area of your life that is bothering you. It's important you see someone who is accredited and who knows what they are doing because there is no legal regulation of people who call themselves therapists or counsellors and especially the latter description is much abused by well-intentioned but not necessarily skilled people.

Counsellors are usually lay people who have completed a training course in a specific subject, such as marriage breakdown or bereavement; psychotherapists are usually trained psychologists with extra qualifications in therapy; and psychiatrists are medical doctors specialising in mental health, who may prescribe drug medication as well as talking therapy.

There are many different sorts of counselling and therapy, including:

Psychodynamic psychotherapy which can help you understand how past experiences, patterns and unconscious sentiments can affect your current behaviour. This is particularly helpful for family and childhood-related issues. It may be a long-term treatment.

Cognitive therapy which works to correct negative responses that are blighting your life. It teaches you to spot the automatic thoughts that bring you down, not necessarily to identify where they started but to change your current behaviour. Treatment is often short.

Person-centred therapy which is all about good listening to help you find the best way through unhappy times. This can include finding your own questions as well as the answers, and gradually uncovering the unconscious.

As well as finding an appropriately qualified professional it is also important your therapist is right for you, so don't be put off seeing several until you find someone you can trust to be sympathetic but objective too. You are not looking for tea and a sympathetic wallow in your difficulties. Rather, you are looking for an experienced professional who is going to re-equip your mental tool box and thought processes so you can deal better, yourself, with the negatives and unhappiness in your life. They should have respect for the effort you are putting into your own case and see the journey as a partnership which needs you both to collaborate.

Alternative and complementary practitioners

There are so many to choose from that if you enter 'alternative health' into an internet search engine you will get more than 45 million hits! Despite the overload of available information it is vital to do your research, so a good starting point is to talk to your doctor who may be able to recommend particular people in your area and will be able to advise you of any potential risk, given their knowledge of your condition. Some surgeries have affiliated specialist clinics, such as homeopathy or chiropractics.

First consultations are often longer and more expensive as they need to take down your history. Some may advise a course of six to eight treatments so it can be a big commitment and you might now know whether it is helping or not until some way into the treatment because sometimes it takes a good few sessions to work through 'blockages' before you feel any relief. While most practitioners are genuine, you do run the risk of being taken for a ride so in the event that you need to find a complementary or alternative practitioner yourself, do your research. Seek personal recommendations, check out credentials and give yourself some boundaries in terms of what you are prepared to spend, what your expectations are and what is the likely duration of treatment. Don't be embarrassed about expecting answers to the following questions because a professional specialist will be pleased to allay any concerns you may have:

- Is there a governing body and are they registered members?
- What training have they had, leading to what qualifications?
- What does the treatment involve?
- When can an improvement be expected?
- How long is the average course of treatment for your condition?
- What is the cost likely to be?
- What other things can you do to help yourself?
- Is there anything you should avoid during the treatment?

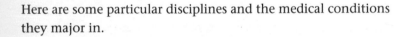

Here are some particular disciplines and the medical conditions they major in.

Acupuncture

An ancient Chinese medicine where the practitioner inserts and sometimes manipulates needles on various points of the body along the meridians (energy channels), the idea being that when these meridians are disturbed and energy isn't flowing freely, symptoms crop up. It shouldn't hurt and the needles are sometimes in and out almost instantly, while other times they can stay in for as much as an hour, depending on the diagnosis. People use acupuncture for all sorts of complaints: skin conditions, chronic pain, digestive problems, painful periods, breathing difficulties, allergies, high blood pressure, addictions and stress.

The Alexander Technique

The Alexander Technique is used to help to teach people about using their body in the most efficient way possible – as nature intended. Breathing is an important part of the technique as poor posture often affects the voice and restricts breathing, as well as leading to aches and pains. Good for complete re-education in how to stand, sit and move effortlessly – which in turn alleviates symptoms and associated stress.

Reflexology

Uses massage to work on areas in hands and, mostly, feet that correspond to particular parts of the body so the right foot becomes a map for the right side of your body and the left foot mirrors the left. A tender point on the foot invariably relates to an organ or area in the body that isn't working properly. The idea is that massage frees up energy channels in the body, which can get blocked and lead to ill health. All sorts of things respond to reflexology. A friend of mine swears by it for arthritis and also sinusitis. Other things that respond well: migraine, hormonal imbalances, breathing difficulties, digestive problems, circulatory problems, back problems, tension and stress.

Homeopathy

Homeopathy works on the principle of treating like with like; explained most simply, it is treating the disease with a very diluted version of what might bring about those symptoms in a healthy person. Giving your case history is important as what you are prescribed will be entirely dependent on what sort of person you are – what your natural disposition is. While homeopathy is recognised, debates continue as to how it works, but it does. It seems to work best on chronic conditions like anxiety, asthma, eczema, digestive problems and allergies.

Osteopathy

The idea is – if the body is correctly aligned, then it's not stressed and can work efficiently; the organs are well supported and protected and the body can heal itself. An osteopath will look at the entire body and try to work out why particular bones, muscles, ligaments and soft tissues are causing pain. Sometimes they use a gentle touch to diagnose and treat, other times they manipulate firmly and quickly to put the body back in line. Common problems treated include sports injuries, back and neck pain, frozen shoulder, sciatica, headaches, digestive problems and depression. Cranial osteopathy is often used to treat babies who might have had a traumatic birth or be suffering from colic.

DIY Health Checks

As well as being routinely aware of the day-to-day wellness of your body you should also carry out some specific health checks on a regular basis; they will only take a couple of minutes. It makes sense to choose a regular time to look for any warning signs and, of course, if you do spot anything amiss, to make an immediate appointment to see your doctor.

Skin

The sooner skin cancer is detected the better and the warning signs to look for are changes in the colour or texture of the skin, in particular any moles or freckles which might suddenly seem darker, bleed, itch or change shape.

Mouth

Any patches on the tongue – either red and inflamed or persistent and white – that fail to clear up after a couple of weeks are a cause for concern, as are bleeding and inflamed gums, which can be a sign of infection. Other conditions pre-indicated by oral problems are diabetes, anaemia and some vitamin deficiency. See your doctor or dentist in the first instance.

Bowels

Your poo says a lot about the health of your gut, and with bowel cancer the second biggest cause of cancer deaths in the UK, it is plain foolish not to keep an eye on what you flush away. Not least because this will make it easy to notice any changes in your bowel habits; any sudden attack of constipation or diarrhoea that lasts longer than a fortnight warrants making an appointment with your doctor, as does the appearance of any black tarry material in your stools which could indicate the presence of blood.

There is enormous variation in people's bowel habits and frequency. The ideal 'Call to Stool' is when you feel you need to go but are not worried you are going to be caught short, when you sit on the loo and it happens without delay and without any straining, when the process is effortless and comfortable and afterwards you feel simply pleasant relief!

Fewer than half of us are regular once-a-dayers and while some people might defecate two or three times a day, others only go two or three times a week. It's generally accepted that food hanging around in the gut for several days is not a healthy thing but, by the same token, there is no guarantee that twenty-four-hour regularity means that all is well, Much better is to consider the type of stool you are passing, and conveniently there is a Bristol Stool Form Scale to check yours against!

- Type One – separate hard lumps like nuts
- Type Two – sausage-like but lumpy
- Type Three – like a sausage but with cracks in the surface
- Type Four – like a sausage or snake but smooth and soft
- Type Five – soft blobs with clear cut edges
- Type Six – mushy stool of fluffy pieces with ragged edges
- Type Seven – watery with no solid pieces

The ideal stool types are three and four with type one having spent longest in the stomach and seven the least amount of time.

Breast Examination

It's recommended that all women over the age of twelve should examine their breasts once a month in the week after their period when the breasts are least tender and, of course, see your doctor immediately if you notice anything untoward.

How to do a breast examination

- First make a visual examination of the breasts while undressed and look for changes in shape, colour and skin texture and also check for any signs of discharge from or changes to the nipples.
- Raise your arms and repeat the visual checks.
- Then while standing or sitting examine your left breast with your right hand while your left arm is raised.
- You should use the pads of three fingers for the examination, moving them in small circles and using different levels of pressure.
- Make the movement continuous over the whole breast and make sure you don't lift the fingers from the skin. Repeat the same process on the right breast.
- Pay particular attention to the area between the top outside quarter of the breast and armpit as this is where most breast cancers occur.
- There are many more detailed and illustrated step-by-step guides to breast examination on the internet.

Testicular examination

Make this examination to spot changes in your testicles a routine on the same day of every month. Your testicles will relax if you carry out the examination after a bath or shower. You are looking for lumps or discharge, a change in size and checking for pain, tenderness or any sort of dragging sensation in the groin.

How to do a testicular examination
- Examine them one at a time, first looking for visual changes in a mirror. It is normal for there to be slight differences in the size or drop of each.
- Use gentle pressure to feel each testicle individually and you should be able to feel a soft oval-shaped ball. Check for any lumps or swelling.
- Next feel the epididymis, which is a duct fixed along the top of each testicle. It should feel soft and slightly bumpy.

You should see your doctor immediately if you find any lump or swelling, even if there is no pain, also if you experience a sense of heaviness or a dull ache in your groin, scrotum, lower abdomen or lower back. You should also seek medical help if there is a sore or small area on the shaft or tip of your penis that doesn't heal. Don't be embarrassed about getting advice; remember, it's better to be safe than sorry!

First Aid

What if you have to react to an incident or emergency in the home and administer some first-aid treatment yourself? We are all capable of taking a painkiller or dabbing antiseptic cream on a cut but how many of us know what to do if something more serious occurs? There are very good basic first-aid courses run all around the country which can take as little time as just a couple of hours, but if you can't find the time to take one of these at least buy yourself a first-aid emergency guide and keep it with your First Aid Kit, which should be stored in a secure cupboard or box well out of children's reach.

The following guidelines are just the basics you should know for treating adults, recommended by the Red Cross.

You should treat **burns or scalds** as quickly as possible under a cold running tap for at least ten minutes, then raise the injury above the level of the heart to reduce swelling, cover with a clean pad or kitchen film and seek medical advice.

If an adult has a **choking** fit, encourage them first to cough and if that doesn't clear the obstruction, make them lean forward and give them five short slaps between the shoulder blades. If that fails, make a fist and place it above their navel, below their breastbone and pull it sharply inwards up to five times with the other hand. Check their mouth and remove anything you can see. Stay calm and repeat both procedures up to three times and then call an ambulance.

If someone appears to be having a **heart attack**, make them sit down, call an ambulance immediately and, if they are conscious, give them an aspirin to chew.

If someone is **unconscious**, speak to them clearly and give them a gentle shake by the shoulders. Check their airway is open by placing one hand on their forehead to steady their head and gently tilt it backwards. Remove any obvious obstruction, such as dentures or a gum shield, and then using the fingertips of the other hand, lift their chin, which should bring the tongue back into its normal position and leave the airway open. Listen for breathing by putting your ear close to their mouth and nose or see if you can feel their breath on your cheek. Look to see if their chest is rising and falling over ten seconds. If they are breathing, put them into **the recovery position** by taking the arm nearest to you, bending it at the shoulder and elbow, placing the palm upwards, so the upper arm is at a right angle to the body. Then bring the other arm across their body, take hold of the hand and place it palm downwards, against the person's cheek closest to you. Keep holding their hand against the cheek and, with your other hand, take hold of the leg furthest away from you, just above the knee, and pull it up until the foot is flat on the floor. When you pull on the knee the person will roll towards you. Finally make sure their head is tilted back and the airway is open. Any vomit or blood in their mouth can then be drained away.

If they are not breathing, call an ambulance immediately and then begin **rescue breathing**. You must initially give two rescue breaths and should make five attempts. Kneel next to the person and make sure their airway is open. Bring your hand down from their forehead and pinch their nose tightly. Take a breath and place your mouth around the person's mouth and blow steadily and gently. Take your mouth away and watch the chest fall. There is no need to rush this procedure. Allow the chest to rise and fall. After the initial rescue breaths, check for signs of circulation – breathing, coughing or movement of the limbs. If none are present, start **chest compressions** which stimulate the heart. Kneel alongside the person and find the inverted V-notch at the bottom of the breastbone. Place two fingers on the breastbone, just above the notch and place the heel of the other hand on the breastbone alongside these two fingers. Remove your two fingers and place this hand on top of your other hand. Interlock your fingers. Lean over the person with your arms straight and press down 4–5 cm. Press fifteen times and aim for a rate of 100 times per minute. Continue to deliver two breaths followed by fifteen compressions until an ambulance arrives. Note: this is for an adult casualty only. Different ratios apply to children under eight.

If not treated promptly, **severe bleeding** can result in shock and, in a small number of cases, prove fatal. The severity will depend on the location, size and depth of the wound. Some parts of the body, for example the scalp, appear to bleed heavily when in fact the blood loss is not significant. When treating a severe bleed, your aims are to stop it as quickly as possible, prevent the onset of shock and minimise the risk of infection. Check to see if any object is embedded in the wound. Do not remove it if there is and press either side of it, building up the padding, when carrying out the following procedure. To stop the bleeding, quickly place pressure directly on the wound using your hand (where there isn't an object), the person's own hand or a clean pad, if available. At the same time, raise the injured limb above the level of the heart. This helps to reduce blood flow by using gravity, and ensures essential organs are kept adequately supplied.

If you suspect **a fracture**, make sure the injured person stays still and supports the affected area with their hands. If firmer support is needed, bandage the injured part of the body to an unaffected part, checking the circulation every ten minutes to make sure it is not too tight. Call an ambulance.

If someone is **electrocuted**, turn off the current at the mains immediately if you can safely reach it. If not, stand on some dry insulation material, such as a telephone directory, and separate the casualty from the electrical source with something that is made from insulation material, such as a broom handle.

First Aid Kit

adhesive microtape

alcohol-free antiseptic wipes

assorted adhesive plasters

bandages (two) for sprains, strains and to keep pads in place

crepe roller bandages

disposable plastic tweezers

emergency foil blanket

eyewash solution

forehead strip thermometer

non-fluffy absorbent gauze

note pad and pencil for noting any information that needs to be passed to the doctor or emergency services

safety pins

scissors

sterile dressing pads in different sizes

sterile eye pads

torch

triangular bandage to use as a sling

tubular bandage

Add to your First Aid box the medications to suit your individual health needs, such as capsule painkillers, dissolvable painkillers, antiseptic cream, hydrocortisone cream, sting/bite spray, antiseptic lotion, calamine lotion, vapo-rub, cough mixture, Immodium, Diarlyte and flu powders. In the absence of any specific emergency items in the kit you can use the following everyday items:

- A bag of frozen peas wrapped in a towel and held on a sprain or strain for ten minutes will help reduce swelling.

- Cling film used to gently cover a burn after it's been held under cold water for ten minutes will act as a protective barrier against infection or fluid loss.
- A credit card can be used to scrape away any visible part of an insect sting and won't cause any further poison to go into the skin.
- A bathroom full of steam from a bath full of hot water should create enough steam to ease an attack of baby croup. If it persists, take the infant to hospital.
- Natural yogurt is really good at easing the irritation of thrush/athletes foot.

Fitness

It's a fact that you can be fit but not healthy and healthy but not fit, which is the sort of irritating, smug thing that very healthy *and* fit people say. They're unlikely to be reading this as they're probably snacking on fruit on their way back from the gym, and they're already very well informed about fitness facts, but if you're anything like me (and I'm not one of those people), you will probably agree that it's quite hard to get a handle on what is likely to constitute being just healthy and fit enough for *you*.

Your basic level of fitness is dictated by your genes, your age and body type, and lifestyle factors such as whether you smoke and what you eat. The good news about it is that it's never too late to start improving your level of fitness and almost immediately you will reap the benefits. Being fitter will almost definitely improve your health and you will feel better generally. Doh!

There are two sorts of fitness – the sort that will help you *stay* healthy and the sort that taxes your body further than that for other reasons such as job, sport or vanity.

Fitness to help you stay healthy

It's really not breaking news that regular exercise will help you to stay healthy, in fact just regular *moderate* activity will do that.

It will make you less likely to get ill and help keep your weight stable.

Moderate activity is considered to be thirty minutes of exercise at least five times a week. Given the benefits that will bring to the health of your heart, your weight and general demeanour it seems silly not to, doesn't it?

You can get technical about what sort of exercise you do but the fact is that simply walking briskly for half an hour or so that you get a bit puffed and sweaty is a simple and adequate daily fitness regime to start with. Throw appearances to the wind and open and close your arms at chest height as you walk, or add even more fitness value by stopping now and then to incorporate a few gentle shoulder shrugs, arm lifts above your head, some side bends or knee lifts up to your chest.

Forty-four-year-old Marie found her simple solution: 'When I first decided to try to get fitter I didn't have the time or money to sort out gym membership or play sport so I decided to start by walking home from work each night, which would take forty-five minutes. I changed into a tracksuit at the office and would ring my husband when I was ten minutes from home. The benchmark I set myself was that the tracksuit would need to go in the washing machine because I'd perspired so much and that I'd only have enough puff to say on the phone, "Put the supper on," or "Crack open the wine."'

If you decide to start an exercise routine to help yourself stay healthy, however simple, follow these few basic rules to get the most out of it.

- First of all seek advice from your doctor if you are unfit.
- Start with what you consider to be an achievable distance or duration of exercise, say five minutes, and build this up over a period of time by a few minutes more each day.
- Wear comfortable and appropriate clothing. It's worth investing in decent footwear and being measured and getting advice from a sports or outdoor walking specialist shop. Fancy Lycra numbers can cost a bomb and won't alter your performance, although the

stretching and pulling that can go on to get into some of the more hard-core outfits could, I suppose, be classed as a warm-up of sorts.

- Don't launch yourself into frenetic movement straight away. Make sure you warm up by either starting to walk more quickly, at a steady comfortable rate for the first few minutes or by doing some gentle skipping or running on the spot. The idea behind warming up is literally to get your muscles warmed and to prepare the rest of your body for imminent exercise.
- Once warmed up use your exercise time to flex more than just your legs by swinging your arms.
- At the end allow yourself a cooling-down period of a couple of minutes of stretching the muscles you've worked to avoid getting aches and pains later.
- You'll benefit different parts of your body if you build in a variety of types of activity, such as swimming, skipping or dancing.

If you are keeping fit just to stay healthy, apart from the thirty minutes of moderate activity five times a week, also be aware of your general activity levels. It doesn't matter what your circumstances or age, it's an easy fix to build movement into each and every moment of the day. Here's just a few ideas:

- Always take the stairs and avoid lifts and escalators. If you must use the latter, walk up it rather than standing still.
- Walk, cycle, jog to work or at least get off the bus a couple of stops before your destination.
- When you walk, walk faster than usual.
- Use commercial breaks while watching TV to some exercises.
- Lie on the floor anyway while wathcing TV and do leg lifts and stretches, alternating sides of the body. It'll irritate the rest of the family like mad but will do you good.
- Walk to the shops each day to buy milk and the papers instead of having them delivered.
- If you have time on your hands, shop daily – walking, of course.
- When thinking of taking up a new interest consider if it brings with it exercise opportunities.

- Walk children to school – it will encourage good road sense too.
- Instead of going to the canteen or pub in your lunch hour at work, go for a walk with colleagues and take some sandwiches and a drink.
- Even better, when the weather is fine, and you need to have a meeting to discuss something, consider walking while talking in a local park.
- Use every opportunity, even when sat in traffic jams in the car, to flex abdominal muscles or tense and relax your pelvic muscles.
- Think physical with the duster. Did you know that half an hour of ironing burns off 45 calories, window cleaning 84 calories, and that the same length of time doing some physical work in the garden equals 159 calories?

Think laterally too about how improving your fitness level with regular moderate activity can benefit other parts of your life, such as your relationships.

Tom and Rebecca decided to make an hour-long walk with their three children part of their weekend routine. 'It's become a real sort of catch-up time for all of us, away from home with all its distractions and chores. Although the kids grumbled at first it's something we all enjoy now, being out in the fresh air together, the cobwebs getting blown away and chatting about all sorts while we walk. We feel we've missed something if we don't do it.'

Extra Fitness

If you set yourself fitness goals you will be doing more than helping yourself to *stay* healthy. You'll be *improving* your health alongside raising your performance in sport or changing your body shape.

Overall physical fitness exercising has five different components. They are; cardiovascular which will improve your stamina; muscular strengthening which will make you strong; muscular endurance which will give you speed; flexibility which will keep you supple; and motor skills which help maintain coordination.

You need to decide what you want to improve and so what sort of fitness activity is going to work for you. Don't buy into the latest fitness fad, think what activities you enjoy. You may need to think back to when you were a child and remember if there was something you did then you found fun. Things to consider:

- Are you likely to be a solitary exerciser?
- Or would you be more motivated in a group or find it more fun?
- Do you need the discipline of a class?
- When in your week are you going to be able to exercise?
- How hard you are going to work at it?
- How long will each session last?
- Over what period of time are you going to maintain the exercise regime and when will you review it?
- How much will it cost financially?
- Which of the five fitness components do you feel you need to particularly improve upon?
- What form will you exercise take?

With some thought you should be able to have an idea of what sort of activity will be appropriate for you. The good news is that most fitness trainers would say an eight-week programme of regular exercise will show your body changing, losing fat and gaining muscle tone, stamina, strength and suppleness. This is not an over-facing amount of time so decide on a plan and determine to review it and your achievement in two months' time.

On your own

There are lots of exercise routines you can do on your own, without joining a gym or leisure centre. Walking, jogging, cycling either on a proper bike or on a stationary one at home, skipping, swimming or working-out to an exercise or dance DVD are all things you can do alone. You just need to make sure you are exerting yourself enough to get the fitness benefits. So for example with walking, try hill walking which will use more energy, or power walking where you walk really fast. Before you set off on your own, though, talk to someone else who does it and get expert advance about right shoes and techniques. Or if you choose to swim, use different strokes so that you give different parts of your body exercise; buy some goggles and get your head down to power through the water rather than glide leisurely up and down the pool.

Gym

A good gym will provide you, whatever age you are or however unfit, with the right environment, equipment and knowledgeable experts to help you get fitter – *if* you go regularly.

Before you sign up for gym membership, spend a week really thinking about the times you will go there and gauge your reaction to that as a reality in your daily timetable. It may be worth checking with your doctor to see if an 'exercise on prescription' programme operates in your area. This is a referral scheme where your GP sends you to a local fitness centre for a supervised exercise programme for eight weeks.

If the gym is for you, familiarise yourself with all it offers: classes, personal-training supervision, the equipment and how it all works. In your assessment ask the trainers to help you devise a programme that will suit your aims and agree when it will be reviewed and adapted as you progress. It's important your trainer is properly qualified.

There are different types and benefits of exercise classes and facilities. **Aerobic** is the best all-round form of exercise for both improving fitness and losing weight. It involves continuous and rhythmic movement, mainly using the larger muscles, and makes you breathe harder, sweat a little and raise your heart rate. **Aqua fitness** is a good option if you are concerned about stress on joints from more traditional impact aerobics and is a good option for older people, those with disabilities and pregnant women. **Resistance exercise** involves lifting free weights, weights machines, callisthenics (e.g. push-ups, chin-ups, sit-ups). This form of exercise will predominantly help to improve the strength and tone of your muscles. Because it will increase the amount of muscle in your body it will boost your metabolic rate, which means that you will burn more calories, so there may be some weight loss too. **Flexibility and Stretching** exercises, such as yoga, t'ai chi, Pilates, work well to improve joint flexibility and will improve posture and suppleness. There are many different sorts or schools of yoga and this sort of exercise is more 'holistic' than others, working towards a mind/body harmony. Most of the exercises involve stretching and bending and many can be done at home alone once you've mastered the moves.

Sport

Sport is a great way to get fit because it also helps improve balance and coordination and is likely to be sociable and fun. You may have been put off sport at school and given it a wide berth ever since, but if you have time for it and want to improve your fitness it's worth investigating all the different options to see if you can kick-start your sporty gene back into life.

It's pretty obvious which sports will be more energetic than others and so burn more calories, etc. Much more important is that you choose a sport you really engage in. The sport ethos is about much, much more than fitness and weight loss. Or so I'm told. This, of course, from someone who likes to read and cook above anything involving bats or balls.

But there's something to suit everyone, from full-on, energetic team games and contact and ball sports, to considered and steadily paced activities such as golf or bowling. Almost all sports are do-able at all ages to a greater or lesser extent, all have associations and clubs that can advise on training and local activities, and all will be multi-layered enough for you to choose how much or how little involved you want to get. You may just want a Sunday morning kick around, or you may want to learn from scratch. If there's something that appeals then take your curiosity to the next level. Always ask how fit you need to be in the first

Joining a gym

place to play a sport as you may be advised to tone up and exercise beforehand.

Fitness and Ageing

I'm trying very hard in this book not to single out particular age groups for specific advice in any area because I just don't think it works like that very often in our lives now. However, fitness is an exception because there might be physical aspects of getting older that mean you should approach exercise more carefully. With the wisdom of your years I'm sure you will have worked that out for yourself!

Time passing may have made you more sedentary, plumper or maybe even turned you into a bit of a stick-in-the-mud, so I do feel righteous in saying that exercise and fitness do have even greater rewards for older people. (Sorry about that if you're rather enjoying your relationship with the remote control.) Not only will it bring health advantages but it will also recharge your energy supplies, and if you're not sleeping well it will probably help there too; plus it should take you out of yourself, which is a very good thing for ageing curmudgeons.

Learning to play golf after retirement transformed seventy-five-year-old Patrick's life. 'I'd resisted learning earlier because I'd always felt I was too busy, which I regret now, I can heartily recommend it for both men and women to take up at any age, because you can either learn one on one or in a group and the handicap system means you can play with others of differing ability. It is good steady exercise, with each full game being more than seven miles of walking in the fresh air. It doesn't require you to be an athlete and it's challenging mentally as well as sociable.'

Mental Agility and Fitness

This is not just for older people. Those in their twenties happily embrace the idea of keeping fit physically but don't spend much time thinking about that other big muscle, the brain, that needs fitness maintenance. As you get older you become more forgetful which is absolutely infuriating when you find you can't recall the simplest things. To keep the mind fit, it's important to ensure you get plenty of sleep, fresh air and physical exercise, but if, as well, you give your brain a bit of a daily workout too you'll find you probably boost your memory power.

Exercise your brain. Get into a regular habit of doing crosswords or word/number puzzles. Don't give up easily on books or articles that are complicated – struggle on with them. Learn a poem verse by verse over a period of days. Look at a picture and then turn it over and see how many facts you can remember about it. Play games that test your skills of recall, such as Scrabble or Trivial Pursuit.

Finding time to exercise

It's important to be realistic about your commitment to the exercise you decide to do to keep fit. There is no point setting an objective to go for a run every morning before work and then beating yourself up about your failure to do so time and time again because you just can't fit it into your morning routine.

If you are a 'lark', get up half an hour earlier, or whatever it takes to carry out your chosen exercise routine; if you're an owl, choose an activity for after work.

Be organised about your kit. Maybe have several sets, keeping one at home, one in the office, one in the wash. This to include washbags and towels. Keep a kitbag in the car in case an opportunity comes up for a run or swim when you are out and about. If the rest of your life is pretty well timetabled, and you're keen on charts, diarise your fitness times and fill in a Fitness Planner, such as the one in *The Life Audit*, maybe charting some goals.

Diet and weight loss

You almost definitely won't be reading this unless you want to lose weight and, first off, what do you think I am going to tell you that you don't know already? There are whole forests of diet books and plans available. Come on, Fatty, you and I both know that the chances are that your overweight probably comes down to the very simple truth that you eat too much of the wrong things and don't exercise enough. (Obviously, apologies to anyone who does have a thyroid problem or other medical condition, and if you suspect that could be a reason for your personal load bearing, then go and see your doctor.)

Some truths you know already:

- Being overweight has a direct bearing on your health.
- It's worth taking some time out to assess your eating and trying to spot any patterns or triggers that encourage bad habits.
- Keeping a food diary and spending some time planning your menus for the week are helpful things to do, leaving you no place to hide from your gluttony.
- Likewise, with an exercise diary.
- Identify why you are eating too much. Is it to satisfy a feeling removed from basic hunger? Is it loneliness, anxiety, depression or even celebration? Refer to the relevant area in the book for advice on fixes to relationships, image, work or leisure, etc.

In the plethora of diet and weight-loss advice the most sensible thing that is said is about the importance of having a *balanced* diet where food intake fuels the energy you expend maintaining your body's vitamin and mineral requirements to stay healthy.

A Balanced Diet

There are basically five different categories of food and getting the balance right does not mean equal amounts of each. Doctors agree that your diet should contain some of each of the following in decreasing proportions:

1. **Foods containing starch and fibre** which are rich in vitamins from the B complex. Bread, potatoes, pasta, rice, noodles and cereals – preferably choose wholegrain varieties that have the highest fibre.
2. **Fruit and vegetables**, fresh, frozen or canned, and salad vegetables too. You should aim to eat at least five portions of these a day to ensure a good intake of vitamins, minerals and fibre. One portion equals one tablespoon of small vegetables, an apple or banana, a slice of large fruit such as melon or pineapple, a small bowl of small fruits such as strawberries or grapes, a tablespoon of dried fruit, a medium bowl of salad, a couple of tomatoes or a glass of fruit or vegetable juice.
3. **Milk and dairy foods** including cheese, yoghurt and milk which are rich in protein, calcium, vitamins and minerals. You should aim for just two to three servings of these each day and where possible choose low-fat varieties.
4. **Fish, meat, poultry or pulses** should be eaten approximately twice a day. Oily fish, such as mackerel and sardines, are especially good for you and should feature a couple of times a week, while lean red meat will provide you with iron and vitamins B12. Pulses include lentils, beans and nuts.
5. **Foods containing fat and sugar** such as butter, cream, oils, ice cream, cakes, biscuits, chocolate, sugary drinks and crisps. These should be eaten in moderation and healthy options sought where possible.

On paper it seems pretty straightforward, doesn't it? But inevitably in each group there are foods that will be better for you than others.

Vitamins and supplements

The science of a healthy balanced diet is to ensure that you get the minerals and vitamins your body needs. Diet is particularly important with regard to vitamins, because, apart from vitamin D and the B vitamin niacin, most can't be made by your body.

Vitamins A, D, E and K can be stored for a short time in your fat and liver cells but vitamins B and C are water soluble and need to be eaten every day as they don't hang around in the body for long.

The following shows you which foodstuffs are good sources of which vitamin and where that benefits the body:

Vitamin A (eyes, nose, throat, lungs and skin) – red and orange foods, such as carrots, pumpkins, sweet potatoes, tomatoes, apricots, mango and dark green leafy vegetables.

Vitamin D (bones and teeth) – mainly sourced from the sun but can be found in small amounts in oily fish and cod liver oil. Oily fish, such as herrings, mackerel, tuna, sardines, and salmon and trout are all good sources of protein and omega three which is good for the heart if eaten twice a week.

Vitamin E (skin, and helps fight free radicals which are molecules that can cause cell damage) – vegetables, poultry, fish, vegetable oils, nuts and seeds.

Vitamin K (helps the blood to clot and the body to make proteins) – sprouts, broccoli, cabbage, spinach, soya oil.

B-complex vitamins (aid metabolism and your blood flow and production) – green vegetables, wholegrains, meat and offal, nuts, vegetable extracts.

Vitamin C (skin and bone collagen production and absorption of iron) – many vegetables and fruit including dark leafy varieties, strawberries, citrus fruit and potatoes.

There is currently a lot of debate about the use of vitamin and mineral supplements but basic good advice seems to be to eat healthily, wellying up intake of those foods that will help any particular problem you have. Take a good multi-vitamin tablet if you want to pill pop and if you are still worried, visit a nutritionist.

Food Labelling

To be an informed consumer, you need to know what you're putting in your mouth. Food labels are there to give you all the information you need. Here's how to read them intelligently.

How to read food labels

Ingredients are listed in descending order of weight. Other words can be used for sugar: fructose, maltose, sucrose, glucose, syrup. 'Carbohydrates' is a catch-all for sugar and starches. Other words can be used for fats – animal fat, non-milk fat, lard, butter, coconut cream or milk, oils of various sorts, cream, egg and egg yolk solids, shortening, whole milk solids. 'Energy' refers to the amount of energy in calories and joules, that you will take in from the product. On average, a healthy woman should have 2,000 and a man 2,500 calories per day. Protein is an important element for body growth and repair, and fibre intake is important for a healthy gut; and finally there is sodium which is, of course, salt and is a serial offender in the Food Police files.

Realising that most of us don't have a PhD in nutrition the Foods Standards Agency has created a simple comparison table of what constitutes a lot and a little of each of the things you should be checking for. This information is per 100 g of a produce, so if you are reading the label of a ready meal, for example, you may have to work in multiples of 100 g.

A Lot	A Little
10 g of sugars	2 g of sugars
20 g of fat	3 g of fat
5 g of saturates	1 g of saturates
3 g of fibre	0.5 g of fibre
0.5 g of sodium	0.1 g of sodium

The quantities given below are a very rough guide to the recommended daily amounts of calories and nutrients for an average man or woman. So, for example, if a ready meal contains 50 g of fat, you know that it has over half the recommended amount of fat for the day if you're a man and more than two thirds if you're a woman.

Men	Women
Energy = 2,500 kcal	Energy = 2,000 kcal
Sugars = 70 g	Sugars = 50 g
Fat = 95 g	Fat = 70 g
of which saturates = 30 g	of which saturates = 20 g
Fibre = 20 g	Fibre = 16 g
Sodium = 2.5 g	Sodium = 2 g

Weight

So if you are confident you're eating a balanced diet, how do you know if you are overweight? The charts on the facing page show where in the weight range you fall.

You can also work out your Body Mass index.

- Work out your height in metres and multiply the figure by itself.
- Measure your weight in kilograms.
- Divide the weight by the height squared (which is the answer to the first question).
- That gives you your BMI.

Underweight is a BMI of less than 19.
Ideal is a BMI of 20–25.
Overweight is a BMI of 25–30.
Obese is a BMI of 30–40.
Very obese is a BMI of more than 40.

The above figures will not apply if you are very muscly or an athlete, pregnant or breastfeeding, or very frail.

How to lose weight – the common sense way
If you decide to lose weight, the following eating, cooking and eating-out best-practice tips will also help:

Men

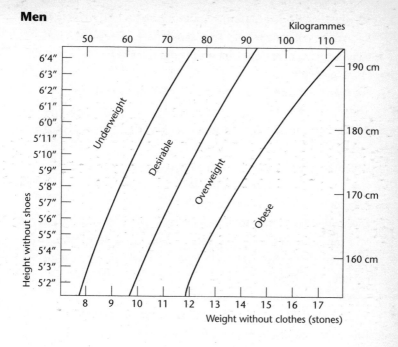

Women

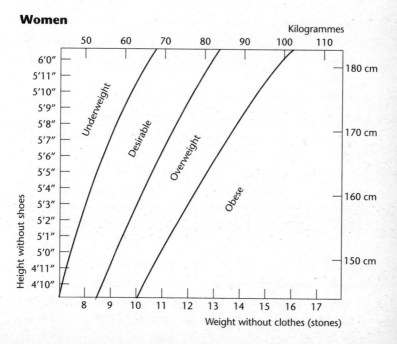

- Serve yourself smaller portions and refuse second helpings.
- Regularise your mealtimes and don't snack in between.
- Whenever you can, eat fruit and vegetables raw.
- Drink plenty of water.
- Try doing without sugar in hot drinks – your taste buds adjust very quickly.
- Avoid frying food; try grilling, poaching, dry roasting, or baking instead.
- Grill and roast meat on a rack so that the fat drips away.
- Use a separator jug so that the fat floats to the top and the meat juices alone can be poured out.
- Make stews and casseroles a day ahead and allow to cool so that you can remove the fat that sets on top before reheating.
- Use non-stick pans and brown meat by stirring over a gentle heat without adding oil.
- Use the light spray oil in cooking.
- Try pureeing fresh fruit with a little honey and spreading it on soft bread instead of using shop-bought jam and butter.
- Also try these other healthier substitutes: frozen yogurt for ice cream, dried fruit instead of sweets, dark organic chocolate in place of full-milk bars, vintage cheese instead of processed, raw nuts instead of salted peanuts, and oat and fruit bars instead of flapjacks.
- Choose low-fat versions of spreads and dressings – but always check the sugar content and overall calorific value.
- In restaurants, always ask for dressings and sauces to be served on the side.
- If you are eating French – choose provençal dishes that have lots of tomatoes, peppers and onions rather than creamy sauces.
- Italian – avoid the pasta with the cheesy creamy sauce, instead opt for pesto sauces and grilled offal or chicken.
- Indian – try the curries of vegetables and pulses or simple tandoori chicken and NOT the korma and coconut-based curries or the deep-fried samosas and bhajis.
- Chinese – forget the deep-fried spring rolls and dumplings – choose instead stir-fried vegetables, dry spare ribs or clear soups.

- English – go for the fish option, preferably without the batter, or some lean roast beef with a big spud and some steamed brassicas. Have the gravy served on the side.

Josh had business lunches regularly at the same restaurant and bravely told the maître d' that, whatever he ordered from the menu, he was always actually to be served plain grilled fish and a salad, and that his wine glass was to be kept topped up with water. 'Of course everyone thought I was mad, but it worked. I'd salivate over something on the menu but be stuck into business talk by the time the food arrived and not notice that it wasn't laden with sauces. I noticed the difference within a week.'

Common sense dieting is all about balance and being informed. So getting adept at reading food labels is crucial, as is having a rough grasp of the relative merits of basic foodstuffs. Calorie counting may feel old-fashioned compared to the latest fad diet, but it's still a useful tool for the down-to-earth dieter. So, here is a table showing you the amount of calories, fat, fibre and carbohydrates in main foodstuffs. Don't get obsessed with any of this information but do use the table as a reference tool to enable you to make healthier choices. (The letter N in the fibre column indicates that there is no reliable data available.)

Specific	Amount	Kcals	Carb	Prot	Fat	Fibre
FRUIT						
Apple	1 medium [112 g]	47.0	11.8	0.4	0.1	2.0
Apricot, raw	1 [65 g]	20.0	5.5	0.2	0.1	1.2
Avocado	1 medium [145 g]	275.0	2.8	2.8	28.3	4.9
Banana	1 medium [150 g]	143.0	34.8	1.8	0.5	4.5
Blackberries, raw	100 g	25.0	5.1	0.9	0.2	6.6
Blackcurrants, raw	100 g	28.0	6.6	0.9	trace	7.8
Cherries, raw	100 g	48.0	11.5	0.9	0.1	1.5
Clementines	1 medium [60 g]	22.0	5.2	0.5	0.1	1.0
Damsons	100 g	34.0	8.6	0.5	trace	3.3
Dates, dried	100 g	227.0	57.1	2.8	0.2	6.5
Dates, raw	100 g	107.0	26.9	1.3	0.1	3.1
Figs, semi-dried, ready to eat	100 g	209.0	48.6	3.3	1.5	11.4

Specific	Amount	Kcals	Carb	Prot	Fat	Fibre
Gooseberries	100 g	19.0	3.0	1.1	0.4	2.9
Grapefruit	1 medium	68.0	15.6	1.7	0.3	3.7
Grapes	100 g	60.0	15.4	0.4	0.1	0.8
Kiwi fruit	1 [60 g]	29.0	6.3	0.7	0.3	1.1
Lemon	1 medium [125 g]	24.0	4.0	1.3	0.3	5.9
Lychees, raw	100 g	58.0	14.3	0.9	0.1	1.5
Mango, raw	100 g	57.0	14.1	0.7	0.2	2.9
Melon, canteloupe	100 g	19.0	4.2	0.6	0.1	0.9
Melon, galia	100 g	24.0	5.6	0.5	0.1	0.9
Melon, honeydew	100 g	28.0	6.6	0.6	0.1	0.8
Melon, watermelon	100 g	31.0	7.1	0.5	0.3	0.3
Mixed fruit, dried	100 g	268.0	68.1	2.3	0.4	6.4
Nectarines	1 medium [140 g]	56.0	12.6	2.0	0.1	3.1
Olives, in brine	100 g	103.0	trace	0.9	11.0	4.0
Oranges	1 medium [160 g]	59.0	13.6	2.2	0.2	2.9
Passion fruit	100 g	36.0	5.8	2.6	0.4	3.3
Peaches	1 medium [110 g]	36.0	8.4	1.1	0.1	2.5
Pears	1 medium [200 g]	80.0	20.0	0.6	0.2	4.4
Peel, mixed dried	100 g	231.0	59.1	0.3	0.9	4.8
Pineapple, raw	100 g	41.0	10.1	0.4	0.2	1.3
Plums, raw	1 medium [55 g]	19.0	4.6	0.3	0.1	1.3
Prunes, semi-dried, ready to eat	100 g	141.0	34.0	2.5	0.4	12.8
Raspberries, raw	100 g	25.0	4.6	1.4	0.3	6.7
Rhubarb, raw	100 g	7.0	0.8	0.9	0.1	2.3
Satsumas	1 medium [70 g]	25.0	6.0	0.6	0.1	1.2
Strawberries, raw	100 g	27.0	6.0	0.8	0.1	2.0
Sultanas	100 g	275.0	69.4	2.7	0.4	6.3
Tangerines	1 medium [70 g]	25.0	5.6	0.6	0.1	1.2
VEGETABLES						
Asparagus, raw	100 g	25.0	2.0	2.9	0.6	1.7
Aubergine, raw	100 g	15.0	2.2	0.9	0.4	2.3
Bamboo shoots, canned	100 g	39.0	9.7	0.7	0.0	1.0
Beans						
baked, canned in tomato sauce	100 g	84.0	15.3	5.2	0.6	6.9
broad, boiled	100 g	81.0	11.7	7.9	0.6	6.5
French, boiled	100 g	25.0	4.7	1.7	0.1	4.1
Red kidney, canned	100 g	100.0	17.8	6.9	0.6	8.5
Runner, raw	100 g	22.0	3.2	1.6	0.4	2.6

Health

Specific	Amount	Kcals	Carb	Prot	Fat	Fibre
Beansprouts, raw	100 g	31.0	4.0	2.9	0.5	5.6
Beetroot, boiled	100 g	46.0	9.5	2.3	0.1	2.3
Beetroot, pickled	100 g	28.0	5.6	1.2	0.2	2.5
Brussels sprouts, boiled	100 g	35.0	3.5	2.9	1.3	2.6
Cabbage, boiled	100 g	18.0	2.5	0.8	0.6	2.5
Carrots, boiled	100 g	22.0	4.4	0.6	0.4	2.7
Cauliflower, boiled	100 g	28.0	2.1	2.9	0.9	1.6
Celery	100 g	7.0	0.9	0.5	0.2	1.6
Chickpeas, canned	100 g	115.0	16.1	7.2	2.9	4.1
Chicory	100 g	11.0	2.8	0.5	0.6	0.9
Courgette, boiled	100 g	19.0	2.0	2.0	0.4	1.2
Cucumber	100 g	10.0	1.5	0.7	0.1	0.7
Fennel, boiled	100 g	11.0	1.5	0.9	0.2	2.3
Garlic, raw	100 g	98.0	16.3	7.9	0.6	4.1
Gherkins	100 g	14.0	2.6	0.9	0.1	1.2
Hummus	100 g	187.0	11.6	7.6	12.6	3.2
Leeks, boiled	100 g	21.0	2.6	1.2	0.7	2.4
Lentils, green & brown, dried, boiled	100 g	105.0	16.9	8.8	0.7	3.8
Lentils, red, dried & boiled	100 g	100.0	17.5	7.6	0.4	3.3
Lettuce	100 g	14.0	1.7	0.8	0.5	1.3
Mushrooms, raw	100 g	135.0	0.4	1.8	0.5	2.3
Mustard & cress	100 g	13.0	0.4	1.6	0.6	3.3
Onions, raw	100 g	36.0	7.9	1.2	0.2	1.5
Parsnips, boiled	100 g	66.0	12.9	1.6	1.2	4.4
Peas, boiled	100 g	69.0	9.7	6.0	0.9	7.3
Mange tout, raw	100 g	32.0	4.2	3.6	0.2	4.2
Peppers, raw	100 g	20.0	0.7	2.9	0.6	1.9
Potatoes, chips						
homemade	100 g	189.0	30.1	3.9	6.7	3.0
oven, baked	100 g	162.0	29.8	3.2	4.2	2.8
Potatoes, new, boiled in skins	100 g	66.0	15.4	1.4	0.3	1.3
Potatoes, old, baked with skin	100 g	136.0	31.7	3.9	0.2	2.7
Potatoes, old, roast	100 g	149.0	25.9	2.9	4.5	2.4
Pumpkin, raw	100 g	13.0	2.2	0.7	0.2	0.5
Quorn	100 g	86.0	2.0	11.8	3.5	4.8
Radish	100 g	12.0	1.9	0.7	0.2	0.9
Spinach, raw	100 g	25.0	1.6	2.8	0.8	3.9
Spring greens, raw	100 g	33.0	3.1	3.0	1.0	6.1
Spring onions, raw	100 g	23.0	3.0	2.0	0.5	1.5

Nutrition values

Specific	Amount	Kcals	Carb	Prot	Fat	Fibre
Swede, boiled	100 g	11.0	2.3	0.3	0.1	1.2
Sweet potato, boiled	100 g	84.0	20.5	1.1	0.3	2.3
Sweetcorn, canned	1 tbsp [30 g]	122.0	26.6	2.9	1.2	3.9
Tofu, steamed	100 g	73.0	0.7	8.1	4.2	0.3
Tomato puree	100 g	68.0	12.9	4.5	0.2	2.8
Tomatoes, canned	100 g	16.0	3.0	1.0	0.1	0.8
Tomatoes, raw	100 g	17.0	3.1	0.7	0.3	1.3
Watercress	100 g	22.0	0.4	3.0	1.0	3.0

NUTS AND SEEDS

Specific	Amount	Kcals	Carb	Prot	Fat	Fibre
Almonds	100 g	612.0	6.9	21.1	55.8	12.9
Brazil nuts	100 g	682.0	3.1	14.1	68.2	8.1
Cashew nuts, roasted & salted	100 g	611.0	18.8	20.5	50.9	3.2
Hazelnuts	100 g	650.0	6.0	14.1	63.5	8.9
Macadamia nuts	100 g	748.0	4.8	7.9	77.6	5.3
Mixed nuts	100 g	607.0	7.9	22.9	54.1	7.5
Peanuts, plain	100 g	564.0	12.5	25.6	46.1	7.3
Peanuts, roasted, salted	100 g	602.0	7.1	24.5	53.0	6.9
Peanuts, dry roasted	100 g	589.0	10.3	25.5	49.8	7.4
Pecan nuts	100 g	689.0	5.8	9.2	70.1	4.7
Pine nuts	100 g	688.0	4.0	14.0	68.6	1.9
Pistachio nuts	100 g	331.0	4.6	9.9	30.5	3.3
Walnuts	100 g	688.0	3.3	14.7	68.5	5.9
Nut-based products						
Marzipan, bought	100 g	404.0	67.6	5.3	14.4	3.2
Peanut butter, smooth	100 g	623.0	13.1	22.6	53.7	6.8
Sesame seeds	100 g	578.0	0.9	18.2	58.0	7.9
Sunflower seeds	100 g	581.0	18.6	19.8	47.5	6.0
Tahini	100 g	607.0	0.9	18.5	58.9	8.0

CEREALS & CEREAL PRODUCTS
Biscuits

Specific	Amount	Kcals	Carb	Prot	Fat	Fibre
Chocolate, assorted	100 g	524.0	67.4	5.7	27.6	2.9
Digestives	1 biscuit	73.0	9.8	1.0	3.3	0.6
Digestives, plain chocolate	1 biscuit	85.0	10.0	1.3	4.4	0.5
Gingernuts	100 g	456.0	79.1	5.6	15.2	4.7
Hobnobs	1 biscuit	72.0	9.6	1.0	3.2	N
Mini Cheddars	100 g	534.0	52.9	11.3	30.2	2.3

Specific	Amount	Kcals	Carb	Prot	Fat	Fibre
Bread						
Brown, average	25 g slice	55.0	1.8	2.0	0.5	1.5
Croissant, plain	1 average [50 g]	180.0	19.2	4.2	10.2	1.3
Crumpets, toasted	1 [40 g]	80.0	17.4	2.7	0.4	1.2
Granary	25 g slice	59.0	11.6	2.3	0.7	1.6
Hovis	25 g slice	53.0	10.4	2.4	0.5	1.3
Malt	35 g slice	93.8	19.9	2.9	0.8	2.3
Pitta	75 g	199.0	43.4	6.9	0.9	2.9
Rolls, brown, soft	1 [43 g]	115.0	22.3	4.3	1.2	2.8
Rolls, hamburger buns	1 [50 g]	132.0	24.4	4.6	2.5	2.0
Rolls, white, soft	1 [45 g]	121.0	23.2	4.4	1.9	1.8
Rolls, wholemeal	1 [45 g]	108.0	21.7	4.1	1.3	4.0
Breakfast cereal						
All-Bran	100 g	261.0	46.6	14.0	3.4	30.0
Bran Flakes	100 g	318.0	69.3	10.2	1.9	17.3
Coco Pops	100 g	384.0	74.0	5.3	1.0	1.1
Corn Flakes	100 g	360.0	88.6	7.9	0.7	3.4
Frosties	100 g	377.0	93.7	5.3	0.5	1.2
Fruit 'n Fibre	100 g	349.0	72.1	9.0	4.7	10.1
Muesli, Swiss style	100 g	363.0	72.2	9.8	5.9	8.1
Porridge with milk	100 g	116.0	13.7	4.8	5.1	0.8
Porridge with water	100 g	49.0	9.0	1.5	1.1	0.8
Shredded Wheat	100 g	325.0	68.3	10.6	3.0	10.1
Special K	100 g	377.0	81.7	15.3	1.0	2.7
Weetabix	100 g	352.0	75.7	11.0	2.7	11.6
Cakes						
Doughnuts, jam	1 [75 g]	252.0	3.4	4.3	10.9	1.9
Doughnuts, ring	1 [60 g]	238.0	28.3	3.7	13.0	1.9
Eclairs	1 [90 g]	356.0	23.5	5.0	27.5	1.4
Fruit, rich	70 g slice	239.0	41.7	2.7	7.7	2.2
Sponge, jam-filled	65 g slice	196.0	41.7	2.7	3.2	0.7
Teacakes	1 [60 g]	197.0	35.0	5.3	5.0	2.8
Crackers, cream	1 [7 g]	31.0	4.8	0.7	1.1	0.2
Crispbread, rye	100 g	321.0	70.6	9.4	2.1	11.6
Flour						
Cornflour	1 level tbsp [20 g]	71.0	18.0	0.1	0.1	trace
Soya, full fat	100 g	447.0	23.5	36.8	23.5	10.7
Soya, low fat	100 g	352.0	28.2	45.3	7.2	13.3
Wheat, brown	100 g	323.0	68.5	12.6	1.8	7.0

Specific	Amount	Kcals	Carb	Prot	Fat	Fibre
Wheat, white, breadmaking	100 g	341.0	75.3	11.5	1.4	3.7
Wheat, white, plain	100 g	341.0	77.7	9.4	1.3	3.6
Wheat, white, self-raising	100 g	330.0	75.6	8.9	1.2	4.1
Wheat, wholemeal	100 g	310.0	63.9	12.7	2.2	8.6
Noodles, egg, boiled	100 g	62.0	13.0	2.2	0.5	1.0
Oatmeal, raw	100 g	375.0	66.0	11.2	9.2	6.8
Pasta						
Macaroni, boiled	100 g	86.0	18.5	3.0	0.5	1.5
Spaghetti, white, boiled	100 g	104.0	22.2	3.6	0.7	1.8
Spaghetti, wholemeal, boiled	100 g	113.0	23.2	4.7	0.9	4.0
Fresh egg pasta	100 g	270.0	49.9	10.5	3.2	1.5
Pastry						
Flaky, cooked	100 g	560.0	45.9	5.6	40.6	2.1
Shortcrust, cooked	100 g	521.0	54.2	6.6	32.3	2.5
Wholemeal, cooked	100 g	499.0	44.6	8.9	32.9	6.0
Rice						
Brown, boiled	100 g	141.0	32.1	2.6	1.1	1.5
White, easy-cook, boiled	100 g	138.0	30.9	2.6	1.3	1.0
EGGS						
Chicken egg						
whole, raw	1, large [57 g]	84.0	trace	7.1	6.2	0.0
MILK AND DAIRY PRODUCTS						
Butter and spreads						
Butter	100 g	737.0	trace	0.5	81.7	0.0
Low fat spread	100 g	390.0	0.5	5.8	40.5	0.0
Cheese						
Brie	100 g	319.0	trace	19.3	26.9	0.0
Camembert	100 g	297.0	trace	20.9	23.7	0.0
Cottage cheese, plain	100 g	98.0	2.1	13.8	3.9	0.0
Cream cheese	100 g	439.0	trace	3.1	47.4	0.0
Dolcelatte	100 g	320.0	0.2	19.2	27.0	0.0
Edam	100 g	333.0	trace	26.0	25.4	0.0
Emmenthal	100 g	401.0	trace	29.0	31.4	trace
Feta	100 g	250.0	1.5	15.6	20.2	0.0
Fromage frais, plain	60 g pot	68.0	3.4	4.1	4.3	0.0
Hard cheese, average	100 g	405.0	0.1	24.7	34.0	0.0

Specific	Amount	Kcals	Carb	Prot	Fat	Fibre
Parmesan	100 g	452.0	trace	39.4	32.7	0.0
Soft cheese, medium fat	100 g	179.0	3.1	9.2	14.5	0.0
Stilton	100 g	411.0	0.1	22.7	35.5	0.0
Cream, fresh						
clotted	100 g	586.0	2.3	1.6	63.5	0.0
double	100 g	449.0	2.7	1.7	48.0	0.0
single	100 g	198.0	4.1	2.6	19.1	0.0
soured	100 g	205.0	3.8	2.9	19.9	0.0
whipping	100 g	373.0	3.1	2.0	39.3	0.0
Ice cream						
Dairy, vanilla	100 g	194.0	24.4	3.6	9.8	trace
Milk, dried						
skimmed	100 g	348.0	52.9	36.1	0.6	0.0
Milk, fresh						
whole	1 pint [585 g]	386	28.1	18.7	22.8	0.0
semi-skimmed	1 pint [585 g]	269.0	29.3	19.3	9.4	0.0
skimmed	1 pint [585 g]	228.0	35.1	22.2	0.6	0.0
soya	1 pint [585 g]	187.0	4.7	17.0	11.1	0.0
Yoghurt						
low-calorie	100 g	41.0	6.0	4.3	0.2	0.0

MEAT AND MEAT PRODUCTS

Specific	Amount	Kcals	Carb	Prot	Fat	Fibre
Bacon						
Gammon joint, raw	100 g	236.0	0.0	17.6	18.3	0.0
Rasher [back], raw	100 g	428.0	0.0	14.2	41.2	0.0
Rasher, streaky, raw	100 g	414.0	0.0	14.6	39.5	0.0
Beef						
Forerib, raw	100 g	290.0	0.0	16.0	25.1	0.0
Mince, raw	100 g	221.0	0.0	18.8	16.2	0.0
Sirloin, raw	100 g	272.0	0.0	16.6	22.8	0.0
Stewing steak, raw	100 g	176.0	0.0	20.2	10.6	0.0
Beefburgers, frozen, raw	100 g	265.0	5.3	15.2	20.5	1.3
Chicken						
Dark meat, raw	100 g	126.0	0.0	19.1	5.5	0.0
Light meat, raw	100 g	116.0	0.0	21.8	3.2	0.0
Duck						
raw	100 g	122.0	0.0	19.7	4.8	0.0
Ham						
Honey roast	100 g	108.0	2.4	18.2	2.9	0.0

Nutrition values

Specific	Amount	Kcals	Carb	Prot	Fat	Fibre
Lamb						
Chops, loin, grilled	100 g	355.0	0.0	23.5	29.0	0.0
Leg, raw	100 g	240.0	0.0	17.9	18.7	0.0
Meat products						
Pepperami	100 g	560.0	1.0	20.0	52.0	N
Salami	100 g	491.0	1.9	19.3	45.2	0.1
Sausages, pork, raw	100 g	367.0	9.5	10.6	32.1	0.6
Offal						
Liver, calf, raw	100 g	153.0	1.9	20.1	7.3	0.0
Liver, chicken, raw	100 g	135.0	0.6	19.1	6.3	0.0
Liver, lamb, raw	100 g	179.0	1.6	20.1	10.3	0.0
Pheasant						
roast	100 g	213.0	0.0	32.2	9.3	0.0
Pork						
Chops, loin, raw	100 g	329.0	0.0	15.9	29.5	0.0
Leg, raw	100 g	269.0	0.0	16.6	22.5	0.0
Turkey						
Dark meat, raw	100 g	114.0	0.0	20.3	3.6	0.0
Light meat, raw	100 g	103.0	0.0	23.2	1.1	0.0
FISH, SEAFOOD AND FISH PRODUCTS						
Anchovies, canned, in oil	100 g	280.0	0.0	25.2	19.9	0.0
Cod, fillets, raw	100 g	76.0	0.0	17.4	0.7	0.0
Haddock, fillet, raw	100 g	73.0	0.0	16.8	0.6	0.0
Kipper, baked	100 g	205.0	0.0	25.5	11.4	0.0
Lemon sole, raw	100 g	81.0	0.0	17.1	1.4	0.0
Lobster, boiled	100 g	119.0	0.0	22.1	3.4	0.0
Mackerel, raw	100 g	223.0	0.0	19.0	16.3	0.0
Mussels, boiled	100 g	87.0	trace	17.2	2.0	0.0
Pilchards, canned, in tomato sauce	100 g	126.0	0.7	18.8	5.4	trace
Plaice, raw	100 g	91.0	0.0	17.9	2.2	0.0
Prawns, boiled	100 g	107.0	0.0	22.6	1.8	0.0
Salmon, canned	100 g	155.0	0.0	20.3	8.2	0.0
Salmon, raw	100 g	182.0	0.0	18.4	12.0	0.0
Salmon, smoked	100 g	142.0	0.0	25.4	4.5	0.0
Sardines, in oil, canned, drained	100 g	217.0	0.0	23.7	13.6	0.0
Scampi, in breadcrumbs, fried	100 g	316.0	28.9	12.2	17.6	1.1
Squid, frozen, raw	100 g	66.0	0.0	13.1	1.5	0.0
Tuna, canned, in brine	100 g	99.0	0.0	23.5	0.6	0.0
Whitebait, in flour, fried	100 g	525.0	5.3	19.5	47.5	0.2

Specific	Amount	Kcals	Carb	Prot	Fat	Fibre
DESSERTS						
Pancakes, sweet, made with whole milk	100 g	301.0	35.0	5.9	16.2	0.9
Yoghurt, Greek	100 g	115.0	2.0	6.4	9.1	0.0
Low fat, fruit	150 g pot	135.0	26.9	6.2	1.1	trace
Low fat, plain	150 g pot	84.0	11.3	7.7	1.2	0.0
SOUPS, SAUCES AND MISCELLANEOUS						
Chutney						
Mango	1 heaped tsp [15 g]	43.0	7.4	0.1	1.6	0.2
Tomato	1 heaped tsp [15 g]	24.0	6.1	0.2	0.1	0.3
Miscellaneous						
Baking powder	1 level tsp	7.0	1.5	0.2	trace	0.0
Marmite	1 level tsp	15.0	0.2	3.6	0.1	0.0
Mustard, smooth	1 level tsp	11.0	0.8	0.6	0.7	N
Pickle, sweet	1 heaped tsp [15 g]	20.0	5.2	trace	trace	0.2
Oxo cubes	1 cube	16.0	0.8	2.7	0.2	0.0
Vinegar	100 g	4.0	0.6	0.4	0.0	0.0
Salad dressing						
French dressing	100 g	649.0	0.1	0.3	72.1	0.0
Mayonnaise	100 g	691.0	1.7	1.1	75.6	0.0
Salad cream	100 g	348.0	16.7	1.5	31.0	N
Sauce						
Brown sauce	100 g	99.0	25.2	1.1	0.0	0.7
Mint sauce	100 g	87.0	21.5	1.6	trace	N
Soy sauce	100 g	64.0	8.3	8.7	0.0	0.0
Tomato ketchup	100 g	98.0	24.0	2.1	trace	0.9
SUGARS, SYRUPS AND PRESERVES						
Preserves						
Jam, fruit	100 g	261.0	69.0	0.6	0.0	0.0
Marmalade	100 g	261.0	69.5	0.1	0.0	0.6
Sugar						
Demerara	100 g	394.0	104.5	0.5	0.0	0.0
White	100 g	394.0	105.0	trace	0.0	0.0
Syrup						
golden	100 g	298.0	79.0	0.3	0.0	0.0
FATS AND OILS						
Dripping, beef	100 g	891.0	trace	trace	99.0	0.0
Olive oil	100 g	899.0	0.0	trace	99.9	0.0

Specific	Amount	Kcals	Carb	Prot	Fat	Fibre
ALCOHOLIC BEVERAGES						
Beer, bitter, draught	1 pint	182.0	13.1	trace	0.0	0.0
Cider, dry	1 pint	204.0	14.8	trace	0.0	0.0
Lager, bottled	1 pint	165.0	8.5	trace	0.0	0.0
Fortified wine						
Port	30 ml	47.0	3.6	trace	0.0	0.0
Sherry, dry	30 ml	35.0	0.5	trace	0.0	0.0
Spirits						
Brandy 40% proof	30 ml	65.0	trace	trace	0.0	0.0
Gin, 40% proof	30 ml	65.0	trace	trace	0.0	0.0
Vodka, 40% proof	30 ml	65.0	trace	trace	0.0	0.0
Whisky, 40% proof	30 ml	65.0	trace	trace	0.0	0.0
Wine						
Red	1 glass [120 ml]	82.0	0.4	trace	0.0	0.0
White, dry	1 glass [120 ml]	79.0	0.7	trace	0.0	0.0
NON-ALCOHOLIC BEVERAGES						
Coffee, instant, no milk or sugar	1 mug [260 g]	2.0	0.2	0.3	0.0	0.0
Tea, no milk or sugar	1 cup [200 g]	trace	trace	0.2	trace	0.0
Juice						
Grapefruit juice, unsweetened	1 glass [200 g]	66.0	16.6	0.8	0.2	trace
Orange juice, unsweetened	1 glass [200 g]	72.0	17.6	1.0	0.2	0.2
Tomato juice	1 glass [200 g]	28.0	6.0	1.6	trace	0.2
Other						
tonic water, low-calorie	1 glass [200 g]	1.6	trace	trace	trace	0.0

Diet support

You can, of course, pay money to sit in a room with other like-minded, overweight people fighting the flab to get group support, or buy any of the hundreds of diet aids or slimming books.

The following are just the headline acts of some of the main players. With groups all over the country, **Weightwatchers** offers an environment of group support for a programme involving eating and activity plans. Foods are given numbers of points and the dieter has a number of points to use in a healthy daily meal plan. The **Atkins Diet** theory is that overconsumption of carbohydrates causes overproduction of insulin leading to hunger, so carbohydrates are limited while protein and fat are encouraged. The **GI Diet** is based on how the Glycaemic Index rates carbohydrate foods depending on how quickly they are broken down and the impact they have on our sugar levels which, when low, can prompt food cravings. The rules of the **Beverly Hills Diet** are that specific foods have to be eaten at the same time or in a certain order over a period of time to achieve weight loss. A week of following the **Cabbage Soup Diet** means eating a soup made up of cabbage, onions, tomatoes, celery and leeks plus vegetable bouillon, supplemented with a few extra foodstuffs, which is the basis of this kick-start weight-loss plan. The **food combining** plan insists on separating certain foods and eating them in a particular combination, with the theory that weight is gained by the way you eat rather than what you consume. The **Scarsdale diet** is a strict plan of low-carbohydrate meals consisting of fruit, vegetables, and lean meat and fish in unlimited amounts. **Slimming World** offers group support throughout the country; this organisation's eating plans use colour-coding and food ratings to help dieters achieve weight-loss targets.

Being overweight isn't just about having a fat bum or a beer belly; it isn't about being large-boned or under-tall. It's also about what's going on elsewhere in your life – or not! So now you've reached here and read everything you knew already, perhaps you'd best turn elsewhere and either right a wrong or find something to fill a void. *Then* address balanced, sensible eating and exercising. You know it makes sense because the biggest truism of the lot is that there is fat and there is slim and slim is definitely better . . . and healthier.

Money

You should know that within a couple of days of finding out information for this section, I managed to save hundreds of pounds. Some of it was obvious and staring me in the face, such as spending a bit of time getting better interest deals; others less so, such as changing my electricity tariff. So I have really benefited from *having* to spend time squirrelling down into my money matters, and that's what it comes down to – spending time. For most of us, effective money management comes down to time and how much of *that* we are prepared to spend sorting out our finances. After this experience – trust me, it's worth it and I won't be sidelining it again.

I've had to make difficult decisions about the money all my life. Having been for most of my career a freelance journalist or television producer or running my own businesses has meant that it's often not been easy to predict my income with any degree of certainty. At the same time, I have never let the lack of a set and regular wage ever inhibit any ambitions to spend money on things I considered important, I've juggled funds, had sleepless nights and had to downshift for financial reasons more than once in my life. Also, as someone who has walked around a property with the bailiffs on a walking possession visit, when they were effectively marking the goods they would take to meet the VAT bill I was struggling to pay, I am someone with a healthy respect for the power of money when you haven't got it! Being in debt is like finding you've put on weight – it happens easily and quickly and it is much more difficult and takes twice as long to get yourself back into solvency. A key part of Life Auditing is facing up to the reality of situations and you don't get any more cold or bare facts than those on your payslip or bank statement. These are the questions the Life Auditors asked themselves:

How much of a worry is my financial position?
Does it colour many decisions I make in other parts of my life?
Does it cause rows with my partner or family?
Do I know my exact financial position?
How often do I balance my books?

Money makes the world go round, so says the song and certainly it buys a whole lot more than just goods and services. It can buy you freedom and choice, education, better health and broader horizons. The power of money extends way beyond the cash drawer and your acquiring of it and disposing of it will go a long way to defining the sort of person you are in many different aspects of your life.

'Rich or dead', was what one friend once said to me, rather glumly as I recall. I think he was going through a bit of a lean period and having money mattered quite a lot to him. But actually he rather bucks a trend that perversely cheers me rather and might cheer you too, that people with lots of money are very often more unhappy about their money (what they do with it, where they keep it, what they'd do without it) than the people who don't have any and who therefore don't have to invest the same amount of energy and angst in it. That said, and I know this is naughty, so don't take me too seriously, I have always had some affection for the sentiment that, 'you can never be too rich or too thin'!

Making money, earning money, saving money, borrowing money and spending money are all really about the same thing. The amount of money you have or need is a tangible measurement of where you are in the course of achieving what you want it to buy – and that can be anything from success and status to new shoes. This in turn means that saving money and lessening any debts is the same as *making* money in that it takes you one step nearer those goals.

But you do need to know the harsh real facts of your financial position and so I'm afraid you should bite on the end of your pencil and learn to love putting numbers in boxes to get to grips with your funds. Therein lies calmness and reassurance. In my direst moments, doing this has shown me that not only are things never as bad as my worst imaginings, but also that where one account or month's finances are desperate, so another one, or the position of the whole, makes up for it.

Kwame was earning good money in the City and enjoying spending it. He was twenty-seven and had worked hard for a good degree so felt the spoils of securing his position were well deserved. A sports car, great holidays, many new clothes and satisfying his love of electronic gadgetry saw off most of his earnings. Although dealing with finance all day, he was, however, being fly in his personal money management. He'd find time to fill in forms for new cards and credit, but many brown envelopes sat around unopened. Then his chaos brought matters to a head.

'I'd missed several payments on a card, not because I didn't have the money, but because I'd not set up automatic payments. Suddenly one day my card wasn't accepted and I found out that in fact my credit record had also been damaged, which might affect future spending and borrowing. On top of that I've now been made redundant, with not much of a pay-off because I've only been with the firm a couple of years, so I've got quite a lot to sort out to keep afloat until I start earning again.'

How to manage your money: the basics

So – we've established it's incredibly important you have a clear and real understanding of your financial situation. That means opening all brown envelopes as soon as they arrive and either sending out cheques and payments immediately or, if there is any juggling to be done, putting aside an 'accountancy' hour when you and your equivalent of a large gin and tonic plough through the bills and payments on a regular basis. Be a grown-up and get your head round it!

Everyone needs to invest time in good personal money management, but if you're **freelance, self-employed, or running a small business** you shouldn't need telling to make sure you keep your books in order, including, especially, your personal takings and compulsory payments for such things as national insurance. If you aren't up to date, the only thing you're banking on is trouble ahead, so go to your accountant, bank manager or small-business adviser immediately and get some help. Either that, or give up on being an entrepreneur and go and get a job where an accounts department does the grunt work – you're living a lifestyle not running a business.

As well as knowing all the actual amounts and dates that are involved in your regular payments, it's important to keep track of other information such as contact details, internet access codes, pins and passwords. Obviously these need to be kept somewhere private and very, very secure but it will make your life so much easier. Be aware, though, of **identity theft**. It is one of the fastest-growing financial frauds. With just the minutest amount of information, such as your social security number, a thief can impersonate you and access your accounts. Shred all financial paperwork.

Your creditworthiness

If you are taking a long hard look at your finances one thing you must do is find out whether you are considered a good credit risk. Banks and other financial institutions you deal with are likely to run a credit check which will show them how you have conducted your financial affairs in the past. It's an automated system, particularly used if you are seeking to borrow because it gives a risk assessment of your creditworthiness from historic financial dealings and information you provide on an application form.

Budget

First off, writing up your budget once a year, for the coming twelve months, is a best guesstimate of your income and outgoings. Give it a reality check every month to see whether you are spot on with your calculations, have room to manoeuvre or are over-spending. Your bank and many of the general finance websites will have standard forms you can adapt to your own use. The essentials of creating a budget are actually pretty straightforward

- Keep a record of all outgoings and incomings during a month.
- Carry that across twelve months.
- Add in quarterly or other regular payments.
- Don't forget seasonal or big items, such as Christmas and holidays.
- Add at least 10 per cent to your outgoings figure for contingencies.

And ouch if there is a mismatch between what comes in and what's likely to go out. Don't bank on expectations of earning more – start looking to spend less and think debt management if you can't immediately cut back. (See page 201.) (Yes, I know what I said about my past – do as I say not always as I do, or did – OK?)

Net Worth

This is my favourite financial chart because at one glance it tells me exactly what money I'd have left in my hot sticky hand to drive off into the sunset with if I sold up everything I owned and settled all my debts. It takes into account all your savings and assets *and* your debts. It's reaffirmation that overall I'm solvent. This is sometimes called a personal asset statement or, in business, a balance sheet. Doing this regularly, to see if things are improving or not, is the best reality check you can give yourself

Net Worth Chart

Date

Assets			Balance £
Fixed assets	£		
House			
Furniture/paintings/antiques			
Electrical			
Fixtures and fittings			
Car			
Other			
Total fixed assets		£	
Cash and bank accounts			
Current a/c (in credit)			
Savings a/c			
Cash drawer			
Money owed to you			
Other			
Total cash and bank accounts		£	
TOTAL ASSETS			£

Liabilities			
Credit cards/store cards			
1.			
2.			
3.			
Total credit and store card		£	
Other liabilities			
Current a/c (overdraft)			
Money owed (less than 1 year)			
Tax owed			
Other			
Total other liabilites		£	
Long-term liabilities			
Mortgage			
2nd mortgage/loan			
Car loans			
HP loans			
Other long-term loans			
Total long-term liabilities		£	
TOTAL LIABILITIES			£

NET WORTH + or - £

in regard to your finances. It's a snapshot of a moment in time for you financially and is a definitive situation report on your financial status if you sold everything, cashed in the premium bonds and started thumbing a lift out of town. It also serves as a good 'what if . . .' reminder if you have any ambitious plans to change your life; after all you can't plan for tomorrow if you don't know where you are today.

Money management: professionals and products

Self-reliance and responsibility are essential, which is why I've emphasised the need to use the basic tools to examine your finances. But sometimes it's good to call in the professionals. There are plenty of regulations policing **financial advisers** and it is one of those professional relationships where you really do need to establish complete trust. He or she will need to know everything about your life to give you the best advice. Imagine holding the meeting in your underpants – that's how exposing the experience can feel. You need to be diligent and informed yourself about the advice you get. They can advise on everything from mortgages to investments, from pensions to loans. They are different to accountants who mainly process existing accounts to comply with tax and other statutory or regulatory requirements. It's very important you trust your instincts and hear that alarm bell ringing if something sounds too good to be true.

There are tied, multi-tied and independent financial advisers. Tied and multi-tied means they are linked to one or more specific financial institution. Independent means they are properly independent and obliged to provide advice and offer products best suited to your own individual requirements, which means they must look at the whole range of options available to you. They need to put in writing why any one product would be a good choice for you, what sort of risk it exposes you to, any fees you will be paying and who gets those fees. The idea is that their advice is completely transparent and you understand exactly what you're putting your money into.

Ask how much commission a financial adviser will be making. You can ask them instead to accept a fee for their services. It's sensible to ask for an estimate of how long a job may take to complete and whether there is an upper limit on charges. You should be offered a statement with your adviser's status and the services they offer as well as a list of their charging structure. Check that your adviser is authorised or accredited, so you have some recourse to get money back if the advice is flawed.

Bank accounts and borrowing

A bank account is the one financial product virtually everyone uses. It's also extremely unusual to change banks, which is bad news for the consumer. The first thing to do when you open a new bank account is to shop around. Current accounts are the basic, everyday account – you don't need notice to withdraw money and they usually come with a cheque book and debit/cashpoint card. You are silly to keep spare cash in your current account as in most cases it will earn you hardly any interest there. You get different interest rates depending on the sort of account you choose. Some require you to put in a guaranteed sum of money every month to get the higher rate. Others offer additional benefits for a monthly fee, like travel insurance. Some are free and all may offer online and telephone banking plus an overdraft facility and a cheque book. You may also want to think about whether it's an ethical bank and where it invests your money.

High-interest accounts, whether they are with a bank or building society, invariably require a period of notice before you withdraw money, often sixty or ninety days. If you need to make an instant withdrawal you may have to pay a penalty. Generally the longer the notice period, the higher the interest they offer and many of the higher-interest accounts require a minimum deposit. Watch out for accounts that attract annual fees automatically charged to your account.

Many banks also offer gold or platinum current accounts with accompanying shiny bit of plastic. Check the benefits and especially look out for insurance cover inclusions for travel, accidental death and motoring breakdown to make sure you aren't double-covered with a separately arranged policy.

Student accounts offer their own separate range of enticing goodies from railcards to mobile phone discounts. Some offer really attractive savings and it's worth shopping around.

Be careful of charges incurred at cash machines, especially the 'convenience' ones positioned away from banks which are increasing in number at supermarkets, stations and petrol stations.

The only sort of **overdraft** to have is an authorised one because you can face hefty charges for going over the limit. For that reason it makes sense to arrange one for slightly more than you are ever likely to need. You won't get penalised for early repayment and only pay interest on what you owe. In fact it's worth asking if you can have an interest-free lower limit, or look for special low-rate deals.

Online banking has several advantages. You can log on from anywhere in the world and check out your account, set up transactions, arrange money transfers and pay bills.

Paying your bills by direct debit will save you money and stress as some accounts offer discounts and it will mean you'll never get penalised for a late payment on a credit card again. Spend time each month checking your bank statements as it's common for accounts to carry on making withdrawals for redundant standing orders and debits linked to lapsed subscriptions, memberships or insurance policies.

Personal loans

Loans are agreed with your bank or building society and, unlike credit cards, your monthly repayment is usually a fixed amount as is the limit on the total borrowing, which should help you stick to your budget. There are unsecured loans; secured loans which may be held against your property, for instance; and special packages for cars or home improvements. However, you're not tied to the bank that provides your current account and it pays to check out the competition between banks and building societies as rates can vary. Don't be tempted to spread the repayments over an excessively long time, and watch out too for any small print that indicates you may be charged a penalty if you want to replay the loan earlier.

Buying on credit

Everyone is offering **credit cards** it seems, from supermarkets to football clubs. Nobody's likely to question their usefulness, especially if you manage to get a zero per cent interest arrangement or loyalty bonus points such as Air Miles every time you use them, plus, of course, you only have to pay interest on the actual amount you owe. However, the downside is that they represent temptation in its neatest form and you may spend more than you can really afford to pay back. Watch out too for any hidden charges or fees for lateness of the monthly repayment.

It may be worth contacting your credit card company and enquiring about a lower rate of interest. Their part of the financial market is so competitive that they may be keen to keep your business.

Most high street stores offer their own **store cards** and will allow you to spend the credit you are given instantly, often with the extra encouragement of a discount on your first purchases. It's worth contacting a store if you intend to buy something expensive to try to find out when they will be holding their next store card promotion because it may well include an extra-special discount enticement. But use the card for that and then cut it up! Watch out for excessive interest charges and for being seduced into spending more . . . just because you can! Having to use real money is a great deterrent for when you've got your impulse-shopping head on.

Buying things on the 'never-never' seems rather an old-fashioned method now but **hire purchase** is still widely used for purchasing cars or large white goods such as washing machines, and other electrical goods such as TVs. You will usually have to put down a deposit and make equal payments over a specified period up to five years. You are effectively hiring the goods until the last payment. **Leasing** is another payment system predominantly used for buying cars where you don't actually own the goods but pay a 'rental' amount instead and have to return the goods at the end of the lease period. With all the above, be careful about getting into debt and taking on repayment schedules you can't meet, with interest rates you hadn't considered. It happens a lot and the gloss soon wears off the shiny new car, appliance, boots when it does.

Personal insurance

We all know someone who seems to clean up on insurance claims. Despite being more accident prone than the rest of us, they replace clothes, glasses, carpets and furnishings with apparent frequency due to the fact their insurance arrangements covered them for the leaking pipe, the careless child, the lost-in-transit calamity. They are either crooks or fantastically well organised in making sure the cover they pay the premiums for really does cover them for all eventualities. The rest of us struggle with insurance. You are safeguarding the future by second-guessing what might happen and it's mighty confusing because there is so much choice and such a lot of small print. What's the key to getting the essentials and avoiding the rest when you can get insurance for just about everything and from just about anywhere: when you buy goods, as you board an aircraft, online and at the supermarket along with your groceries. It is also a very exact science so always read that small print carefully and answer the questions on forms accurately as the premiums are worked out with staggering exactitude against the risk you and yours are presenting.

Because there are so many companies vying for your business, shopping around for the best and most economic cover can be very time-consuming although there are websites that offer to search for you. Don't ever automatically renew your insurance – and if you do decide to change insurance policies make sure there is no gap between the end of the old policy and the start date of your new one.

There is a vast differential between the levels of **life insurance** cover you can get for your life insurance and it is worth checking regularly to see if rates have fallen for the level of cover you want.

Life insurance is a popular subject for financial journalists to cover in the money sections of the weekend papers so keep an eye out for them or visit one of the main personal finance websites. **Level Term Insurance** provides life insurance protection that remains level for the amount of time you select, i.e. ten, fifteen, twenty years. Once the term period is selected it can't be changed.

Pensions

This is an enormous area and is constantly changing. It is vitally important that you look ahead to your future pension provision and have in place some firm plans. There are different sorts of pension plans available and there are various tax advantages. Many people also like to have an ancillary plan as well to supplement their pension, such as buying a property to let, savings accounts or selling their home and downsizing to a smaller property to release some equity.

If you are currently spending some time sorting out your finances it is worth double-checking both the state or private pension expectations you have and the exact date you become eligible for them. There are qualifying contributions you will have had to have made, but also concessions you may be able to apply for if you haven't done so.

Equity release schemes are becoming increasingly popular to access money tied up in property, for older people. The principle is that by remortgaging your house or selling part to a specialist company you can get cash in hand instead of leaving it in the building itself. There are different sorts of equity release

Insurance and pensions

plans and it is extremely important to shop around and find the right one for your circumstances, especially if you think you may want to move at a later date into sheltered housing or a residential home.

Investments

First of all, I sort of suspect that if you have got investments you won't be reading this. Certainly I have to say that if you haven't and are just reading it to consider whether you should get some, then don't feel left out for not knowing your way around the many different investments, bonds and trusts. The basics of being debt free, having a high-interest account to put cash in when you've got it and having pension provision and a level of life insurance you are happy with, is pretty good going. Well done you!

However, people do, of course, invest in all sorts of things to make money: specific tax beneficial savings accounts, property, premium bonds, shares, new businesses, horses, West End plays, wine, etc. As well as taking a punt on getting good returns there are also often tax savings to be made. What's hot and what's not, what's legal and what's dodgy is constantly changing So you really have to do your own research and make sure it is up to date, observing the following common sense guidelines. The Sunday newspaper finance sections are good sources as are some of the general finance websites. Things to bear in mind:

- Don't be seduced by the thought of the big win. Everyone should make investment decisions based on the amount of risk they can afford and that they can live with.
- Lifestyle issues should also be taken into account, such as women wanting more flexibility and to be able to realise their investment because they need or want to take a career break to have children.
- Also you may be concerned that your investment is ethically sound or won't be invested in anything that could harm the planet, in which case look for SRIs. Socially Responsible Investments.

Stocks and shares are a fascinating way to invest money although the maxim, what goes up can also come down, really does apply. You must do loads of research if you are a stock-market virgin.

- Stick to what you know.
- Be watchful of companies you and your friends think are great. You might want to check out that instinct to see if it's a good investment.
- Don't, though, get sentimental or attached to your investments.
- Keep informed by reading in detail the financial pages in the weekend papers.
- Spread your risk.
- Think long term – at least three years.
- Stay realistic – remember what goes up can come down too.

 You can share deal over the internet, work personally with a stockbroker or even join a stocks and shares club. There are plenty of regulations to protect you and loads of good websites with masses of free information.

Debts

A collection of debts is aptly described as a burden and unless you are incredibly astute at juggling your earning and borrowing it's hard to ever think about investments or savings for the future while you are carrying any loans. Apart from the puppy dog zero per cent deals designed to entice you to use a particular bank or finance house, you will be paying added interest on your loans, which in the case of some store cards can be over 30 per cent. Spend time reorganising your borrowing to the lowest-interest accounts you can find.

Trouble repaying debts

It's important you take the following steps if you are struggling to cope with your debts. Own up by talking to the lender involved. Do this as early in the day as you can and even though you may be very tempted to keep the problem quiet. They are more likely to be prepared to negotiate if you let them know *you* know there is a problem at the outset, plus you are more likely to be able to keep your 'good' creditworthiness. With the negotiations remember that financial institutions have an obligation to deal with you on a fair and reasonable basis and are duty bound to consider extended repayment schedules or even a break from making repayments altogether if you come up with plans to meet the debt in the future.

Your plans should include a realistic budget that will identify your priority debts, such as rent. Get help doing this from a friend or member of the family who knows you well enough to stop you fooling yourself. If you get a court order about your breach of debt repayments, get advice and make sure the court is told of any mitigating circumstances, such as losing your job, or your wife running off with the window cleaner, because they may be more lenient and agree to a time order, which might change either the amount of the repayments or the interest rate you are being charged.

The most important thing is to face up to the problem in the first instance and if you are anxious about the prospect of coming clean with your lenders take advantage of the plentiful free and impartial advice that's available from Citizen's Advice.

Maximising your income

Your income is likely to be easier to calculate than your outgoings. Income might include:

- Your basic salary
- Guaranteed overtime
- Pensions
- Child benefit
- Income support

- Tax credits
- Other benefits
- Maintenance

Make sure you really understand your payslip. Not for nothing are deductions called that. You need to be Miss Marple to work out what they are all for. If you get a pay rise consider converting it straight into savings. You survived without it previously and putting even just a bit of it away each month should be a relatively pain-free way to accumulate funds.

How to make tax and benefits work for you

First things first – check your tax code and especially check that you are making the most of any and all the benefits you might be entitled to, or which you may need to discuss with your employer.

Make sure you are using any tax-free savings allowances and claiming back the tax on savings if you are a non-tax payer. Make the most too of tax-free pension contributions and, of course, file your tax return on time to avoid fines or penalties.

Consider making any charitable donations you make go even further by giving via gift aid so that the charities get a tax rebate. You can pass on the same benefits by Payroll Giving through your employer.

If you can manage to, putting aside state benefits is a neat way to save a set amount. Take child benefit paid direct into your bank account. Round down the amount you get per month to a tidy figure and set up a direct debit to transfer this sum to a higher-interest account. Do the same thing with cash from tax credits or tax discounts.

How to make more – sunlighting and moonlighting

Second-job cash is useful either to meet your cost of living or to provide funds for something you are saving for. The difference

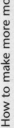

How to make more money

between sun and moon lighting is that moonlighting is when you have an evening job after your day job and sunlighting is when you carry out two daytime jobs. (See page 117.)

Don't be phased by this as an option; evening work is not just for students any more. It's increasingly easy to find flexible working patterns and two part-time jobs may well be both more lucrative and more interesting and fulfilling than one. Before you take on any extra work do check your contract of employment with your main job as some have restrictions on the type of other work you can carry out officially. You will need to discuss your plans with your employer if you want to change any aspect of your working practices to accommodate the second job. Think too about tax and other financial implications and talk to your local tax office.

Sell your stuff!

Sell unwanted things and pocket the cash. It may be cleared-out clutter, unwanted gifts or heirlooms whose sentimental value isn't enough to keep them out of any of the various second-hand sales outlets at your disposal. There are loads of ways to do it. If you've got something you need expert advice on try a **dealer**. Do a bit of research and get an idea of the item's value before taking it to several dealers. There is likely to be a specialist dealer if the item has particular historic or curiosity value. They are a better bet than a general dealer as they will have a client list and will be able to pay a decent price for it knowing they will be able to sell it on quickly. Seek help from the dealer trade organisations.

If you suspect something might be really valuable, it is probably worth approaching an auction house which will give you a free estimate of your item's value without obligation to place it with them for sale. Some will do this from a photo so you don't have to lug a piece of furniture into the showroom. If you do decide to let them auction it, take into account their commission charges and VAT. Again, seek a specialist sale date when similar items will be going under the hammer. Be prepared, in some cases, to pay insurance and for illustrations in the sale catalogue.

Look in your local paper for adverts for large **car boot sales** as they are likely to attract more people. Do a recce the week before to see what prices people are putting on items. On the day pack your car with your items for sale, take refreshments and plenty of change. You'll need a wallpaper table, which should be the last thing you put in the boot, and a large plastic sheet to cover everything in case it rains. Clothes will sell best if they are freshly washed and neatly ironed and presented either folded on the table or hung on a clothes rail.

eBay are the twenty-first-century equivalent of the car boot sale and the original **online auction house**, and are the biggest, with thousands of item categories, but there are many others and if you are buying not selling, sometimes the smaller sites are better because they attract fewer buyers and so there is less competition.

As long as you have a valid email address, anyone can sell items in online auctions. You first have to register and then fill out some simple secure online forms with credit and debit card details to confirm your identity. The instructions are very straightforward to place your item under auction, usually for

seven days, and the percentage listing fee and final value fee based on the closing bid are all clearly explained.

Use your biggest asset – your Home

As a homeowner you may need one day to raise money against the property by releasing equity in it with a remortgage; or you may want to help **increase its value** so you can buy a better property next time. These considerations may well colour your home improvement plans.

Make sure any work you do or get done is good quality. A bodged job not only looks awful and won't last, but when it comes to selling your house it will set off alarm bells with potential buyers and just make the whole thing more of a struggle. If the gloss paint is all gloopy, they could be thinking, 'Lord knows what state the roof is in!' And remember that poor construction or building work on any extension or conversion will give buyers a bargaining advantage in any negotiations over price. So however much you or your partner feel confident about your DIY skills, be realistic about when to get the experts in.

Any work you get done, make sure you keep the paperwork that goes with it. You'll need the guarantee for things like a damp course, and the signed-off approval that shows you have complied with Building Regulations. If you don't have the paperwork, it could stall or even stop the sale going through.

Adding an extra bedroom is always a good bet and if you really want to guarantee more money, add an en-suite bathroom while you're at it. Always plump for plain white porcelain bathroom fittings. Similarly with kitchens, if you are thinking of resale potential then opt for simplicity and neutrality, which luckily is often the cheapest option. Central heating is a good way to add value to your house too. A well-done loft conversion that doesn't involve dodgy ladders is another asset. New windows are good news but choose them carefully. Weigh up the pros and cons between traditional sashes that may be in keeping with your property and modern double-glazed units that are likely to be more secure and energy efficient. Always check out whether you're in a conservation area before you replace doors and windows. Or indeed whether you need planning permission if the house is listed. It's a big and expensive job so do your research first and make sure you really are adding value, not taking it away. Parking is often a deal breaker so if you can, make a proper space for off-road parking, lay some gravel or think about building a garage. Check first, though, with your local council to see whether you need planning permission.

Best times to sell your home
You have to think about the type of home you have and what time of year it is shown off in its best light. This, combined with

when a likely purchaser will have a house move or purchase on their mind, should give you a good idea of when to go to market. For instance a cosy cottage with an open fire will be most seductive in the thick of winter with a log fire burning during visits from prospective purchasers. A seaside home or one with a fantastic garden will sell best in the summer months. A good-sized family home will sell quickest in the spring so that parents can plan to start their children at new schools in the following September, and a holiday second home will be sought in the New Year as people start to consider where they are going to spend their holidays. Likewise, if your property has a downside, such as close proximity to a sports stadium or a large school, consider when the neighbourhood is quietest when deciding to sell.

Making money from your home

Taking in a lodger is a quick way to earn money from a spare bedroom although you will pay for it with a level of loss of privacy. If you really don't mind intrusion, taking in bed and breakfast guests could be an option. The great thing about offering B&B is that you decide when to put the vacancy sign up and don't have to do it all the time. You will not be awash with regulations if you only have a couple of paying guests at a time.

What about your home's suitability as a **location for a film, advert or TV** series? The most likely attribute it's going to have to have is a unique or curious aspect, be in an unrivalled position or be distinctive in its period, although flats and council houses are sometimes also sought. You can earn from a couple of hundred a day to thousands depending on the property and the amount of disruption from the film crew and cast. Some location finders are happy to have your property on their register for free. Nothing ventured, nothing gained.

You don't need to aim for the stars, though, because you may be able to make money simply by cashing in on your home's desirability as a **short-term let**. If it's near a sporting venue or a big annual event, you could rent it to participants or spectators and, depending on size, because even the smallest flat could be

Property

let-able, earn up to several thousand pounds for a short period of time.

Or maybe you are based near a railway station or airport and have some driveway or off-road space that could be let as a parking space to a regular commuter.

Turn your hobby into cash

If you think you are good enough at something to turn it from a spare-time pastime into a nice little earner, first of all check out the competition by getting their catalogues and comparing quality and prices.

To be able to sell things by mail order from a website is a great way if you can make it work, so look at the competition's sites too and get quotes from web designers and engineers to create your own. Check out the law about selling goods online, register to process money via credit cards, and get advice from your 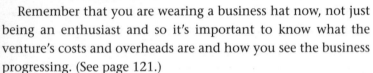 bank or a business adviser.

Remember that you are wearing a business hat now, not just being an enthusiast and so it's important to know what the venture's costs and overheads are and how you see the business progressing. (See page 121.)

Minimising your expenditure

I can feel you tensing already – but belt-tightening doesn't have to be all doom and gloom. The key to cutting your outgoings, whether on your mortgage or your weekly food shop, is to get really well-informed. Do your research and shop around. Use the information in this section as a starting point and try to work up some enthusiasm for the project – there really are great savings to be made.

Denise and Matthew had both just retired when they carried out the Life Audit to help them make some plans for the future. They took up the challenge of looking at every aspect of their

Money

expenditure to see if they could cut it down, which would improve the scope of lifestyle choices they could make elsewhere. 'We took one area of cost at a time and started up a sort of mythical savings account, and began theoretically banking the savings we were able to make. We looked at everything from spending less on groceries to getting new quotes for insurance. Do you know, on this one thing, it was our current insurance company that came up with a better deal saving us more than £300 a year. Up until now we've always just automatically renewed the policy! Cutting back financially sounds such a miserable thing to do – but actually doing it this way became quite good fun. If only we'd done it years ago think how much we'd have saved.'

Your Home

The roof over your head is likely to be your biggest expense both in terms of a capital outlay to buy it or for rent, and in keeping and maintaining it. It will also, probably, eventually be your biggest asset and it's helpful to have an up-to-date idea of its value by getting a valuation once every few years or when you are making other financial plans. It's an essential part of the net-worth exercise, for example.

The Mortgage

As with insurances, pensions and loans there are very many different types of mortgage. When you're shopping around for a conventional mortgage, have some questions written down and check them out with any offers being made to you.

- Do you absolutely understand what's being said in amongst the financial jargon?
- Are there hidden costs or penalties? For instance will you be penalised if you want to pay off the mortgage early with a lump sum?
- Does the person selling your the mortgage stand to make a hefty commission from the deal?

The biggest single question is probably which type of mortgage to go for.

Standard mortgages are still what most people have and they can be either repayment or interest only. With a repayment mortgage you are paying off the interest and a little bit of the capital with each monthly payment. With an interest-only deal, you are only paying off the interest and need to have some other means (often another type of investment) to pay off the actual lump sum you originally borrowed at the end of the agreed term.

You can get **fixed rate** or **tracker rate mortgages**. A fixed rate will usually be for a set period, often two to five years, and if you're anxious about your budget these are often a good idea though you will, of course, miss out if interest rates fall. A tracker rate will follow the movements of the Bank of England base rate – so you could immediately benefit from any fall, or conversely suffer from a rise.

Flexible mortgages mean you can vary your monthly payments depending on your circumstances; you could make a lump-sum payment or maybe not pay anything at all for a period, all depending on what you have agreed as your borrowing limit. The benefits are obvious, particularly if you come into some money, as you can pay off a great lump, reduce the length of time you're borrowing and consequently save on lots of interest payments.

Endowment mortgages work by saving money into a policy with the plan that this investment will be able to pay off the lump sum of the mortgage at the end of the agreed term. They have had bad press in recent years as many of these investments are falling short of the necessary sum.

A **current account mortgage** can be quite complicated but the basic idea is that it's like a giant overdraft (which some could find rather depressing) combining your mortgage with your bank account. But the upside is that, because everything is in one pot, when you get paid or when any money goes into your account, it instantly reduces the size of your mortgage and consequently the amount of interest you have to pay.

You need to research the options carefully because there are **all-in-one** and **offset mortgages** as well which take into account any other borrowing like credit cards or loans. Again everything is in one pot, which makes sense, but you need to be very vigilant and keep an eye on what's going in and coming out.

The big thing with any mortgage is to regularly check out the other deals available. You may be tied into your current mortgage for a fixed term but always investigate what else is out there as sometimes another competing company will pay the penalty for you in order to get your business. Don't feel over-faced by the hassle. Get stuck in and make sure you are getting the best deal; put your mortgage provider through their paces to see if there is a better deal to be had. Not least because if you can reduce your monthly payment you could carry on investing that saving into the mortgage and so pay it off in a shorter time. This is an increasingly popular option when compared with the returns on other investments. Some companies also offer cash-back deals where you get a percentage of the mortgage back in a one-off payment.

Keep an eye on your lender's website for special-offer deals or use its online mortgage calculator to flag up any new advantages you may have in switching to another type. Periodically get quotes from other lenders and if you get offered a better deal go back to your lender and give them a chance to match or better it. Diary this sort of checking to remind you to do it.

Most newspapers have weekly up-to-the-minute round-ups and comparisons and some financial websites are particularly good at making recommendations in the consumer's interest.

Look out for fees that may be charged for mortgage change arrangements. In the first instance look for and use a service which offers a no-obligation remortgage check. These should be free unless you take up one of the deals offered, when a fee of a small percentage of the loan may be charged.

Other, potentially money saving, ways to buy

Shared equity is a state-funded scheme organised by the government with high street banks and mortgage lenders offering first-time home buyers help to buy a property. Basically you buy shares in the property with the government and the building society or bank owning the rest, on which you pay rent. As time goes on and you earn more, you can commit to more shares, eventually becoming the outright owner.

Housing associations are about providing affordable homes to people who might otherwise struggle to pay commercial rents or to get on the property ladder. There are new schemes coming out all the time, designed to help people buy a home in partnership with an association.

Sweat equity is a marvellous expression and actually it can apply to many areas of finance and money where you are able to put in effort or energy instead of straight cash. Self-build projects run in conjunction with local housing associations or charities are promoting the idea as a good way for people to get on the property ladder. People either have or acquire building skills and work together to build several houses with the value of their work built into the value of the development, giving them a share in their home from the outset. Your local authority may have details of local schemes in your area, or contact one of the large housing associations to find out more as all schemes are different.

Rent

You pay your money into the well-known renting black hole and it seems pretty fixed, but it is worth checking out whether the amount you are paying is fair in the current market.

Stephanie and Raoul had been renting a flat for a couple of years when a friend took on a similar property in the same street for far less. 'We hadn't noticed that the rental market had changed because so many people had bought properties to let out and there was a shortage of good tenants. We went to our landlord and threatened to hand in our notice to leave and he reduced our rent by a third immediately to encourage us to stay.'

An assured shorthold tenancy is the most common sort of formal agreement and means that the landlord has the right to repossess his property at the end of the term. It used to be the case that it was for a minimum of six months but now the tenancy can be for any period – and not necessarily short at all. The written agreement is made and signed by the landlord and the tenant and will agree the rent, how often it should be paid, when it might be reviewed, and it should describe the accommodation accurately. If the rend is to be paid weekly then the tenant should have a rent book.

Maintenance and Running Costs

How much you need to put aside each year for the maintenance of your home is very dependent on the age and basic condition of the property. Work out the cost of the annual tasks and keep on top of repairs and renewals yourself if you can because while interest rates might be low and mortgages cheap, the cost of properly maintaining a private home professionally can be five times the rate of inflation! Having a cushion of money for household maintenance will also save you money since it means you won't be reliant on expensive loans for those essential repairs.

Water rates are one of those expenses it's easy to forget when doing your budget or cash flow because they are usually payable twice yearly and the only possibility of saving money is by getting a meter that could show a lesser payment.

You can save by switching energy suppliers of **gas or electricity**. There are several price comparison sites but carry out a check once a year as the best deals change all the time.

Switching to energy-saving light bulbs will save you money before you even turn them on because they last eight times as long as standard ones. Making sure your hot water tank is well lagged, always selecting a 40°C wash cycle in the washing machine, and waiting until you have a full load, will all save money.

Changing a few personal habits can save you cash, for example showering rather than bathing, switching appliances and electrical equipment, such as TVs, off at the mains rather than leaving them on standby, and turning down the heating thermostat in your home by just one degree.

Shopping around for a different **phone** service in the same way you do for better electricity or gas suppliers can save you up to 90 per cent on the cost of your phone calls, depending on the number of calls you currently make. It's not a complicated process and you won't have to change your number.

There are also clever cyberphones on the market which can save a fortune on long-distance calls. They aren't expensive but you do need a broadband connection to make free calls to someone using the same phone and software. Other calls made on these phones are also cheaper.

The thought of negotiating the maze of **mobile phone** options may leave you feeling faint but it's worth persevering with and equipping yourself with the following information to make it easier.

- Write down your telephoning habits.
- Make a note of the number and length of your calls.
- How many texts do you send?
- Clock what time of day you make them.
- Are they to other networks or to landlines?

This will at least give a starting point for what sort of deal would suit you now.

Having **home insurance** will be a condition of your mortgage when you take it out although it does not necessarily have to be with your mortgage provider unless you have agreed a special deal that includes it. The figure you are insuring for is the full rebuilding cost of your property and you can either take that from the valuation report that was made before you bought the property or go to an online rebuilding cost calculator. With all house insurances look out for hidden extras and ask for any you really aren't fussed about to be removed and the premium reduced. These can include legal expenses, accidental damage or cover for items when they are away from the property.

Many **contents insurance** policies are index linked so, providing contents are valued accurately the first time, the value of your possessions should rise automatically. Even so, you should review your list of contents every couple of years and let the company know if you've made any significant purchases. Increasing your cover does not necessarily mean you will have to pay a higher premium. You may also need specialists to come in and value things like antiques. Remember when doing an initial valuation to go into every room, including the garage and attic if you have one, and list literally everything you would want to take with you if you moved, and what it would cost to go out and buy new equivalents of each item. When you make expensive purchases keep receipts and take photographs. Don't forget to include large collections of CDs or books. If you still feel insecure look for an unlimited cover policy.

When you're looking at clothes and linen, you do need to deduct some value for wear and tear. Apparently the average wardrobe is worth approximately £4,000, a tenth of the average household contents, and if you have a particularly posh frock or designer suit it might be worth naming it as an individual item for insurance. Read the small print and make sure you're complying with any clauses such as if the company insist you have a particular type of window lock. It's not worth trying to get away with a different sort because in the event of a claim, the insurance company will want to know that everything they stipulated was in place. And if it wasn't, they won't pay up. If in doubt about details, ring up your insurance company and ask them.

If you are going off to university or have a child doing so, it's worth seeing if you can arrange cover for their belongings on your contents insurance. Some policies may automatically include up to 10 per cent of your total cover for your teenager away from home, others may add cover at just a small cost. It's an important consideration because theft is a hazard in student accommodation with home entertainment electronics and mobile phones lying around.

Home insurance

Appliance insurance is real glass-half-empty stuff and it is astonishing that we don't bat an eyelid at the shop assistant trying to sell us extended appliance insurance when we are buying that brand new washing machine or tumble drier. What clever sales psychology to get us accepting the inevitability of something brand new breaking down even before we've got it out of the door.

Think carefully before buying into the sell. Would you not be better putting the premium cost away into a special household repairs and renewals, high-interest bank account?

Even if you do decide to sign up you will have a cooling-off period when you can cancel and it might be worth going home and carrying out a bit of research into the repair costs you could expect to pay using local service companies. Come to think about it, why not talk to a friendly local repair man about which makes are the most reliable before making your purchase in the first place?

Also do look for bargains on auctions or clearance sites for white goods and other electrical hardware.

Transport

This is likely to form a large part of your spending, unsurprising when you think that buying a car is probably the second largest purchase you make after buying your own home. It is perfectly possible to get a bargain but this is one area where it particularly pays to have done your research. There are some key points to remember when **buying a car**.

- Do your homework on prices before going to a car dealership to buy a car and be prepared to haggle.
- Consider going to a car auction.
- You don't have to go to an actual live auction if, like many people, you are nervous about bidding. Be your own car auctioneer and set up your stall or shop for a new vehicle online.
- Never accept a dealer's finance package without comparing the deal to online or other high street car loans.

Shop around for the best price on a **car service** and don't feel hidebound to go to a franchised dealer, because restrictive warranties are no longer allowed; however, you may find that the dealer *can* offer a better service and price because he has computer diagnostics and specially calibrated tools for your make of car.

Drive in the highest gear possible without making the engine scream and **save fuel**. Fill your car with petrol in the morning as sun and raised temperatures later in the day cause petrol to expand a little so you'll pay for more than you are actually getting. This latter will make probably the tiniest of difference but, hey, if you are in penny-counting mode – might as well, and it's not easy to keep an eye on petrol costs – there can be wide fluctuations and differences. Consider too having a car converted to LPG fuel or even having an electrically chargeable car if you only make short journeys. You'll be being a better citizen and may even avoid paying any congestion charges. (See page 237.)

Be clever in the way you use the car. If there are regular same routes you and others carry out, such as the school run, work commute, or weekly shop to an out-of-town shopping centre, set up your own car pool with others and take it in turns. Or look into joining a car-sharing scheme if you only occasionally need a vehicle.

Look into different ways to get from A to B on any long trips by using **public transport**. There are bargains to be had by taking trains or coaches but remember to take into account the journey time, when you can travel and any transfer or connection issues. Also look for live information about disruptions and accidents. Consider using public transport for commuting and find out the cost of season tickets. Don't forget cycling or walking to work or on short journeys.

General expenditure

There are ways to manage all areas of your outgoings and one key way, which applies to loads of things, is to **shop online**. On average online purchases are much cheaper than the high street and online shopping is fantastically convenient with goods being delivered straight to your door. The downside is length of delivery and difficulties with returning faulty goods. A way to safeguard against this is to check out returns policies and always choose sites that list customer service telephone numbers and a headquarters address.

In terms of security the web should be as safe as the high street but always check there is a padlock symbol at the bottom of the screen when entering your payment details, which means your details are encrypted and therefore not visible to anyone else. Regular web shoppers agree that online shopping and dealing is really worth it when you know exactly what you want, as in electrical or white goods. Its time-saving factor in terms of finding out information and comparing prices is unparalleled. Share good experiences of online shopping and cost-comparing with friends and colleagues to create your own favourites list.

Online or offline there are hundreds of ways to drive down your spending and borrowing and increase your earnings, savings and investment. All you have to do now is dismantle the items on your budget one by one.

Food shopping

This is the stuff of life – the stuff you put into your mouth and others'. It includes the packet of wine gums you buy in the motorway services, the Starbucks coffee on the way into work and the Good Boy choc drops for your hound.

This is such a variable figure and depends on your circumstances, whether you live alone, love cooking or choose convenience food. It is, however, an area where you can probably reduce your spending with more planning and a bit of strategy. (See page 266.) Try these ideas:

- Don't ever go shopping when you are hungry or miserable because you'll only make impulse or comfort purchases. If you can avoid it don't take the kids with you because it's hard to say no to the sweets, biscuits and novelty yoghurts they'll clamour for.

- Plan the meals for six days of the week, looking for ways to stretch two meals out of one. Use the seventh day of the week to use up all the leftovers. (See page 266.)
- Prices vary in different supermarkets but you are likely to have to take into account convenience and hassle factor. Do your own comparison exercise on half a dozen key items to suss out where the best buys are.
- Try own brands or the basics ranges and see if you honestly can tell the difference.
- Shop late in the day to get priced-down bargains of near sell-by-date foods.
- Avoid buying pre-packed food by choosing loose vegetables and fruit.
- Buy exactly the number of slices of cooked meats you want from the deli counter.
- Try to cut down on your meat intake as that is often the most expensive component of a meal. Cook vegetarian dishes a couple of nights a week.
- Don't buy bottled water; use a filter jug instead.
- Do your food-ordering online if you can and on a Monday for Tuesday delivery, when it carries the cheapest tariff. You will be astonished how much less you spend by not browsing the aisles, and having a focussed list.
- Work out your weekly regular food and drink purchases and look for ways you can bulk buy. For example, if there is a particular wine you like, compare prices and look for a bargain. Look out for bin-end sales, and another thing worth remembering with wine is that wine clubs often have fantastic bargains because of their buying power.

- If you have a freezer think about buying jointed whole animals, such as a lamb in spring, when the meat is at its best. You'll pay less.
- Keep your eye in for a bargain offer either with the Bogof (Buy one, get one free) deals on things you regularly use or by collecting coupons for usual purchases.

- Collect too any loyalty points at your supermarket and make sure you transfer them into something that really will benefit you, such as air miles or money-off vouchers.

Eating Out

If you really want to try a smart restaurant, go for lunch instead of dinner and opt for the chef's specials, which are often part of a set-price meal. Either that or try any tapas or bar canapé menu to savour the atmosphere and style of cooking. National and local newspapers regularly carry adverts for eating-out special offers and can be tremendous value. They are usually two meals for the price of one or early dining deals. You can also get family-discount vouchers at some restaurant chains.

- When ordering still water ask for a jug of tap with ice.
- Always check your bill to see if the tip has been included as an optional, or not, gratuity. Be discerning about giving it if it's not included and most importantly don't pay for it twice.
- If you are likely to have a couple of glasses of wine at a wine bar don't buy it by the glass; buy it by the bottle instead.
- Frighten yourself by multiplying the cost of your daily latte across a year and see if it prompts you to wait until you get into the office, or to invest in a decent coffee machine and make your own before you leave home in the morning.
- Either make your own packed lunch or look for combination deals where you get a drink, a sandwich and some crisps for an all-in price.
- When motorway-travelling avoid buying your refreshments at expensive service stations. Plan ahead and find local pubs, garages and shops within a couple of minutes of motorway junctions or, of course, take some refreshments – it wouldn't have occurred to my parents' generation to buy a snack when travelling. They were always prepared with something to eat and drink.

Children

Children cost! A lot! The sooner you can get them money-wise and ultimately confidently self-sufficient the better, so starting a saving habit early is a good idea. When they are toddlers, children's bonds and other tax-free investments can be organised for them and then they can start getting actively involved themselves in saving at primary-school age with first building society accounts. Don't pay in the money without them. Get them used to making the counter transactions and checking the statements with you and do shop around for the best deal and enticements.

If they are interested in sport, as they get older several soccer and sports clubs have affinity savings accounts for fans who then have the added bonus of closer involvement at a different level with the team they support and knowing that their investment is also helping their club.

In their teenage years you can start them thinking long term with goals, such as a car or to go travelling after school, to save for in a high-interest account. They can have cash card independence with weekly pocket money translated into a monthly allowance.

Rather than shelling out for the latest **toys** or film-related merchandise and watch it being discarded within days, join a toy library where your children can borrow toys and games and exchange them for something new when the novelty wears off.

There really are some great online mail order sites for cheap **children's clothes**, which are a boon if you want to avoid trailing pushchairs, toddlers or, for that matter, sulky young teens around the shops. For other **children's equipment** look in the classified ads of your local paper for second-hand goods. There are always loads.

For **family trips** look out for special family offers or 'kids go free' deals at big attractions such as Alton Towers. Often these are outside the busy months when it's quieter too, so there's less queuing.

What about organising a **babysitting** rota amongst your friends to cover nights off? If one couple are more social than others, create an IOU system where other good deeds, such as getting a weekly shop in, collecting the kids from school, also have a comparable value.

Schools and universities all have plenty of guidance and advisers helping parents navigate their way through the process of education-funding. There are also plenty of savings schemes tailored specifically to help meet fees in the future. After all, if you currently have babes in arms, who knows what the funding model will be in eighteen years' time? At the moment you can save money each month in children's bonds and get the returns paid tax-free after ten years. There are other long-term schemes which will pay dividends in the end but which mean your money is tied up for at least five to ten years. It's worth investigating opportunities for any separate awards or bursaries your child might be eligible for, especially if they have a particular talent.

Entertainment

Don't invest in brand new equipment or kit for that **hobby or sport** you've taken up until you are absolutely sure you intend to carry on with the activity. Look out for short-term inducement memberships rather than having to pay fees and commit to a whole year at the gym or leisure centre.

If the quieter pursuits are more your thing, there are colossal bargains on the internet for **books, CDs, DVDs and games** although the high street are fighting back with their own special offers and promotions and some are tied into sites so you can compare prices before you head out to buy.

Most big **cinemas** have a cheap-night deal in the middle of the week when tickets are reduced, or some offer a season-ticket deal with allows you to buy entrance to so many films at a reduced price.

Instead of going out to the cinema, plan a viewing night at home with friends. Get in the latest DVD and make a big bowl of popcorn. Renting DVDs or videos from the library is much cheaper than from hire shops.

Clothes

Cyberspace clothes sales are fantastic places to sell unwanted clothes or pick up designer bargains and fashionistas won't need to be told that prices have tumbled on the high street. Cloning of designer and catwalk creations is a sophisticated business now and makes buying top-price top names a waste of money . . . unless you just have to have it . . . !

Find a good local dressmaker and fabric store and order your own bespoke wardrobe picking up on those style features you like.

A **clothes swapping** party is a no-cost way to update your wardrobe, and with a few basic house rules will be fun for you and your friends too. It's best to confine the invitations to same-size friends and ban old clothes or anything that is in any way damaged or noticeably worn. Bring loads of items and don't forget accessories such as hats or bags. If you are doing it with close friends, a free-for-all is probably the best bet, but if you don't know everyone that well, categorise your clothes and give them points, i.e. skirts five points, tops three, etc. Have a full-length mirror in the room. Have to say my husband said he wouldn't have married me if he'd known I'd ever think this was a good idea. (This is the only section he's read so God knows what he'll think about the rest.)

If your work and lifestyle allows you to be a serious non-suit-wearing person but then you suddenly find yourself in need of whistle and flute for a one-off formal occasion such as a wedding or function, look in your local **charity shops** for something half decent. Formal men's clothes don't tend to sell as quickly as women's clothes and you will often find top-quality tailoring for very little. Second-hand, vintage and charity shops are all good sources of cheap pieces and have the added advantage of throwing up some really individual stuff.

Beauty

The first thing I have to say, and I know I may sound like a puritan now, is when you are lured by an expensive beauty product, analyse what it is about it that attracts you. For instance some upmarket cleansing regimes include thick cleansing creams which are wiped off and the skin buffed with a special muslin cloth. With the best will in the world, muslin can't be *that* unique that it's not worth trying the same principle with a face flannel or muslin baby square and a tub of a cheaper version of cream cleanser.

In any event, before you buy, ask the girls at the beauty counters in big stores if you can be made over with the range they sell. It will be free, allow you to see how it looks on you, but with no obligation to buy, and if you book it before you have a special night or lunch out it will be as good as paying for a make-up session in a salon.

It's reasonable too to ask for **samples** of any skin creams or foundations to see how your face might react. These can be expensive but if the money is going to go anywhere it should be invested there. Make the savings on everything else by buying cheap brands or by carrying out **DIY beauty treatments**, such as waxing or pedicures and manicures.

Extend the life of drying-out wand make-ups, such as mascaras and lip sticks: plunge the reservoir end into a jug of hot water and add weeks to its life. Cut the ends off tubes and find loads of cream or gel left.

Ring your local college and see if they run courses for beauticians or hairdressers and have **model nights** when members of the public get their students' services for free. Large salons may also have trainees and be looking for willing guinea pigs.

Christmas and holidays

Christmas is a huge black hole for many of us. Make sure you don't end up spending more than you intend, by putting aside a couple of days early on to get most of your shopping done. During the year have a special notebook, or page in your diary, to note down things people say they'd like or present inspiration you might have. Most of the money-saving tips listed under food shopping will apply to your Christmas shopping for festive food. Make your own Christmas cards, or even better get your children to do it with blank cards and envelopes. Choose a simple design or buy a stamp, gold pain and glitter and organise a production line with the whole family helping. Then deliver as many as you can by hand!

Holidays can be hugely expensive but they offer loads of opportunities to economise. Never accept a hotel room rate as advertised. It's known as the rack rate in the trade and is often able to be discounted. Call in advance and ask what's the best price they can do, including corporate rates if you can say you are on business.

There are plenty of websites where you can get last-minute deals and some too where unsold **flights** and holiday deals are auctioned with low reserves. Don't only look at budget airlines for bargains because the nearer you are to departure date the cheaper other airlines get too.

You can stay in some fantastic locations in **youth hostels**, from cliff-top houses overlooking surfing beaches to city-centre heritage sites or eco-friendly hostels in national parks. Youth hostels no longer offer spartan utilitarian accommodation and instead have an increasing number of family or twin-bedded rooms at incredibly cheap prices.

What about signing up to become a **home sitter** and staying in homes all over the country? The agencies that deal with this are constantly on the lookout for mature, responsible people aged forty plus who can provide good references.

The idea of a **house-swap** is that for an agreed period, two households swap homes and consequently get free holiday accommodation. There are a number of different companies, mostly web-based, who organise this. You could, of course, arrange it informally yourself – but if in doubt, it's probably a good idea to go through a company for peace of mind. You can swap with anyone in the world and your homes don't necessarily have to be similar in size or type. You post your own details on a website with an indication of a country or area you would like to visit. And it becomes a honing process, with each side looking at all the options until you find the perfect swap. It may all feel deeply risky, handing over the keys of your home to complete strangers, but the idea is that if you are in each other's home, there is an in-built incentive to be respectful. Do unto others and all that. And you should have spent some time corresponding, swapping photos and information before the holiday, so you will already have built up some sort of relationship and element of trust. Most companies charge a fee to register.

Money through the ages

Finally for this section, in spirit with the ethos of this book, wouldn't it be great if you could look back, reclaim and bank all the money you have frittered away or mis-managed in the past? As you get older it's easy to kick yourself for being so stupid, especially with the probable non-earning years of old age looming. This was sent to me and I have tried to trace its origins but failed, so apologies to its creator for not crediting them.

> There are a recognised Seven Financial Ages of Man. The Unburdened Years up to eighteen when our parents are usually funding most aspects of our life. Then, from eighteen to twenty-four, when we spend most of our disposable income on ourselves and leisure, we enjoy what are known as the Burning Years. The Learning Years follow until we are thirty-four, and are given over to building our careers and starting our families. We then head into the lucrative Earning Years for the next ten years when our incomes reach a peak. We know what to do with our hard-earned or ill-gotten gains at this great age until we are fifty-four and in the Discerning Years of quality spending. We wake up to the prospect of retirement some point before we are sixty-four in a period identified as the Concerning Years. It's then downhill in the optimism stakes as we spend life onwards in the Yearning Years, wishing we'd planned and invested more and spent less.

Hmm . . . well, actually, I rather take issue with the last statement. I'm not sure how future generations will cope but many of today's oldies seem to be naturally thrifty. Something to do with being brought up in wartime with rationing, I suppose. Anyway I note that they diligently switch off lights and power at the mains, make two cups of tea from one teabag, turn the heating down and, of course, when they feel a bit shivery, put a jumper on and get over it!

Citizenship

Here's something to think about . . . apparently, twenty-five years ago, 60 per cent of people in their thirties were involved in a community activity of some sort. Today just 6 per cent of us are!

Life Auditors were anxious to work out what they could do to make the world a better place and wanted answers to these questions:

What does good citizenship mean?
How can I get more involved?
How can I be better informed?
Will my contribution make a difference?
Who and what organisations and advice can I trust?

Considering how good a citizen one is feels a bit like sitting outside the headmaster's study, knowing he's going to say 'could do better'. Even defining what I mean by good citizenship made my brain hurt. In *The Life Audit* I suggested a broad brush that could encompass *anything* you did to make the world a better place, *anything* you did without *self*-interest as the spur and *any* way you enhanced somebody else's life at however minuscule a level.

It's easy to be blinkered about the bigger picture when your personal life is busy and the kids, your job, your partner, your aged mum or just that spot on the end of your nose are all demanding attention. But if, and while, you are considering your citizenship, bear in mind that you are in fact a citizen of several communities – **local, national and global**. Being a good citizen may be about putting a smile on your next-door neighbour's face; it also might mean deciding to buck a trend that deprives a poor farmer on the other side of the world of a fair wage. Keep these examples in mind because, unlike other parts of life, being a good citizen is not about seeing the benefits or getting tangible feel-good payback. What it is about is knowing that at least you are doing *something* which is a darn sight better than doing nothing – check?

Even if you can't see how your actions can make any difference to the bigger picture, a good vibe has to start somewhere and it might as well start with you, and him, and her and them and then – blimey, collectively there's a swell (a good collective noun for a group of good eggs?) of people who together might, just might, make a big difference. The trouble is, the zeal of some good citizens can be intimidating when one's own efforts are rather humble, and I also struggle with the 'green is cool' thing, for example, which seems embarrassing and rather patronising. But I have to say there isn't one good reason *not* to try to make the world a better place and it seems stupid and selfish not to do what one can. But merely being aware that one should be a responsible citizen, and having a social conscience in a passive way about the rights and wrongs of the world just isn't good enough – sorry. It's the doing, the speaking out, even just the smiling at someone that counts. A community-links project have launched a campaign called We Are What We Do – www.wearewhatwedo.org – which, I think succinctly says what is in the Good Citizenship tin. **We are what we do** – which is *everything* from the minute you get up to the minute you go to bed, because everything gives you an opportunity to be a good citizen. How many tricks are you missing? It's also really crucial to emphasise that this is not just a duty thing. So many Life Auditors found this one of the most rewarding areas to consider. It's deeply personal but for that reason it's also really worthwhile. Making a difference on a local, national or international level will make you feel better about everything. The two key concepts are **integrity** and **engagement**. You'll need to think hard about what those mean to you, but here are some starting points.

It all begins with you

Might I suggest, before we solve world peace, we start with the inner you? The inner you holds all your opinions and prejudices about lots of other external things and people, and it's a good starting point for testing how comprehensive and refreshed your integrity is about being a good human being and citizen of the communities and world you live in. These are some things you might find it useful to consider:

- Identify the benchmarks that you set your standards by.
- Include any political beliefs, moral stances, views on others in society and your personal manners.
- Spot the dyed-in-the-wool opinions you wheel out and dish up in discussions.
- Work out where those mindsets came from: your parents, your education, the company you keep, your circumstances, a life experience?
- Consider when any of them were last challenged.
- Or tested by you being in a certain situation or meeting others who were.
- Do your opinions sit comfortably in the life you lead?
- Do you often find yourself ranting at others, society, the world not living up to your expectations and standards?
- Are you sure it is them and not you that is out of kilter?
- Are you hanging on to ideals that need adapting to today's world to make them viable and are you resisting those changes?

Keep taking your opinions and any firm views out for an airing and give them a shake up to sanity-test their relevance to the world you live in. Interrogate yourself and allow yourself to be a bit insecure about where you are coming from. Don't let yourself trot out the party line because . . . you always have.

Speaking of party lines, let's use politics as an example of how to keep yourself a scrubbed-up good citizen mentally and intellectually. Enormous understatement coming up but I'll say it anyway: almost everything is political. Politics plays the major part in the way the world revolves socially, economically and morally, at its most global and at its most local. You may find politicians dull as ditchwater or think them devious careerists, but *politics* itself is important because of the role it plays structuring society. So I make no apologies for using it instead of, say, 'parenting' or 'the work ethic' as the subject to illustrate how you can give your opinions a health test.

If you always read one newspaper that affirms your political persuasion, take yourself out of this comfort zone and buy a paper that supports another party. Read its opinion columns to see what it is exactly you disagree with or whether there are some views you share. In fact with most newspapers and periodicals available on the web, it should be an easy and quick thing to do on a regular basis and reading at least two leader columns a day is a mature way to keep your opinions informed and up to scratch.

Of course you'll probably not agree, but at least try to *understand* what their motivation is for beating that drum or flying that flag about said issue. Where are they coming from in taking that stance? Spot any areas you like to pontificate on and make sure your reasons for doing so, and your sources, are valid. Are you up to date with developments about that issue? Do you have any big hates about people involved? For example who do you think are the villains of the piece? Have you ever met one of them or heard first-hand accounts of why they do whatever it is that makes you see red? And who are the victims, are they culpable at all? Do you put your helping hand where your mouth is or are you talking theoretically?

The next step: being neighbourly, especially to strangers

So that's the inner you, the starting point of being a good citizen. Where next? Well, what about the woman next door, the man on the tube, the rail guard, the woman at the post office, or that person – there, that one, the one walking towards you. What about the possibility of actually saying good morning? You don't have to sound like someone out of a 1940s B-movie. It isn't necessarily a freakish thing to do. Just say it as it is.

Engage eye contact, move mouth into smile shape and say, 'Morning,' or 'Evening,' or 'afternoon'. Or even just 'hello'!

It is depressing that lots of people don't exchange pleasantries any more. They move through their days in bubbles of aloneness. Squished up against each other on public transport, standing in queues, pushing past each other in shops, serving people or being served with hardly any social or kindly exchanges. You don't even have to say anything because an open friendly face or a smile can speak volumes.

Now . . . what about actually being *helpful*? Offer that seat to an elderly person, carry that heavy case up the station steps (thank you, thank you, lovely young man at Slough), knock on next door's and say you are going to the out-of-town supermarket – can you get them anything while you're there – you were just wondering? No – OK, that's fine! Isn't it a lovely day? Or of course, windy, rainy, etc.

Oh dear, am *I* sounding preachy, worthy? I may be and so sorry but it's not because I think everyone *has* to be matey and it's not that I'm confusing being a good citizen with just being a good person. It's just that moments like that one at ghastly Slough station, when I was heaving my case up two flights of stairs and that lad offered to help, really did make my day and made the society I live in less lonely and full of suspicion and more – well, civilised. The fact that he was Asian made it feel all the more significant and generous on his part. It was the week after the London bombs and there were dozens of people on the platform, all not looking at each other and certainly not at me puffing and sweating. He didn't need to do it but he did and I bet it wasn't a one-off gesture. See what I mean about everything being political? Dozens of the contributors to *The Life Audit* listed the little kindnesses from strangers as the things that enhanced their lives and made them feel good. Equally it's the mean-spirited acts of rudeness or ungraciousness that can make your soul die.

Community action – act local

If you struggle with spontaneous smiling at strangers or neighbourly cold calling, you could join any number of community schemes to do your bit locally. This way too you'll probably make new friends, discover a new interest or even indulge a hobby. There is scientific evidence that people involved as volunteers in **community activities** are usually healthier and happier. Focussing on others, it would seem, brings personal rewards. If you're not sure who the people are who might appreciate some support or what are the issues that need campaigning for in your neighbourhood, look in your local newspaper or at the local library. An example to get you thinking . . .

It was the headline news in the local paper that the village shop was about to close down that galvanised a small community to get together and work out a way to keep it going. An organising committee started fund-raising, applying for rural grants and setting up a serving rota and within a month they had opened up for business with basic goods in a caravan parked on the village car park. Three months later it was in a brand new wooden building, had broadened its product range and services and had opened a post office counter too. Retired district nurse Joan said the success of the campaign had meant more than just managing to keep a local amenity going. 'It really brought the community together and made us realise how important it is to work together to help each other.'

If there are no identifiable local campaigns, national organisations run **Good Neighbour schemes** where you can choose what you want to volunteer for: from human and civil rights to disaster relief to prisoners and ex-offenders. If you want to volunteer for a charity or non-profitable organisation to donate time or offer expertise, there are many charities where you can register your details to become a volunteer.

Think too about whether your employer might be keen to encourage you and colleagues to take part in some community campaign or charity work. From their point of view it could be good PR to show they are giving something back. Check what issues are currently topical in your locality. Look especially for ones that might be a match with the company's ethos or the skill-set of its employees and talk to the boss to see what company energy, time and resources can be allocated.

The Big Scale: beyond your back yard

What about the bigger picture? It's a growing trend, it seems, for some people, more often than not high achievers, to reach a point in their career and question the contribution they are making to society. Quite often this coincides with an ambitious plan to travel and retrain to help others. If this is you, best not to chuck up your job immediately but to look instead for a compromise period. Talk to your boss about taking an extended holiday or sabbatical. This may be seen as a good thing for the company with you possibly acquiring new skills, such as in leadership or communication. Research potential placements thoroughly, considering accommodation, support, training, medical back-up and, of course, money.

Remember, your good citizenship doesn't only have to be directly helpful to people. There are umpteen projects, campaigns, needy things that are non-human. Clearing ditches, conserving nature, stewarding historic buildings and churches, archiving and building dry stone walls are just some of the things Life Auditors got involved in, sometimes even for annual holidays. Go back to those questions about what integrity and engagement mean for you. What fires you?

Sam had worked with several volunteer groups on environmental projects in his area, such as ditch-clearing, but was interested in finding something a bit more mentally engrossing. So he was pleased to hear about a local botany group looking for volunteers to join them to monitor some woodland over the course of a year. 'It involves a couple of hours each weekend and then half a day once a month when I join the others to collate what we have found out. It's been fascinating studying nature and seeing what is threatened and what is thriving. I'm going to continue the interest. I've made some good friends too.'

Politics, again

For many Life Auditors, **environmental** and **developmental issues** and **ethical consumerism** were the biggest global issues they felt they could engage with. Climate change is natural and has been happening forever. The British Isles, for example, have been tropical, then desert, then tropical again, covered in rain forest, submerged under water and then, about 15,000 years ago, the ice age hit. Since then the earth has been warming up – natural global warming. These changes have always taken thousands if not millions of years – but now climate change is speeding up because since the beginning of the Industrial Revolution, about 200 years ago, man has been making his own contribution to global warming.

We all hear about the Greenhouse Effect – but, like global warming, there's a natural and an unnatural version. Naturally occurring gases like carbon dioxide insulate the earth, sort of protecting it in a blanket, maintaining a civilised temperature and they have been at constant levels for thousands of years. But now we are producing man-made greenhouse gases and the balance has been thrown. Every time we generate energy, and that means turning a light on or starting the car, we invariably burn fossil fuels – coal, oil, gas – and send more of these gases into the atmosphere. The gases, in effect, thicken the protective layer around the earth, trapping the heat from the sun – and the earth heats up.

Put simply: as a consequence of the earth heating up, extreme weather conditions become more and more common. Ice caps melt, coastlines erode, flooding increases, pollution and associated diseases increase, drought, pests and famine become more prevalent.

After climate change – and as a result of it – shortage of water is the second most critical problem for the world this century say the United Nations Environment Programme. One person in five currently has no access to safe drinking water yet the rest of us are increasing our consumption year on year. In twenty years' time there will be a significant shortfall in the amount of water needed for the world's agriculture, which will affect development and cause conflict in many places.

The upshot is – we need to address climate change and we need to curb the gases we're expelling. Use less energy and less gas goes out into the atmosphere.

It's easy to think that it's everybody else's problem. What's the point in being careful when you fill the kettle if a great big factory next door is belching out smoke? But it really is the truth – and an important part of my own notion of citizenship – that if everybody made a single effort, the world would be a better place. Here are a number of easy things you can do to do your bit, and save money while you're at it.

- While you're brushing your teeth, turn the tap off.
- Put the plug in your sink or bath – never let hot water just pour down the drain.
- Have a shower rather than a bath which uses five times more water.
- If you only want to make a single cup of tea, don't boil a whole kettle full of water. Put lids on saucepans and then turn them down once they're boiling.

- Turn the light off when you leave a room.
- Use energy-saving light bulbs.
- Invest in good heavy curtains for their insulating properties and close them as soon as it starts getting dark to keep the heat in.
- Get on top of draughts – seal the gaps.
- Check the temperature levels on your heating and hot water. You probably could get away with turning them both down a bit. Your hot water need be no more than 60°C.
- Put on more clothes (a jumper, maybe!) rather than turn up the heating and if you don't use a room, make sure the radiator is turned off.
- Insulate your loft – about 40 per cent of heat goes out through the loft and walls – and get quotes for cavity wall insulation. There are some very good deals around.
- Don't leave things like your TV on standby – it uses exactly the same amount of energy as if it was on.
- Don't put warm things in the fridge – let them cool down first.
- Time your heating to come on half an hour before you get up and to go off half an hour before you go to bed. Or if your house is well insulated, experiment and turn if off earlier.
- Is your boiler really old and inefficient? A new one could save you money in the long term.
- Consider switching to a green electricity supplier that uses renewable resources.
- When you're buying new white goods or a new car – do your research and buy one that is energy efficient such as LPG or electrically powered.
- Drive less. If it's practicable, use public transport, walk or cycle.
- There are lots of national organisations now that operate car-share schemes and you may also want to try your local county council, which probably operate a scheme as part of a government initiative to go green and cut down on traffic emissions.
- Service your car regularly, check the tyre pressures and make sure you're not lugging round extra weight. All these things affect the efficiency – and fuel consumption – of your car.

You can make a difference

One of the most important things you can do is get used to thinking about **reusing and recycling**. Minimise your impact as much as you can. Have you noticed how in service stations they sell a single pear or apple in a polystyrene shell with a plastic cover on top? Ridiculous. When you go to the supermarket and buy a red cabbage do you put it straight in your basket or put it in one of those plastic bags first? Why do you do that? It's complete madness. Unless it's really muddy, and I bet it's not, it really doesn't need to go in a little plastic bag, does it? And do you find yourself throwing away piles and piles of junk mail and pizza delivery menus every week? If you want to stop getting this, contact the Mailing Preference Service.

- Have you got a cupboard or corner in your home that is stuffed with old supermarket carrier bags? Do you take them out with you to use again or just get another one and shove it in the cupboard when you get home? Do you eventually stuff them all in the bin or recycle them? Have you thought about not using them at all and taking a proper shopping bag out with you? There's a radical suggestion – use-a-shopping-basket and instantly be a better person!
- Make a positive point of looking at packaging and choosing to buy things that have used recycled materials. Buy recycled loo paper and kitchen roll. When you're de-cluttering, always take things to be recycled or to a charity shop.
- More than likely your local council run a recycling collection scheme. If in doubt, ring them up and ask.
- It's a good idea to use rechargeable batteries but you can't throw them away as you would normal batteries. They contain hazardous metals so either take them to your local tip where they should be able to dispose of them safely or send them back to the manufacturer.
- Mobile phones – take your old one to a phone shop and they should be able to recycle it for you.
- Set your computer printer to print double-sided and buy recycled paper. Recycle your computer.

- Instead of chucking old furniture and household appliances, see if there's a scheme local to you which helps to set up and furnish their home, who otherwise couldn't afford to. Old spectacles? Don't throw them away but donate them to a charity who can give them to someone in a developing country.

If you've got a garden, one of the most sensible things you can do is make your own **compost**. The first thing you need to do is buy or make your compost bin. The idea is to build up some heat to give bacteria and micro-organisms the right environment to break down the softer material, then in come worms and insects to get to grips with the bigger stuff. So whatever your bin is made out of, it needs a lid and to be in a sheltered position where the sun can warm the contents. It takes about three to nine months for compost to mature and you need to get in there and stir it up every now and then. You can put in grass, old fruit and vegetables, horse, chicken or pigeon manure, egg shells, shredded paper, old straw and animal bedding, fur and old leaves, plant clippings and teabags. But nothing meaty, fishy or likely to attract rats. Nothing revolting like dog or cat poo, no weeds like dandelions, no nappies, dairy products or coal ash. It's just common sense really.

Make sure any garden trimmings are nicely shredded and always put in a good mix – not an enormous layer of anything at a time, and every now and then, a bit of water. You want it to be warm and wet and don't mix it so often it doesn't have a chance to stew in its own juices. When it comes to taking the compost out to put on the garden, go to the bottom and use that oldest stuff first.

Be an ethical consumer
When you're 'consuming' you have more power than you may think. You can choose to positively pay for things that you know are ethical, for example Fairtrade goods – and you can choose to boycott and not buy things you don't believe in. This was a biggie for many Life Auditors.

Recycling

Fairtrade – a worldwide labelling initiative – guarantees a better deal for producers. When you buy something with a Fairtrade label on it you know that the people who produced the coffee, bananas or whatever, are getting a proper price for their efforts and that their business is consequently a sustainable one. The farmers are being treated with dignity. They're not being shafted – for want of a better word – by a faceless multi-national.

The key thing is – do your research and take responsibility for the choices you make. No one's perfect and it's pretty much impossible to be entirely wholesome but think about the component parts of your life and where things come from. You may already buy organic carrots from the supermarket but are you aware of the criteria some supermarkets impose on their producers? Did you know that a huge percentage of the organic carrots the farmers grow have to be chucked because they aren't straight enough to fit into the plastic bags? And how far have those organic carrots travelled? When you realise that actually they've come 400 miles on the motorway, in lorries spewing out petrol fumes, they may not be such an ethical choice. Surely much better to find some locally grown carrots – a bit muddy and bent. And what about organic green beans from Egypt? Think about the madness of it. Air travel is an environmental disaster: according to one source, for every 4,000 miles travelled by one person, a tonne of carbon dioxide pollution is produced.

And what exactly does organic mean? It may be governed in the UK by the Soil Association but do other countries have the same rules?

Find out what food producers are local to you and check them out. Obviously local doesn't necessarily mean it's great but do your research and try to find out where your food comes from and how it's produced. **Farmers' markets** are the obvious first port of call. Get there early and get to know the producers of local cheeses, buy vegetables grown in season in nearby fields! Maybe you have a local farmshop or a grocer in your area who supports good, local producers.

More than likely buying ethically is a bit more expensive but what is the real cost – to your health, the environment and someone else's quality of life? And it's not just food where you can use your purchasing power to make an ethical point. From bricks, to paints, to sofas, to bed linen or nappies, golf balls to gifts – there will be an ethical option whether you're building a house or shopping for Christmas. Go on the internet and type ethical products or specify ethical whatever it is you're looking for into a search engine and you will be presented with dozens of credible sites either selling wares or recommending and offering links.

Ethical money is now big business and consumers increasingly want to know where their money is invested. When you take out a pension or join up with a new bank, you can choose to invest ethically and know that you're not supporting an oppressive political regime or arms dealer. Maybe you want to steer clear of any association with animal testing, tobacco producers or pornographers. Ask questions and look out for the options – ethical investing is one of the fastest growing sectors of the last ten years.

You can actually select a financial adviser who specialises in ethical or socially responsible funds which, in typical finance-speak, are called SRIs.

You could choose a **charitable credit card** – which means that a small percentage of your spend goes to a charity, and some of them even give a lump sum to the charity when you take it out. Lots of charities have them so ring up and find out.

Make your donations to charity tax efficient by opting for gift aid which means that the charity can reclaim the tax. You could also consider asking your company to set up a payroll scheme whereby some of your salary goes to charity. It's deducted before tax, so you will hardly notice it and the charity will receive more.

Call to arms . . .

There are many big and little things you can do to make the world a better place and, without wanting to sound preachy, the truth is most of us are all staggeringly self-interested these days.

Ethical consumerism

241

We go from A to B in our own hermetically sealed units and little lives, too busy or guilty or frightened to look up and notice the community or lack of it we live in. Where we live, the good fortune we enjoy and the opportunities we have are often lucky accidents of our birth, as is much of the suffering of others, who were unluckier than us. It doesn't take much to do *something*, however little, not just to assuage guilt, but to make a positive contribution to everyone's world. It's important! Really important!

Home

When you are faced with big life issues, such as 'keeping love alive' or 'how to spite the boss', there is nothing quite like retreating into the elbow grease of household management. Its chores and demands are safe and definable, you know when they need doing, you see results after doing them and the methods you use either work or they don't. There are no fuzzy, maybe areas. I like that! It's not that I am a particularly fastidious housekeeper and at times really rubbish, actually, but I do like a good gumption. I tell you this so you understand where I'm coming from here. So, deep breath and pinnys on.

Your home has to provide down-to-earth needs for you and your family. Make sure you're realistic about your circumstances. It may be that those dreams of the thatched country cottage with roses around the door will have to wait a while because you can't afford it or because work or other commitments mean you need to live in the heart of a city. Don't make the mistake of hankering after a domestic set-up that is inappropriate – look at your life as a whole and choose the best dwelling for you right now. More than anything these are the practical things that matter:

Is it a safe and secure shelter and sanctuary?
Does it provide you with privacy?
Does the cost of your home fit your budget?
Do you have the time and money to meet its maintenance needs?

Then, there's everything else – the personal stuff, and that's incredibly important too, of course. If *Through The Keyhole* were to visit, would there be 'in-character elements' that would reflect you and the interests and loves in your life, or are the rooms full of things you neither like nor need, that say nothing about the person you are and contribute nothing to the life you lead?

Think about the contents of your home – your stuff. As William Morris said, 'Have nothing in your house that you do not know to be useful or believe to be beautiful.' True happiness is when a useful object is *also* a thing of beauty, and design and substance come together. The beauty bit is, of course, a bit subjective, although some goods that seem to have achieved it to universal acclaim do get mentions from me. If your contents make your home feel cluttered then be inventive about storage and, better still, be brutal about getting rid of some of them.

Think of what your home and contents mean to you and how they fit the way you live. Ask yourself these questions:

Does your home feel like a sanctuary?
Does its functionality complement your lifestyle?
Does it reflect your style?
How does living in your home affect you – make you happy or depressed?
Do you love all your belongings or appreciate their usefulness?
Do you mind doing the housework?
Which people, products, routines help get it done?

This section of the book will consider the practical issues of home-keeping and has heaps of good advice on the basics of cleaning. This is not because I am a clean freak but more because doing things the right way will minimise the time they take. The rest of the chapter is structured on a room-by-room basis and also covers the exterior of your home, including the tricky spaces such as garage and garden shed. It finishes with a look at managing the paperwork that keeps a home running. I want to start with general cleaning basics and then tackle the chores and typical contents of each room.

Cleaning

Oh how happy am I writing this . . . tra la la la. Here's the deal: a clean, tidy and well-maintained house lets you get on with the rest of your life while a house that you obsess about keeping clean or tidy will rule your life.

Speaking personally, I am big on the sense of liberation and peace of mind a tidy house bestows, though reading what follows may lead you to believe I am bordering on the obsessive. I'm really not. I just believe organisation and routines to take care of what needs to be done are the way ahead. Get the job done quickly and properly and then move on to more interesting bits of life. If you want to introduce extra obsessing into the rest of your time, that's your choice but maybe you should look to what's missing elsewhere . . .?

Who does what

Before we go any further, can I say first off (oh dear – here I go) that I think it's bonkers for people to get hung up about who does what with regard to housework and cleaning. Haven't we moved on from all that? Along with who earns what and who nurtures the children. No, I know lots of people haven't – well, they jolly well should have. It makes no sense in today's world and it just doesn't work like that any more. This issue could go into the Relationships section, what with all the rows it causes. It may be *just* housework but why do people ignore its importance in making for a harmonious life and position themselves so firmly in terms of what they consider to be their own responsibility? I'm talking here mainly about blokes who do nothing and women who do everything and feel like martyrs. I've heard lots of stories in which either all the housework falls to one person and others in the household are breathtakingly untidy or everyone is so busy that it just doesn't get done at all and chaos rules. As with any other aspect of life and work, keeping a house tidy and clean takes a bit of organisation and some time. *If* it falls naturally that one person has more time to do chores above other commitments then that's all well and good, but if people in a household are all being busy most of the time then it makes sense to share responsibility for what needs to be done. We are talking about support services for the household here – just because we may all have a chance to *have* it all, does not mean that just one of us has to *do* it all. So, here's the drill on how to reach an agreement everyone in your house can live with. And a note to those of you who live alone: you should be feeling very smug – sometimes the greatest luxury is only having your own washing-up to deal with.

- Agree a definitive list of things that need to be done in each area of the house.
- Decide the standard that the job should be done to.
- Collectively match people to jobs according to when they are around to do them. Don't put up with any nonsense about someone being better than anyone else at dishwasher-loading – yeah right! Now you've agreed a standard, individual performances don't come into it.
- Without wishing to sound like a cleaning-rota Nazi, have a tick-box system to flag up if something doesn't get done. Let's assume not because they couldn't be bothered but because events elsewhere overtook them. It still needs doing and so someone will have to – they, I am sure, will reciprocate when someone else needs extra support.

Doesn't feel like rocket science to me. Indeed it seems mighty equitable and if someone in your household won't join in, or is happy for others to take responsibility for this, then the issue really is one of relationships not housework. You may decide to let it be or that there is a fair pay-off in another area of your life but if you feel fed up about it – and I have to say I'm with you – it's just plain unfair. Support Services are support services and it's just mean and selfish for someone not to pull their weight.

That includes **children** helping too. As toddlers they can be got into the habit of putting toys away at the end of playtime and from seven they can be making their bed, dusting and sweeping and helping lay the table. From eight it's not unreasonable to ask a child who is a whiz on a PlayStation to know which buttons to press on a washing machine after loading in their uniform or sports kit. Size of said child dictates when they can do bedlinen-changing but at the age of nine my two lads with their long arms were quicker at putting on duvet covers than me. (That said – one of the greatest acts of kindness you can do for your teenager, along with all the intellectual parenting you might want to apply to their adolescence, is to let them treat their own room as a pig sty, as long as it's not unhygienic, and very occasionally when they are away to go in and muck it out for them.)

 Create a master checklist to identify the daily, weekly, quarterly and other chores. Use it too if you have **paid-for cleaning help** (see page 76) to be clear about your expectations. List jobs, products to be used, and a comments box. Use this to flag up specifics you want doing – especially useful if you are out at work when they come. Do every job *yourself* to your satisfaction and time how long it takes so you don't have unrealistic expectations of what's achievable. If you are someone to whom it matters *how* things are done, be anally pedantic detailing procedure and products. Others may think you are mad but it's better than expecting them to be telepathic while simmering with rage at their methods versus yours. How are they to know it's the old *pink* toothbrush you use to clean the grouting around the shower? It's in their interests and yours that the job gets done to your satisfaction and this way they'll be clear on what you want.

There are some items that need specific cleaning and maintenance, and they are covered room by room, but here are the basics . . .

General housework

- Open windows for half an hour a day whatever the weather to air rooms.
- Always start cleaning at the top and work down – i.e. cobwebs first, carpets last.
- Dust, plump cushions, change sheets, etc., before vacuuming.
- Organise and get on top of jobs such as window-cleaning, carpet-shampooing or taking soft furnishings to the cleaners. Schedule these chores to make sure they happen.

Dusting

- Work out how often you need to dust – with my windows open lots and living right on a road, I should do it once a day – ho hum.
- Use a soft cotton cloth *very lightly* moistened with sprayed water and dust using a circular motion, follow with a dry cloth. *Or* buy a pair of cotton lint-free gloves and get hands-on using the same principles.
- Lift lamps, etc., and dust underneath.
- Use a soft artist's brush to get into any finicky places.
- Dusting doesn't require 'products' so you don't *need* to use spray polish. However, the following do other things. Using beeswax furniture cream a couple of times a year will nurture solid wood. A glass cleaner on, er, glass table tops will make them super shiny. Special anti-static cleaning cloths for TVs, computers, etc., will – stop static.

Mopping

- Mop hard floors at least once a week, more if they are in an area of much foot traffic, or if you have pets and, like my long-haired dog, their fur blows like tumbleweed, gathering disgustingly around chair and table legs.
- Pull furniture out from walls.

- Sweep or vacuum first, using a low setting.
- Mix detergent, or special wood-cleaning detergent if it's a wooden floor, into hot water.
- Mop with long sweeps from side to side, lifting the mop to avoid sloshing muck back over a cleaned area. Rinse the mop out in the bucket and squeeze the excess out every few strokes.
- Get up as much liquid from the floor as you can and leave to dry without walking over it.

Sweeping and Vacuuming

- Choose brooms with angled heads.
- Use soft and synthetic ones for inside, coarse and bristly for outside.
- Sweep towards you out of corners from one end of a room.
- Then sweep the dust into neat piles to be collected by a dustpan and brush.
- Understand the workings of your vacuum and know when to empty the bag and wash the filters.
- Learn to use all the different nozzles and suckers on curtains, upholstery and for places hard to get at.

Window-cleaning

- Don't clean windows on a sunny day because they will dry too quickly and leave smears.
- Wash woodwork and surrounds with detergent.
- Lightly spray window cleaner and polish with a lint-free cloth.
- Use vertical movements on one side of the glass and horizontal on the other so you can see which side has smears.
- Or use a squeegee and weak soapy water and start from the top of each pane drawing the rubber blade down at an angle and wiping between each stroke.
- Finish with one horizontal stroke along the bottom.
- Distilled vinegar and newspaper are also effective window-cleaning materials.

General housework

- You can stop windows misting with condensation by rubbing them over with a tiny bit of washing-up liquid on a dry cloth.

Cleaning Silver

- You shouldn't put silverware into the dishwasher because some foods and other metals can cause tarnish and corrosion.
- Use a soft toothbrush to get into crevices.
- There are creams and dips and impregnated commercial cleaners – they all do the job so it's up to you which one will make this chore less grim. Claridge's hotel in London say the cream ones are best.
- Or put silver to be cleaned into a pan of water in which you have heated a crumpled-up piece of aluminium foil and simmer for ten minutes, then wash in soapy water and dry well.

Cleaning Kit

Keep all your cleaning things in a caddy, bucket or basket so that you can cart them from room to room rather than keeping or leaving bottles all over the house. If you are currently peering at the stacked array of squirty sprays and gumptions under your sink thinking they just won't all fit in one receptacle, clear the draining board and get them all out on top to see what you have. There are so many specialised house-cleaning products on the market you may well have many that in fact could double up. You may have chosen them because of the whizzy dispenser, the smell, the promise of result without elbow grease or just because it was a cleaning product for something you hadn't thought about cleaning. In actual fact you could get away with just three cleaning agents for the whole house:

- A mild abrasive cleaner for scrubbing surfaces that won't scratch.
- A non-abrasive cleaner for surfaces that are shiny and might scratch.
- Washing-up liquid for almost everything else, used in various strengths of dilution.

The above could be supplemented by some bleach for disinfecting and distilled white vinegar and bicarbonate of soda. These last two were staples of old-fashioned house-keeping and can easily be used to make your own cleaning fluids, adding a couple of drops of essential oils, such as pine or eucalyptus, to make them smell fresh. This is a good way to trim household costs and has the added benefit of reducing the amount of chemicals you're sending into the environment.

All-purpose anti-bacterial cleaner – Rinse a used spray bottle thoroughly and fill with two-thirds water. Add one to three tablespoons of liquid bleach (depending on how strong you need it to be) and one tablespoon of washing-up liquid. Gently mix and fasten lid. Always rinse off with fresh water and cloth.

Window cleaner – Mix one-third white vinegar with two-thirds water and use in same way as a commercial cleaner. Using newspaper instead of a cloth works too.

Stain remover – Bicarbonate of soda mixed to a paste works wonders on all sorts of stains and in fact is a real star in the cleaning cupboard, working miracles on problems from blocked drains to making stainless steel shine.

Air freshener – There are loads of ways you can scent your home, from gently heating a pan of water with some cinnamon and cloves in or leaving some orange slices to dry in the oven as it cools down after cooking, to putting some drops of essential oils on some cotton wool out of sight on a radiator. Or you can make your own atomiser by mixing 20 drops of essential oils, such as bergamot, lavender, sandalwood and verbena, to a tablespoon of water then adding 30 ml of vodka, and after a couple of days, 30 ml of distilled water. Pour into a spray bottle and shake before use.

If you are worried about your exposure to chemicals and don't want to make your own cleaning products, there are alternative environmentally friendly brands available.

It has to be said that in amongst a lot of gimmicky and well-marketed but ineffective cleaning products there are also some great ones that do exactly what they say on the tin with record speed and minimum effort and so save time and grief on some of the nastiest cleaning jobs. If you are not taking the minimalist route, the following is a standard cleaning kit I use:

Acidic kitchen cleaner
Alkaline bathroom cleaner
Bottle brush
Brush
Bucket
Caddy or bucket with a handle to carry cleaning goods
Cloths – change daily as apparently average one contains million times more bacteria than is found on a loo seat!
Dusters
Dustpan
Feather duster or modern fluffy fibre equivalent (with a telescopic pole if you have high ceilings)
Floor detergent
Hoover
Metal cleaner for silver, copper or brass
Mop
Mop bucket
Rubber gloves
Scourer
Stiff brush for mats
Thick bleach – use with care
Washing-up brush
Wood polish

Room by room

I should warn you at this point that, at times, I may seem rather anal with the specifics that apply to each room. It's a bit like exposing one's knicker drawer, revealing how one organises and cleans one's home . . . so, for the record, some of what follows lapses into extraordinary detail, but that's the way I like it.

Kitchen

A kitchen is usually the hub of a home where domestic and social life come together. Therefore it needs to be efficiently ordered and equipped, it also needs to be kept clean and germ-free because it is the main area for food preparation and probably eating, but at the same time needs to have a warm ambience and comfort.

People can get very territorial about kitchens. The main cook and potwash may take umbrage at mess, or flatmates can become bitchy about the misuse of *their* butter on *their* fridge shelf. So, when it comes to kitchens, and probably bathrooms as well, actually, it's a really good idea to have some house rules and routines. Encourage collective responsibility because the kitchen is a room where the regular observance of good practice means important hygiene and safety issues will be dealt with as a matter of routine. If you have children start them young by getting them to help so that they learn about food storage and preparation.

Cookers, microwaves, hobs

- Whenever you cook, give the appliance a wipe over with a damp cloth when you have finished and it has cooled down. (Don't use an abrasive cleaner on anything with a shiny or glass finish.)
- Depending on how often you cook, the hob and oven will need a more thorough clean at least once a month. Doing this regularly will mean it should never become a ghastly job with the regular heat turning spilt food into permanent cement and smoking the house out.
- Try to mitigate cooking mess by using large enough pans and trays, by covering food while it's cooking whenever you can, by taking extra care when lifting things out of the oven, and by lining the grill pan with foil to make easy disposal of resulting fat which can smoke and even catch alight if left until more cooking is carried out.
- Should you burn something in the oven, remove the offending charred remains outside and try sprinkling some salt on any burnt remains in the oven to get rid of the stink and allow you to carry on cooking.
- When cleaning a hob, detach as many removable parts as possible including knobs and handles although be careful to put them

back on correctly and double-check that you haven't inadvertently turned on a ring, plate or the oven.

- When cleaning the oven, read the instructions carefully on a proprietary cleaner – some work best when the oven is warm and most need to be left for a bit of time to be effective. Put plenty of newspaper down and be careful not to breathe in the fumes. Before getting down to this horrid job, heating an ovenproof container full of water inside the oven for half an hour will create steam that will help the cleaning process.
- Or save up for an Aga or Rayburn – burnt food just burns away with no smell.
- When using microwaves always cover the food to avoid splattering. To clean, remove the rotating plate and don't forget to check the roof where most food explosions will have made the most impact. A useful tip is to wet the cloth you intend to use on your microwave and then place it inside to cook for one minute. You won't be able to handle it for a while so leave the door shut. When it's cooled down use the cloth to wipe down the interior and you will find that the resulting steam has helped soften stuck-on food debris making it easier to shift.

Sinks

The sink is where many a drama is played out and the state it's left can cause plenty of rows. It's probably the most used fixture in your kitchen and it's important it's kept clean as if its surfaces look clear and spotless and it will make your kitchen instantly appear more spick and span. Whether your sink is enamel, porcelain or stainless steel there are plenty of cleaners on the market specifically to do the job, although a mild general-use detergent will cut through the grease and a splash of bleach left in a sinkful of water for half an hour will disinfect effectively. Keep your sink drain unblocked by using a draining disc over the plughole to stop scrapings and vegetable peelings being washed away. Never pour melted fat down the drain, because it will set when it cools and block the pipes.

To **unblock a sink drain**, put the rubber cup of a plunger over the plughole and pump up and down, creating suction in the pipe to shift the blockage. Covering the overflow will add to the pressure. Follow this with a heavy-duty chemical drain cleaner, available from most high streets. If this doesn't work you need to tackle the U-bend pipe under the sink. Put a bowl underneath the U-bend and unscrew the U bit of piping. Rinse it and the blocking muck out thoroughly – but not in the sink above!

I do appreciate that giving 'instructions' on **washing-up** may seem both daft and patronising, but I am amazed by how many people really don't understand the basics. I watched the daughter of a friend of mine, who was in her twenties, trying to clean a greasy pan under cold running water. And – just checking, but did you know the flat side of a washing-up brush can be used as a scraper – I didn't and it can!

Buy a decent draining rack for the draining board so that items air dry quickly. Air drying is actually better than hand drying with a tea towel (apart from cutlery) as it saves time and is germ free. Washing-up doesn't need to be a hateful chore – try changing your mindset.

Mike actually enjoyed hand-washing dishes. 'I think it's a very satisfying job. It's companionable, because someone usually helps and if they don't it's quite an undemanding, contemplative, ordered sort of chore. Plus, you achieve results and see them quickly.' These are his washing-up instructions (I know! But see, I'm not the only one!).

How to do the washing-up

- First scrape off leftover food and stack the dirty dishes near to the bowl in order of washing, which is the least dirty first, so glasses followed by cutlery then plates, bowls and general crockery, finishing with the cooking utensils and pots, pans and ovenware.
- Squirt some washing-up liquid into the sink and run the hottest water you can bear, which will be greater if you are wearing rubber gloves.

- Be particularly careful with anything with a non-stick surface, avoiding scouring pads and leaving to soak any sticky substances.
- It's good to rinse hand-washed items in fresh hot water or under a hot tap before stacking on the drainer.
- Apart from cutlery which will have water spots on if you don't dry it, leave the washing-up to dry completely and then put away. And polish up glasses with a soft cloth.
- Use a solution of biological washing powder to get rid of stains on stainless-steel cutlery and bring to a simmer in a pan to remove burnt-on food.

There is heated discussion up and down the country about the wrong and right way to load a **dishwasher** and if you have a dishwasher bully in your household it may be best to let them get on with it. These, though, are the basic rules of dishwasher loading:

- First thing is, however tempting, don't put in anything precious, ancient, fragile, hand-painted, made of thin plastic or with joined-on bits such as bone or bamboo handles. My sister spectacularly once put her knife block into the machine – it came out looking like a crazy piece of contemporary wood sculpture.
- Dishwashers are fantastic for getting things spotlessly clean and sterile but loading is a bit of an art form. Check your instructions but, usually, the top shelf is for the least robust items, such as glasses, while the bottom, which gets hotter, is for more soiled things, such as pans and plates. Load from the back to the front, the top before the bottom.
- Washing stainless steel with silver or silver plate will cause tarnishing.
- Rinsing off beforehand can improve the wash and may be sensible if you don't have a full load and the crocks are

going to sit around for a while but I have to say it does seem a bit of a waste of time and effort to me.

- Spin the arms that distribute the water to make sure they have a clear path, close the door and let it get on with its work.
- Once a week run the dishwasher empty on a hot cycle with either one of the proprietary dishwasher cleaners or a cup of white vinegar that will cut through grease and get rid of residual smells.

Worktops and tables

All kitchen surfaces need wiping down daily to get rid of crumbs and any food debris left after food preparation. Do it after every meal and last thing at night with a damp cloth, and once a week give a really good wash with a cloth and disinfectant. Always use a chopping board and have different ones for meat, bread and vegetables. Plastic ones can go in the dishwasher to be sterilised, wooden ones need a scrub and to be scalded with boiling water to get rid of all their germs.

Fridges and freezers

Using your fridge effectively and safely is pretty much common sense with just a couple of basic rules to follow:

- It should be about 4° C and it's worth buying a fridge thermometer if you don't have a built-in temperature display. Freezers should be minus 18° C.
- Never put hot food into your fridge because it will raise the ambient temperature and affect everything else that is chilling.
- Once in the fridge always put cooked meat above raw so that no blood can drip on to the dish.
- As a general rule, store bottles and jars on door shelves where the temperature will fluctuate with the door opening and shutting. Dairy produce should go on the top shelf with fresh meat or fish

being put as near to the bottom as possible. Follow any manufacturer indications for specific uses of fridge drawers. Keep fruits and vegetables separate as they can spoil each other and in some cases taint the taste. For instance carrots will become bitter if kept with apples. Never put bananas in the fridge – they'll turn black.

- Always put newer items behind old ones that need using up, and have a sort out each week to cull anything that's gone off.
- Do a weekly clean at the same time, wiping over the shelves and fridge walls with a damp cloth and detergent or bicarbonate of soda. Don't forget the door seals that can be home to a disgusting build-up of gunk. Finally rinse off well – a splash of white vinegar in the water will help remove stubborn stinks.
- A small dish of bicarbonate of soda in the bottom of the fridge will also eliminate smells.
- Label everything you put in the freezer with a date and don't let things sit there for months. Check freezer life of bought foods.
- Unless you have a self-defrosting model you will need to defrost your freezer every couple of months.
- Run down your freezer stock and put any remaining frozen foods into a picnic cool box with ice packs while you clean it.
- Switch the freezer off and unplug from the mains then place a bowl of hot water inside to speed up the thawing process. Put an old towel underneath the freezer to mop up the resulting defrosting water.

Appliances and utensils

Be careful not to be seduced only by good looks if you need your appliance to do its job efficiently too. Be realistic about buying the latest 'foodie' gadgets that won't get used, will gather dust and make you feel guilty. Ask yourself if you have the space to store it and how often do you think you would actually use it? Read consumer reports and get word-of-mouth recommendations to find beautiful appliances that truly do the jobs they are meant to do. There are some manufacturers that really do the business. One of them is KitchenAid, an American company who have been making food mixers since the thirties. The design is a classic – it hasn't changed at all and the mixer is so robust, so simple and strong, you know you really only need buy one of these in your lifetime. The food writer Nigella Lawson has brought out a Living Kitchen range – from bowls to measuring spoons to colanders – that has been designed to be both beautiful and useful. Her All Purpose Cooking Pot, satisfyingly huge with a steamer on top, is a real joy to use. On a final note – beware of too much stainless steel and shiny chrome; it will drive you mad with the number of fingermarks and other smears it attracts. To keep it pristine don't ever use an abrasive cleanser, instead buff up with a soft cloth and a hint of window cleaner, distilled white vinegar or even the teeniest amount of baby oil.

Other kitchen tasks

- Wash **oven gloves and aprons** once a week, change **dishcloths and tea towels** daily.
- Old-fashioned though it sounds, using **lining paper** makes cleaning the particularly curious scuzz that finds its way into the corners of drawers a less unpleasant job.
- You only need to have to deal with a **bin** load of maggots once to become a fanatical bin emptier and cleaner. Rinse out weekly with disinfectant and leave for half an hour or so to dry and air outside.
- Use strong **bin liners** and store the unused pile at the bottom of the bin so they are ready at hand when you remove the full sack.
- If you keep your tied rubbish where it is prey to foxes or other animals ripping it up at night, keep a spray bottle full of diluted bleach and give the bags a squirt.
- Keep **waste disposal** units clean by running for extra time after grinding has finished and at the end of every day, then pour in a very diluted solution of bleach and leave it overnight.

Basic 'Batterie de Cuisine'

This is culinary French for the assortment of cooking implements and appliances you have in your kitchen. What you have or should have in your cupboards will depend very much on your lifestyle, and whether you love cooking – this is my basic essential kit, but remember I'm a keen cook. The italicised items are the basic basics for the pragmatic rather than the passionate.

Baking trays; loaf tin, cake tins, muffin trays, etc., plus liners
Carving fork
Casserole dish
Chopping boards – minimum two
Coffee grinder
Coffee maker
Colander
Cooling trays
Corkscrew
Electric whisk
Fish slice
Food processor
Frying Pan – small large
Garlic press
Grater
Ice-cream scoop
Juicer
Kettle
Knives – small, serated, medium, bread, carving
Knife sharpener
Ladle
Lemon juicer
Masher
Measuring jug
Misc. containers with lids for fridge leftovers
Mixing bowl – small, large
Nutcracker
Nutmeg grater

Pastry brush
Peeler
Pepper and salt mills
Pestle and mortar
Pizza cutter
Poultry needles
Preserving pan
Rice cooker
Roasting tin
Rolling pin
Salad shaker
Saucepans – small, medium, large
Scales
Scissors
Sieve
Skewers
Slotted spoon
Slow cooker
Spatula
Steamer (or steamer insert)
Tea strainer
Thermometer
Timer
Tin opener
Toasted sandwich maker
Toaster
Tongs
Whisk
Wok
Wooden spoons

Conversion Tables

All these are approximate conversions, which have been either rounded up or down. In a few recipes it has been necessary to modify them very slightly. Never mix metric and imperial measures in one recipe, stick to one system or the other. All spoon measurements used throughout this book are level unless specified otherwise.

Weights

1/2 oz	10 g	6 oz	170 g
3/4	20	7	200
1	25	8	225
1 1/2	40	9	250
2	50	10	275
2 1/2	60	12	350
3	75	1 lb	450
4	110	1 1/2	700
4 1/2	125	2	900
5	150	3	1.35kg

Oven temperatures

Mark	1	275°F	140°C
	2	300	150
	3	325	170
	4	350	180
	5	375	190
	6	400	200
	7	425	220
	8	450	230
	9	475	240

Measurements

1/8 inch	3 mm	5 inches	13 cm
1/4	5 mm	5 1/4	13.5
1/2	1 cm	6	15
3/4	2	6 1/2	16
1	2.5	7	18
1 1/4	3	7 1/2	19
1 1/2	4	8	20
1 3/4	4.5	9	23
2	5	9 1/2	24
2 1/2	6	10	25.5
3	7.5	11	28
3 1/2	9	12	30
4	10		

Volume

2 fl oz	55 ml
3 fl oz	75 ml
5, 1/4 pt	150 ml
1/2	275
3/4	425
1	570
1 1/4	725
1 1/2	1 litre
2	1.2
2 1/2	1.5
4	2.25

The store cupboard

Keep these minimum basics in stock and you've always got something in for supper. Supplement with fresh meat and fish and loads of vegetables and those store cupboard or freezer treats that you adore and that can be added to tart up basics. Use your freezer to stock up and get into the habit of cooking more than you need. That way you can stockpile made-up meals or stock. Never throw away cooked leftovers that can freeze down. Even a tablespoon of casserole can be thawed and added to a jacket potato as a filling for lunch. (Nothing that has been cooked and frozen before should be re-frozen.)

Cooking basics – stock cubes; vegetable bouillon powder; olive oil; vinegar (red and white wine and balsamic); Maldon salt and pepper; herbs and spices, tomato puree; Tabasco; soy sauce; Worcester sauce; pesto

Condiments – mustard (Dijon and English powder); tomato ketchup; pickle

Dried foods – pasta; rice; noodles; lentils; couscous; flours; bicarbonate of soda; baking powder; breakfast cereals; oats

Tins, jars and packets – tuna; corned beef; tomatoes; baked beans; olives; anchovies; roasted peppers; long life milk

General – tea; coffee; sugar (brown and white); honey; jam

Fridge – milk; butter; cheese (Cheddar and Parmesan); salad leaves; tomatoes; bacon and dry cured meat (ham or salami)

Freezer – frozen peas; sliced loaf; ready-rolled pastry; fish

Non-fridge perishables – eggs; bread; potatoes; onions; garlic; oranges; apples; lemons

Booze – red and white wine; sherry

Without buying anything else, the above would make the following main-course dishes – pasta with sauces (tomato, onion and garlic), risotto, special fried rice, salads (Niçoise, Caesar, etc.), omelettes (cheese, ham, etc.), frittata, quiches, soups, savoury batters, cakes, traybakes, antipasto, stuffed jacket potatoes, fish pie, plus all-day breakfast and cheesy chips! All these recipes serve two people easily or will stretch to four with additional bread and vegetables or salad.

Tomato, onion and garlic sauce

Fry a **chopped onion** and **crushed garlic clove** in a **tablespoon of oil**, until soft. Add a **400 g tin of chopped tomatoes** and a **tablespoon of tomato puree**, stir while bubbling until reduced to thick sauce. Season and serve with **Parmesan** to grate. You could also add a splash of red wine, a pinch of dried basil, some chopped ham and salami or diced leftover cooked meat at the bubbling stage.

Baked risotto

Pre-heat the oven to 150C/300F/Gas Mark 2. Fry a **chopped onion** and **crushed garlic clove** in **30 g of butter** until soft. Stir in **225 g of Arborio rice**, add 800 ml of **chicken stock**, bring to the bubble, cover and cook in the oven for 20 minutes. Stir in **50 g grated Parmesan** and serve. You can add all sorts of fish, meat or vegetables either by cooking them off separately and stirring them in at the end or by adding and heating through thoroughly towards the end of the rice cooking time.

Special fried rice

A really easy rice dish. Fry a **chopped onion** in a **tablespoon of olive oil** until soft, add **50 g each of peas and any other vegetables** you want to use, fry for a couple of minutes and push to the side. Pour in a **tablespoon of oil** mixed with **two beaten eggs** and as it begins to heat stir it into the vegetables so it sets in threads. Turn the heat up and add approximately **250 g of cooked or tinned meat or fish** before adding **350 g of cooked rice** and stir fry to heat through. Season and serve immediately with soy sauce.

Frittata

Fry a **small onion** in a **knob of butter** and a **splash of olive oil**, in a small frying pan until soft, add a **large cubed cooked**

potato and stir for a couple of minutes to heat through. Add a handful of **chopped salami, ham or cooked bacon** and then pour over **four beaten eggs**, seasoned and mixed with a **tablespoon of grated cheese**. Stir the mixture a couple of times and then leave to cook for a few minutes over a low heat. Once it has set, sprinkle over some more **grated cheese** and put under the grill until the cheese is bubbling. Leave to cool.

Quiche

Pre-heat the oven to 200C/400F/Gas Mark 6. Line a small flan tin with **shortcut pastry**, cover with kitchen foil and baking beans if you've got them, and bake for 10 minutes. Remove foil and scatter over base **4 rashers of lightly cooked and chopped bacon**, pour over a seasoned mixture of **2 large beaten eggs** and **150 ml of cream** and bake in the oven for about half an hour or until the filling is cooked. Cool slightly or serve cold.

Soup

Melt a large knob of **butter** and a **tablespoon of olive oil** in a large pan and fry an **onion**, a crushed **clove of garlic** and any mixture of **chopped raw, tinned or frozen vegetables** up to 700 g, stirring, for five minutes. Add **1.5 litres of chicken or vegetable stock** (beef if onion soup), bring to the boil and then let simmer for 45 minutes (half an hour if it's only onions and add a pinch of sugar). Your call whether you zap it in the food processor to puree it or eat it chunky. You can add all sorts to soups: splashes of sherry, wine, brandy, croutons, croutons with melted cheese on top, cream – the list is endless.

Savoury batter

Pre-heat the oven to 200C/400F/Gas Mark 6. Drop an **egg** into **100 g of sifted plain flour** with **a tablespoon of milk** taken from 250 ml. Beat together, adding the rest of the milk gradually, mix until smooth. Stir in **two tablespoons of grated Parmesan**. Put **chopped cooked bacon** and drained

chopped tinned tomatoes into shallow dish and pour the batter over. Sprinkle with **grated Cheddar cheese** and bake for 40 minutes. Variations on this include using only vegetables instead of bacon and tomatoes or six sausages, previously browned but not cooked through.

Fish pie

Pre-heat the oven to 200C/400F/Gas Mark 6. Bake **500 g fish pieces** in **300 ml milk** with flecks of **butter**, salt and pepper, covered with foil, for half an hour. In a saucepan melt **75 g of butter** and stir in **a tablespoon of flour**, the milk the fish cooked in and a further **200 ml of milk**, whisk over the heat until it thickens, and season. Mix **two chopped hardboiled eggs** and **2 chopped anchovy fillets** with the fish and add to the sauce. Squeeze in the **juice of half a lemon** and pour the mixture into a baking dish. Top with **800 g of mashed potato** and put back in the oven for 30 minutes to brown. You can add prawns and other shellfish, capers, chopped gherkins, peas and parsley to your pie mix and grate some cheese on top too if you want.

Caesar salad

Whisk together an **egg yolk, 2 crushed cloves of garlic, 2 anchovy fillets, a teaspoon of Dijon mustard, 2 tablespoons of white wine vinegar, a tablespoon of white wine**, some salt and pepper. When smooth add **125 ml of olive oil**. Lightly toast **2 thick slices of crusty bread** and cut into cubes, mix with **crunchy salad leaves**, such as Cos, Little Gem or Iceberg, and **4 chopped cooked and cooled rashers of bacon** and **a tablespoon of grated Parmesan**. Toss with the dressing.

Being Frugal

Meat is usually the most expensive ingredient in a meal, so when I buy meat I buy the biggest cuts I can afford, preferably bone-in (to make stock) and if we are having a lean week I can always get at least five or six meals out of it – if I can stop the family having thirds. The principle is really simple and applies to most meats. Adding leftover gravy (always make twice as much as you need), fried onions, tomatoes and garlic, or noodles, ginger and soy sauce will all give distinct and different flavours.

Meal One – roast meal
Meal Two – with salad and bread
Meal Three – chopped or minced and mixed with gravy as potato/pastry-topped pie (Monday pie)
Meal Four – chopped and mixed in with risotto rice, pasta, noodles, or mashed potato (as a hash with an egg on top)
Meal Five – added to soup

Monday pie
Fry an **onion** and **crushed clove of garlic** in a **splash of olive oil** until soft. Add **chopped cooked meat** and heat through, stirring all the time. Mix in any **leftover vegetables**. The whole mixture of cooked meat and vegetables should come to at least 500 g. Stir in a **tablespoon of flour** and then add any leftover **gravy, tinned tomatoes or stock** until the mixture is covered. Bring to the boil, then turn the heat down so the mixture is just bubbling, season. Meanwhile boil **1 kg of potatoes** and mash. When meat and vegetable mixture has reduced to a thick consistency, put into shallow dish, pile the potato (or put pastry) on top and bake on the top shelf of a hot oven for 15 minutes.

A word on **shopping** – it really pays, in terms of saving time and money, to do it in an organised way. Create a master list of your staples either on your computer or photocopy it and have a fresh copy each week in the kitchen to tick things you see you're running out of. Order the items in relation to the supermarket layout or get into internet shopping if you can – it's fantastic, certainly for all the heavy household things. Get phone numbers of local shops and see if they mind if you ring your order ahead or even if they will deliver. Shop for ethnic ingredients in ethnic supermarkets where you'll get the real McCoy and usually in bigger, cheaper sizes. Don't forget to add to your list household cleaning products and personal and other items that you need to buy regularly, such as stamps, matches, magazines, birthday cards, etc. Impulse purchases can be a real drain on the household budget so be as disciplined as you can in the planning, and spare yourself the temptation.

The kitchen drawer

Finally let me pay brief homage to the kitchen drawer, holder of old candle ends, bits of string, carrier bags, various pens and blunt pencils, odd screws, batteries, Christmas cracker prizes, and just about anything that falls under the heading miscellaneous which you don't want to chuck because one day you just might need it . . . I think every kitchen needs and probably has a drawer like this and while you could invest in a flexible, expanding, drawer-tidy system, every kitchen needs a space dedicated to small incidents of chaos. Let it be.

Bedroom

It's the place you sleep, dream, make love, start and end each day. It's a place of rest and relaxation, fantasies, hope and sanctuary. It's also possibly home to a pile of clothes that need washing, last Sunday's newspapers and the dregs of yesterday's first cuppa that hasn't made it downstairs yet. Lack of space may also mean you use a corner of it to house your computer or the exercise bike. This room often has to have a dual personality: aesthetically calming and restful for sleep, while doubling up as a place for doing – dressing room, office, even gym. But, it doesn't necessarily have to be like that. Here's a really creative solution: are you sure your bedroom has to be dual function? Parents to three lively toddlers, Brenda and her partner, Tom, decided to ignore the convention that usually ends up with parents having the main bedroom. 'The kids' toys caused chaos downstairs and we were always tripping over them so it made sense to let them have the larger room upstairs and for Tom and me to use a combination of the smaller rooms to provide areas for sleeping, dressing and as a study.'

If your bedroom absolutely *has* to house work, exercise or other paraphernalia, try to keep surface areas clear apart from when you are working, and if possible shield off the space with a screen or tuck the gear into an alcove behind a blind. Plan the use of bedroom space carefully, including your storage needs. Don't forget the less obvious storage opportunities, such as under the bed and on the back of the door. It's important to get lighting right if you need practicality alongside a calm ambience. Use dimmer switches to change moods, have specific lights for specific jobs, i.e. bedside, make up mirror, and get interior lights fitted in wardrobes. Unless you like to wake to natural light, fit a compact black-out blind and then curtains can just be decorative. The room should be uncluttered and well ventilated. It's important to air the bedroom fully each day given that you spend approximately eight hours, breathing in oxygen and breathing out carbon dioxide.

Beds

Whatever sort of bed you have, your mattress could well be the most important thing you buy in your home. You'll either love it and look forward to climbing on to it each night or it will blight your life and leave you creaking every morning. Mattresses come in lots of different sizes and the rule of thumb is that a 4 foot 6 inch (double) will just about do a couple although the larger width of a 5 foot (kingsize) is better.

If you are **buying your first bed**, shop around and try different sorts of mattress. You can usually buy bed base and mattress separately and it's advisable to spend as much as you can afford on the mattress. (It will need replacing every ten years.) You should always test one before buying it, so don't be embarrassed in the store by asking to lie on it for at least ten minutes, without your coat and shoes on, to gauge whether you need a softer or firmer base. It needs to support your body yet yield to your shape and be especially comfortable in whatever is your usual sleeping position. If you and your partner have different requirements, consider buying zip and link beds with different specifications. Try this simple test to see if you are getting enough support. Lie on your back and put your hand in the small of your back. If you can move it easily the bed is too hard but if your hand feels trapped then it is too soft. Slight resistance is what you should aim for. Allergy sufferers could consider a latex mattress. Specialist manufacturers also make feather, water and even hair mattresses.

Mattresses do need looking after and it's sensible to use a fitted mattress protector which can be easily washed regularly. You should turn your mattress quarterly, both bottom to top and flip-flop to alternate sides, turning the downside to face upwards. Latex mattresses don't need turning. Hoover your mattress at the same time to remove accumulated dust and dust mites and if possible drag it outside once a year on a fresh sunny day for a really good airing.

Mites and bugs go with the bedroom territory because of the amount of soft furnishing and fabric combined with somnolent bodies shedding skin cells and moisture during the sleeping hours. This can be as much as a quarter of a pint of moisture a night and up to 1 lb of skinscales a year – yeuch! This can make life miserable for allergy or eczema sufferers. There are various specialist products that can help, with treated dusters, cleaning systems and sprays and washes.

'Don't let the bedbugs bite' may be an affectionate night-time kiss-off but ignore this pest at your peril. *Climex lectularius* is a nasty little mite that loves clutter, and warm un-aired soft furnishings. You have been warned!

Pillows and Duvets

A good-quality pillow should last about ten years and although sleeping with just one is meant to be good for the posture, most people prefer to have two pillows each. Down is the softest and is made from goose or duck down. The pillow will be very light but may not be suitable for people wanting greater support. Goose is more expensive than duck. And Hungarian geese are the top dogs. If you are having to use several pillows because you find it helps your breathing or prevents night acidosis, try lifting the actual head of the bed with a folded paper wedge to see if that helps instead.

Because of dribbling, smearing mascara, neck sweats, etc., it makes sense to use pillow protectors underneath your pillowcases. Plump your pillows every day with a good shake out and box in the ends before shaking again. Most pillows can be washed but it's not something you should do too often. Read the care instructions carefully and allow plenty of time for drying, especially with down and feather. Some can be tumble dried and will benefit too from being pegged out by the corners on the line on a good drying day. Shake frequently and make sure the filling is completely dried. The smell of damp feathers is disgusting.

Duvets provide a great warmth to weight ratio and create hardly any dust, compared to blankets or bedcovers. It's sensible to buy a duvet that is at least 45 cm wider and longer than your bed. They're given a tog rating with the higher the tog the warmer the duvet: 13 to 15 is snug for the winter while a summer duvet can be as low as 4.5. You can get combi duvets where a 4.5 and a 10 tog can be buttoned together or used separately. The best-quality duvet fillings will feel lighter but still have a high tog value. A box-constructed duvet keeps the filling evenly spaced. Always check and follow care instructions; while most duvets are washable you'll probably need to use the high-capacity washing machines at the launderette. As with pillows, give your duvet a good shake out every morning and air it outside occasionally if you can.

Bedlinen should be changed and washed weekly, though if the weekly timetable defeats then at least change pillowcases and sheets. Aim to have at least two complete sets of linen for each bed. Colour-code your sheets and duvets with marker pen on tape labels to identify if they are single, double or kingsize, or tie them together in bed sets with ribbon. As ever, follow the care instructions on your linen but as a rule try not to overload the washing machine or tumble drier to ensure maximum cleaning and minimum creasing and wear.

There is a distinct hierarchy in the linen stakes. The most luxurious and expensive (very) material for sheets, pillowcases and duvet covers is linen, preferably Irish linen, and a pair of linen sheets can last twice as long as your mattress or pillows, twenty years or more, getting softer with each passing year. Most people, however, will have cotton or cotton mix sheets and the higher the thread count, which is the number of threads woven per inch, the better. Claridge's linen has a thread count of 300.

It's much easier to iron linen when it is still slightly damp, or you can use a light mist of water or a mildly scented linen spray. Fold larger items, such as sheets or duvet covers, in half, hem to hem, ironing each side before folding in half again horizontally until the item becomes manageable enough to be folded vertically. Iron carefully around any plastic poppers on duvet openings. Fitted sheets are difficult to iron thoroughly but creases tend to disappear when stretched over a bed. To fold fitted sheets, place your hands into the corners of the bottom or top of the sheet with the right side facing you. By putting your hands, still in the sheet corners, into the other end's corners, fold the sheet in half. With the corners tucked into each other, place on a flat surface and smooth out before folding the two sides and corners into the middle, twice, and then in half again to get a neatly folded sheet to store on top of your flat sheets in the airing cupboard. Pillowcases should be ironed flat on either side and then folded lengthways, before widthways, for storing.

Always wash your duvet cover inside out with the poppers or buttons done up to avoid getting all the other washing trawled up inside it. When putting it back on the duvet, undo the poppers, reach right up inside it and grab the two top corners in both hands. While still clutching the cover, grab the top two corners of the duvet itself and shake the cover down over it, right side out, moving to take the two bottom corners of the cover and duvet together and shaking it out before doing the poppers up and smoothing it out over the bed.

How to make a bed

Always aim to make your bed before you leave the house in the morning. A made bed is one of those things that instantly tidies up a room and is a welcome sight especially at bedtime. It need take only a couple of minutes and Claridge's say a total bed change to the highest standard can be done in three minutes exactly.

- First smooth the bottom sheet over the mattress and tuck in the bottom end.
- Go to the head end of the bed and by lifting the long side of the sheet out from the bed up to a quarter of the way down, tuck under the top edge before letting the sheet drop and pulling it into a smooth diagonal fold, tucking it neatly under the mattress.
- Repeat on the other corners making sure the sides are firmly and snugly tucked in.
- Place your pillows on the bed and then lay the top sheet, if you are using one, right side down on top, with the hemmed edge covering the pillows.
- Next lay your duvet over the top with the uppermost edge lying neatly along the bottom edge of the pillows.
- If you are using blankets, instead of a duvet, put them with the top edge placed about 25 cm from the headboard and tuck them in all along the sides and bottom using the same method as above.
- Fold the top sheet back down over the blanket edge and tuck in.
- If you are using a flat bedcover this can also be tucked in if you want to.
- Duvets are usually left untucked and extra covers or bedspreads can be folded back over the end of the bed.

Bathroom

You can tell a lot about someone from their bathroom. It's where everything gets laid bare, literally, and where the most personal of functions happen. It's also bacteria's favourite room in the house and provides an ideally humid atmosphere with damp towels, cloths and mats for the mildew and mould to multiply in perfect conditions.

Although a simple cleaning solution of diluted washing-up liquid will do many jobs in the bathroom there is a difference between kitchen and bathroom proprietary cleaners. In the kitchen they will have acidic properties to cut through grease while in the bathroom they should be alkaline to deal with limescale.

Bath and Shower

- Get into the habit of cleaning your bath and shower every time you use them; not only will you be naked and able to slosh water around enthusiastically, but also the steam and condensation from the hot water will help loosen any dirt and make it easier to deal with.
- You can find non-rinse cleaners but, if not, the rinsing is important to avoid stains left by detergents or deposits for the next bather to find in their bath water. In hard-water areas you may want to wipe dry too with a soft cloth, including around taps and showerheads, to avoid limescale marks.
- Pull shower curtains out to fullest length to dry before bunching back against the wall.
- Once a week give the whole bath and surround or shower enclosure a good clean, including the plughole.
- Tackle any stains on the grouting with some bleach and an old toothbrush.
- Use a limescale remover around the taps, showerhead and plug.
- Buff with a soft cloth to make it shiny.
- Polish up the chromeware with a specialised cleaner or use a squirt of window cleaner to make it shine.

Loos

Loo-cleaning is one of the grimmest household chores; however, if it's done daily it should never get too bad. It *should* be done daily because this area really can harbour nasty germs and bacteria, not to mention smells! Keep the rubber gloves and cloths you use for cleaning the loos separate and what I do is chuck daily cloths used for this into a separate bucket to which I add diluted bleach once a week before washing separately.

If you have a **blocked loo**, before you call in a plumber it's worth having a go at fixing this problem as the solution can be as straightforward as clearing a blocked sink – and it uses the same tool and method.

Place a large cupped plunger over the narrowed opening at the bottom of the bowl. You may need to bail out some of the water, but leave enough to cover the plunger cup. Pump it up and down vigorously about a dozen times to shift the blockage.

Towels and Bathmats

Although you can buy linen towels or ones made from synthetic fibres, most towels are made of cotton, Egyptian being considered the best. Their absorbancy is dependent on loop length and fabric weight. Look for towels with over 600 gsm and mats of 1500 gsm. Also consider the **huckabuck towel**. I'm a fan. Not often seen in bathrooms now but very sensible if you want to put out a fresh hand towel in busy loos each day but worry on eco/laundry grounds that it's not a sensible or responsible thing to do. Huckabuck towels are hard-wearing, tea-towelesque linen cloths for hands and a week's worth wouldn't even make a washing machine load. They will need ironing, though, to look lovely.

If, as most of us, you share your bathroom with others, you will know how variable **bathroom etiquette** can be! I think bathroom blindness is pretty much a man thing. Why is it that so many just don't seem to see the stubble rim, skidmarks and raised loo seat left behind for others to sort. Apart from making sure cloths and cleaning products are discreetly available and not in an unsavoury state to encourage good behaviour, there are tips from the bathroom front line which might help.

'If someone in your home has the bad manners to always leave their wet towels on the floor, don't pick them up!' says mother of three boys, Marion. 'Instead hide away the dry towels and let them learn the hard way how miserable it is drying with a damp cloth. I actually even used to use the abandoned towels to stand on when I got out of the shower – just to make sure they stayed suitably wet, of course! Unfortunately for the rest of us, it took until the towel had become horribly musty for one of my sons to get the point – but we got there in the end!'

Susan, mother of three boys, started their *training* very young with that well-known mothering technique, fibbing; 'I told them that leaving the loo seat up after having a pee was bad luck and that if their favourite football team lost that week's match, it could be their fault. I'm not saying they *really* believed me, but they certainly weren't prepared to take the risk, it worked like a dream. They put the seat down from habit now.'

Dining room

Or, dining *area*. General housework rules apply to the maintenance of this space but there are aesthetic considerations too, so here are some guidelines to apply, if you entertain much. Remember, people don't come to your house for dinner because they are hungry so the setting, including the *table* setting, is all part of the atmosphere you create for a social occasion. If you are tight for table space, consider making a separate, larger MDF table top that can be placed on top of your table to accommodate more people.

Crockery, Cutlery and Glasses
The following is a basic list, elements of which you can ignore or which you can add to if you serve lots of courses or eat or cook speciality dishes that call for specific crocks, such as Knickerbocker Glories or perfect Martinis. As a basic rule, aim to

have a minimum of six of each set of plates, forks etc. Most households need more mugs and more everyday glasses. Your choice of crockery and cutlery will depend on purse and taste. Always check out manufacturers' factory shops if you are keen on a pricey range. My hero in glassware are Riedel glasses. This is a range of thin blown plain glasses of different shapes and sizes, all designed to match different grapes, and they are universally agreed to be fantastic, making even poor wine taste miles better.

Dinner plates	Steak knives
Breakfast/starter plates	Butter knives
Side/salad plates	Soup spoons
Cups and saucers	Dessert spoons
Cereal/soup bowls	Dessert forks
Mugs	Teaspoons
Serving platter – two sizes	Serving spoons
Serving bowls – three sizes	Salad servers
Sauce boat	Cake slice
Teapot	Three-pronged fork
Coffee pot	General use glasses
Sugar bowl	White wine glasses
Jug – two sizes	Red wine glasses
Dinner forks	Hiball glasses
Dinner knives	Champagne flutes

How to lay a table

Place setting is fairly straightforward with just a couple of international differences.

- Cutlery is placed face up apart from in a formal French setting.
- Knives and spoons go to the right of the plate.
- Knife edges face towards the plate. (In France a knife rest may be provided so the knife can be kept for the cheese course.)

- Forks go to the left of the plate unless the dish is forkable food only, in which case it goes on the right.
- Dessert cutlery goes above the plate with the fork below the spoon and its handle to the left and the spoon's handle to the right.
- If you are being very formal, and have space, you can place dessert cutlery inside your main-course cutlery either side of the plate.
- Your bread plate is placed on the left-hand side of the setting with your butter knife on top, unless in France where no plate is used.
- Napkins go either on the left on the bread plate or in the centre of the setting.
- Glasses go to the right, above the dinner plate, with water, white then red glasses in proximity to the plate.

Sitting room

This is another communal area that may have various functions and the first thing to do is determine what those are and then make sure the areas in the room accommodate them properly. They might include:

- Watching TV
- Reading
- Listening to music
- Doing paperwork or homework
- Pursuing hobbies

You can demarcate areas of the room by dividers or screens or changes in flooring. Consider screening off from view the paraphernalia of, say, work, for example, if the room needs to be used to relax in, in the evening.

The sitting room is also where you are likely to accumulate clutter in the shape of knick-knacks and old magazines. See the room with fresh eyes and get rid of anything superfluous. This room has to work hard for everyone, needs appropriate lighting and most importantly, needs plenty of storage, which you can create and find everywhere.

- Choose coffee tables, lamp tables, window seats and pouffes with hollow innards for storage.
- Use back-to-back bookcases as a room divider. They don't need to be floor to ceiling.
- Adjust shelf heights to get maximum number of shelves.
- Use the space behind the sofa for a low table or book case.

As your family or interests change so the uses of the sitting room may change, which means it is important to have an annual cull of its contents; this is a good opportunity to empty the storage areas, clean them out and reorganise.

Home office and domestic administration

It's time to reclaim the dining table! Not all of us have the luxury of a separate space to use as an office. If you don't, it's even more crucial to be disciplined about domestic admin. Whether you are working from home or just have an area for doing paperwork and domestic administration, these are the things that will make it all more straightforward.

- A walk-around phone with a speaker facility so you can get on with other things while waiting for call centres to deal with you or while talking to mad Auntie Edna.
- If you are buying a new printer for your computer, consider one with an integrated photocopier and scanner. They are not overly expensive and very useful.
- If you have space, try to have two surfaces so you can spread out. A corner will provide this.
- Have a good stock of paper and different size envelopes and stamps.

- Plain postcards with your address on are invaluable for writing brief notes either to send separately or to accompany payments or returns.
- Simple filing systems – either ring binders with dividers or cardboard accordion ones, available with chronological, alphabetical or blank compartments. Personalise your system to make it work for you. Each member of my family and even the dog has got his or her own filing section. The main thing is to keep it up to date and the random information and data filed away so you know where it is when you need it.
- A key contact address list for other members of the household as reference.
- A hole punch, a stapler and spare staples, paper clips, scissors, Sellotape in a dispenser, pencils with rubbers on top, three highlighter pens in different colours, Post-it notes, a stationery spike.
- A diary system that family can also access, either on the computer, pinned to a wall or in a big desk diary.
- Keep all paperwork filed and to hand.
- Set aside the same time every week to do your domestic administration, such as paying bills, filing, even doing your online shopping order. (See page 219.)
- Always back up your computer at the end of a session.
- Keep a note of all your passwords somewhere very, very safe. (Yes, I know this will be frowned upon but I did say *very, very* safe.)
- Mark on bills, letters, etc., the date they were dealt with, and if you had direct contact with a service, who you spoke to. Always try to get a contact name.
- Keep the following personal documents in a fire-retardant container; birth certificate, marriage certificate, passports, wills, insurance policies, driving licence counterfoil, vehicle registration details, share certificates, copies of credit cards.
- You may be advised to place the originals of some of the above, such as wills, with your solicitor or in a bank safe-deposit box.
- File too guarantees and instruction manuals. Attach to them a photocopy of the receipt for the goods.
- Always check credit card and bank statements and then file them.

Home admin

You need to keep financial paperwork and receipts for just under two years from the end of a tax year, and if you are a business for just under six years, for Inland Revenue purposes, along with anything to do with your house and mortgage.

- At the end of each year go through your files and decant that year's paperwork into a separate box to be stored somewhere safe and dry.
- Double-check bank standing orders, direct debits and subscriptions. At the same time go through the file of all guarantees and instruction manuals and bin any that no longer exist.
- Schedule renewal and service dates in your diary and at the beginning of every year transfer and update the list to the current year's calendar.
- Don't just think about *formal* paperwork; create a filing system for magazine cuttings, photos or catalogues too, to give you inspiration for home and personal projects or plans.

Utility room

Or the corner of your kitchen, basement, bathroom or garage – wherever you do the laundry. Here's the basic kit. You may have or need all or just some of what follows:

Airer
Bucket for soaking
Cold-water starch or starch
   spray
Colour run remover
Fabric conditioner – fluffs up
   fabric, reduces static and can
   make ironing easier although
   watch out for a build-up
Hand-washing detergent
Iron
Ironing board
Ironing water

Laundry basket
Machine-washing detergent
   – biological has enzymes
   that help remove dirt at
   lower temperatures and can
   be better for white cottons
   and heavily soiled items
   – non-biological – doesn't
   contain the enzymes and is
   suitable for general
   washing
Pegs
Pilling comb

Pre-wash stain remover –
soaking or spray
Sewing kit of black, white
and neutral thread,
needles, scissors, needle

threader, pins, thimble,
spare buttons
Tumble drier
Washing machine
White pressing cloth

Washing and drying

Know your symbols or photocopy the washing-symbol list and
put it up near your washing machine.

The washing process by machine or hand	🔲60C	Cotton wash: normal maximum washing conditions can be used at the appropriate temperature, in this case 60ºC.
	🔲	Synthetics wash: a single bar beneath the washtub. Reduced (medium) washing conditions apply.
	🔲	Wool wash; a broken bar beneath the washtub: Reduced (minimum) washing conditions to be used. Applies specifically to machine-washable wool products.
	🧺	Hand wash: do not machine wash.
	⊠	Do not wash.
Chlorine bleaching	△CL	Chlorine bleach may be used.
	▲	Do not use chlorine bleach.
Ironing	⊐	Hot iron: temperature of 210ºC (390ºF) may be used.
	⊐	Warm iron: temperature of 160ºC (300ºF) may be used.
	⊐	Cool iron: temperature of 120ºC (230ºF) may be used.
	⊠	Do not iron.
Tumble drying after washing	⊡	Item may be tumble dried
	⊡	Tumble dry on a low heat setting.
	⊡	Tumble dry on a high heat setting.
	⊠	Do not tumble dry.
	⊔ line dry ⧙ drip dry ⊟ dry flat	

As ever, it's worth doing your **preparation** if you want to get results. First of all sort by colour, then by hot, cooler, more delicate wash, etc. Next tackle stains by soaking or with a pre-wash spray and turn anything that might fade inside out, especially denim or sweatshirts. It's a good idea to put really **delicate clothes** inside a special mesh washing bag or a pillowcase and *always* wash whites separately with no other colours at all. Wash things that go together, together – even if the top to a skirt hasn't been worn. That way they'll fade together. Don't overload the machine – it needs to be able to agitate the clothes properly.

Unless you are very good at **hand washing** consider having sweaters you value dry-cleaned. This has been the best advice I've been given, and saved many a woolly. When you are hand washing, use tepid water and a special detergent and leave the item to soak for five minutes before swishing it around without rubbing and then rinse at least twice. Squeeze the excess water out (try rolling it in a towel to absorb more of the water) and dry flat if the article is at all likely to lose its shape; or if your are confident you could give it a gentle spin in the machine.

If environmental or cost issues concern you – try washing everything on a low-temperature wash with half the amount of washing detergent. You may be surprised – I was. Unlike the advert you really couldn't see the difference and I didn't need to swap two packs for one because it lasted double the time.

There's a science to **drying**. Shake everything before hanging it out and hang washing outside on a line if you can. Straighten side seams, especially on trousers, and peg shirts by their tails, tops by their hems, trousers and skirts by their waistbands, socks by the toe and linen by the hems after folding large items in half horizontally. Bright sunshine will naturally bleach and brighten white items which is great, but it will have the same effect on coloured clothes so turn them inside out. Check the washing line is kept clean and keep your peg bag indoors to avoid them getting rusty.

If you have to dry clothes indoors use an airer or consider having hanging room in your airing cupboard and dry clothes on their hangers. Tumble drying is convenient but expensive, and apart from helping to make towels soft on a coolish temperature, is not particularly good for most fabrics. Neatly fold laundry as soon as it's dry to lessen ironing.

Ironing

Ironing things when they are very slightly damp is easiest, if you can hang them to air afterwards; and it's a good idea to iron things which need the coolest setting first, working up to having a head of steam on heavier fabrics.

There is a difference between ironing, which means sliding the iron across fabric, and pressing, which is when you press the iron down on one area and then lift and move it to another area, without sliding. Pressing is more suitable for tailored or delicate clothes and using a pressing cloth will stop the fabric becoming shiny.

If you live in a hard-water area you may need to use distilled water in your iron. If the iron's soleplate gets sticky, let it cool and either apply a commercial soleplate cleaner or mix a paste of equal amounts of bicarbonate of soda and water, leave it on for quarter of an hour and wipe off. Blast fresh steam, with care, through the holes to clean away any residue.

How to iron a shirt

This should take about two minutes to do properly:

- Use starch and lots of steam if you want a crisper finish.
- Start with the collar and cuffs, wrong sides first, from outer corners in.
- Next iron the yoke, shaking it on to the board from its bottom seam so that it is flat and one thickness.
- Then lay the sleeves, one at a time, flat and parallel to the board and iron both sides.
- Next spread the shirt back over the board to iron.
- Then iron each side of the front, sliding the iron between the buttons.

Ironing

- Do up the top, middle and bottom buttons.
- Turn over so shirt is face down along the board.
- Folding the shoulder too, bring one sleeve horizontally across the back and then vertically down from the shoulder.
- Repeat the other side.
- Fold the bottom third of the shirt up, and again.
- Turn over and straighten.

Car Maintenance

Being on top of car maintenance will keep your vehicle running efficiently and cleanly and help avoid big expensive repair bills by allowing you to spot problems before they become too serious. Your basic car safety, breakdown and maintenance tool kit should include:

car jack	spanners or socket set
cloths	spare fuses
duct tape	spare light bulbs
fire extinguisher	spare wheel
first-aid kit	torch
foot pump	tow rope
pliers	tyre pressure gauge
recovery service contact details	warning triangle
screen wash	water
screwdrivers	wire and string

Your best source of information about the maintenance schedule for your car is the manual that came with it and even if you are a man and don't think you need to read it, you do. Take it to the loo and read it cover to cover. Women, on the other hand, shouldn't be intimidated at the prospect of understanding the workings of the engine under the bonnet. Bored, maybe

– afraid, no. These are the basics that need to be done – some by yourself, some at service time in the garage. That handbook will say when!

- Regularly check the windscreen for cracks or chips
- Check your lights, tyre treads and tyre pressures
- Check your oil and water levels every couple of weeks
- Oil and filter change and chassis lubrication
- Check your anti-freeze level
- Inspect belts and hoses under the bonnet, replace if necessary
- Wheel balancing and alignment
- Brake inspection
- Shock absorbers – push down on the car corners, if the car bounces on release they may need replacing
- Replace air and fuel filters
- Flush and refill the cooling system
- Check air-conditioning

DIY and Tool Box

What you do and don't do yourself is more down to inclination than ability. There are books, TV programmes, in-store advice centres and short courses to learn every aspect of home maintenance and DIY. Although some basic tips are included throughout the book, such as how to unblock a sink, etc., I'm not going to include many other maintenance How to . . .s because the margin for error and potential for catastrophe are too great. So to replace a boiler, hang a radiator, even wire a plug, look for a specialist website or book with step-by-step instructions and, preferably, pictures!

The difference it makes, **having the right tool for a job**, is almost unquantifiable – it makes every maintenance or DIY job easier and quicker, and that applies even if you just want to bash in a couple of picture hooks. Whether you are a student leaving home for the first time or a new retiree about to launch on a project of home improvement, invest some time getting tooled up with the right kit. Always buy the best quality you can afford and take advantage of special offers, even if you don't need the tool in question that minute. Look after your tools by cleaning them after use and storing them properly; that way they will last you a life-time. My father, now seventy-six, still uses the fretwork saw he was given when he was ten years old. He helped me compile the following list and has put together tool boxes for my husband, brother-in-law and both my sons, who all have varying needs and skills with regard to tools. So I consider him my personal expert in this field. If you are a student, by the way, just collect the basics – a hammer, spanner and screwdrivers – you may have trouble making friends if you arrived at Halls and are seen unpacking a pipe detector, wallpapering table and sanding tools.

adjustable spanner
Allen keys
brushes
chisel
drill and drill bits for wood,
    metal and masonry
edge roller
filler
glue gun
hacksaw (junior and large)
insulating tape
level
light lubricating oil
medium hammer
nails and hooks
no-nails adhesive
paper brush
paste
penetrating oil (WD40)
pincers

pipe detector
plaster powder
plastering trowel
pliers
plunger
power duct tape
rawlplugs
sanding block
sanding tools
sandpaper
scissors
scraper
screws
set of screwdrivers (one with a
    built-in current sensor)
set square
small ball-backed hammer
spanner
Stanley knife
staple gun

step ladder	tape measure
straight edge ruler	wallpapering table
super glue	wood saw

Dad, having been taught 'how to do things properly' is not fanatical about **power tools** for every job. He says they give a better finish and certainly save time but sometimes their bulk and the need to access a power supply means they aren't appropriate and that anyway you should know how to do the job without them. Twenty-five-year-old Suzanne, however, says that getting well acquainted with an electric drill and saw has changed her life! "Now I never feel pathetically helpless about putting up shelves, pictures or flat-pack furniture. I don't know why I thought they would be difficult to use – they are no more difficult than using my hair straighteners."

 Remember too that most tools can be hired and this makes particular sense with larger or one-job-specific equipment that can cost a lot to buy. DIY basics for preparation and project planning:

- Know where your local tip is.
- Suss out the trade-paint and decorating suppliers (trade paint dries in half the time, is cheaper and less goes further than normal paint).
- Find too the plumbing and electrical wholesalers where you can buy items more cheaply and be put in touch with professionals should you need them. New legislation means that many electrical jobs in the home have to be done by a qualified electrician.
- Make sure your first-aid kit is well equipped and that you know exactly where your local accident and emergency unit is.
- When you are carrying out a project approach it methodically by thinking it through and time phasing the various stages of the job.
- Write down the tools and the materials you will need.
- Take your measurements. Take them again!

Tool kit

Here's an example of this using **Putting up a Fence** as the project, courtesy of Dad. (You may spot where I get some tendencies from!)

1. **Measure** the length of the fence
2. **Establish length of fence sections** and mark where each support will be located
3. **Prepare materials list**
   Number of fence sections
   Number of fence supports
   Concrete to fix fence supports
   Screws/nails
   Paint/protective finish
4. **Prepare tool list**
   Tools to prepare ground holes for support posts
   (Manual post-hole borer – to be hired)
   Spade to mix concrete
   Wood saw
   Hammer
5. **Prepare holes for fence support**
6. **Establish fence supports**
7. **Assembly of fence sections**
8. **Finish off and paint**

Design and decoration

If you want to completely redesign a room, do as professional interior decorators do and create a colour sheet which should include a floor plan drawn to scale on graph paper – one square to 10 cm is realistic. Draw a bird's-eye view of all fixtures and fittings, including radiators, shelves and pieces of furniture. Then staple small swatches of upholstery and curtain fabric and paint colours on the page, put it in a transparent folder to carry with you when you go shopping. The other crucial thing is to remember to get your measurements right so you don't over or under buy. These calculators will help, and remember to always measure twice so you cut or buy once!

Paint Calculator

DISTANCE AROUND THE ROOM (doors and windows included)

	9m	10m	12m	13m	14m	15m	16m	17m	18m	19m	20m	22m	23m	24m	26m	27m	28m	30m
2.15m	2	2	3	3	3	3	3	3	4	4	4	4	4	5	5	5	5	6
2.45m	2	2	3	3	3	3	4	4	4	4	4	5	5	5	6	6	6	6
2.75m	2	3	3	3	4	4	4	4	4	5	5	5	5	6	6	6	7	7
3.05m	3	3	3	4	4	4	4	5	5	5	5	6	6	6	7	7	7	8
3.36m	3	3	4	4	4	4	5	5	5	6	6	6	7	7	7	8	8	8

PAINT VOLUME GIVEN IN LITRES

Wallpaper Calculator

DISTANCE AROUND THE ROOM (doors and windows included)

	9m	10m	12m	13m	14m	15m	16m	17m	18m	19m	20m	22m	23m	24m	26m	27m	28m	30m
2.15-2.30m	4	5	5	6	6	7	7	8	8	9	9	10	10	11	12	12	13	13
2.30-2.45m	5	5	6	6	7	7	8	8	9	9	10	10	11	11	12	13	13	14
2.45-2.60m	5	5	6	7	7	8	9	9	10	10	11	12	12	13	14	14	15	15
2.60-2.75m	5	5	6	7	7	8	9	9	10	10	11	12	12	13	14	14	15	15
2.75-2.90m	6	6	7	7	8	9	9	10	10	11	12	12	13	14	14	15	15	16
2.90-3.05m	6	6	7	8	8	9	10	10	11	12	12	13	14	14	15	16	16	17
3.05-3.20m	6	7	8	8	9	10	10	11	12	13	13	14	15	16	16	17	18	19

WALLPAPER QUANTITY GIVEN IN ROLLS

Curtain fabric calculator

- For pencil pleats you will need 2.5 times the width of your track or pole.
- For plain gathering tape you'll need 2 times the width.
- Add to this figure 1.5 cm for each side hem plus each seam allowance on any joinings of fabric you need to make up the width.
- Divide this total by the width of your chosen fabric to see how many widths you will need and round it up to the next full width.
- Multiply this by the drop plus your heading and hem allowances to find the total number of metres needed. Add on extra fabric to allow for any pattern repeat.

Blind fabric calculator

- Divide the width of your window by the width of your fabric, rounding up to the next full width.
- Multiply this by the drop plus heading and hem allowances, allowing extra material for any pattern repeat.

The Garden

Taking up gardening can be a bit like joining a gym. You set out with grand plans and great expectations of your own ability and commitment and then find that the reality falls miserably short and you've wasted a bomb on getting all the right kit which you've hardly used. It's easy to get all fired up with enthusiasm for turning your humble bare plot into a mini-Kew, only to run into a plague of aphids, a summer of drought or an easterly gale in May. That's not to mention a falling off in your own interest levels as the sown seeds take ages to show just two leaves, never mind metre-high spires of coloured blooms. So for this reason it makes a lot of sense to step cautiously into the garden when you set out and not to invest in a full set of expensive gardening tools. Buy best budget basics in the first instance, applying these criteria:

- As you hone your gardening style invest in better quality.
- Think comfort with regard to use. This particularly applies to handle-lengths on spades and forks.
- Tool handles are shaped like a D, T or Y. Handle the tools before you buy, to make sure they suit the size of your hands.
- Coated blades will make for easy cleaning.
- Tread on the top edge will make use easier on the feet.
- Get smaller than standard size tools if they are only going to be used in flower borders.

Here's what you need:

fork	accidentally mow over the cable
gardening gloves	
hand tools – trowel and fork	rake
lawnmower – if you've got grass	secateurs/shears
plug-in residual current device – to cut the power if you	spade
	watering can

Always clean your tools after you have used them, scraping off any mud and wiping with a damp, then dry cloth. Occasionally sand down or use a pot scourer to properly clean shears or secateurs and store with the blades shut. You can buy a sharpening stone or have your tools sharpened at some garden centres. Hang large tools on wall racks and keep hand tools in a dry damp-proof bag or basket to prevent rust.

Structural Stuff

The custom of 'beating the bounds' has existed for more than 2,000 years for communities to mark their boundaries and key features. You don't need to make the family dress in pagan weeds and beat the hell out of your laburnum bushes but perambulating your plot once a year and marking your assets is a good way to assess the state of your bricks and mortar.

- Paint external woodwork once every three years, ideally in the spring.
- Paint masonry every five years to keep it protected.
- Gutters and drains need clearing out at least once a year. If you are going to hire a ladder to do this, see if your neighbours want to share the cost and check their gutters too.
- Check on an annual basis for any roof tiles that have shifted.

Using professionals

There are times when you'll bring the professionals into your home to carry out those bits of household management or maintenance that you can't or don't want to do. These can be tricky relationships to get right. Despite being the commissioning party because the deal is happening in your manor and you're paying, it's extraordinary how vulnerable and 'at the mercy of' you can feel. Look to the good-practice guidelines (see page 76) in Support Services on how to achieve a happy and healthy relationship between you and those who help out with everything from cleaning to building and plumbing.

- If you want appliances installed, research the makes and brands you prefer and get retail costings.
- Ask if there is a trade discount they can access by buying materials and equipment on your behalf. You should agree the job, timescale and cost and whether there is VAT included, a penalty fee for missed deadlines, overtime or out-of-hours loading.
- Check they are insured and ask what guarantees and warranties there are on parts and the installation.
- Be sure to specify clearing up, snagging or later inspections you expect.
- Keep lines of communication open and establish a regular time and format for catch-up and debriefing when they can report on progress and you can air any concerns.

Remember first and foremost that mutual respect is important. That and, in my case, gratitude to those who clean and tidy behind me when I've been too busy to do it before they come (!), and to the builders and plumbers who, despite looking at me as though I'm a mad woman, have knocked down walls, installed showers and made good despite my minimal budgets. Their professions often get a bad press for not delivering on time or to budget or just not living up to expectations – but in my case, my home helps are great. Would I dare say anything else?

Safe as Houses

Well, that rather depends on how security conscious you are or whether you have a great woofing, 9 stone Newfoundland dog like I do. There is fantastic belt, or should that be bolt, and braces advice from locksmith organisations about the hundreds of locks and bolts, alarms and deterrents you can use to keep your home and belongings safe from intruders. Here are the basics on home security:

- Check with your insurers what they require you to have in place. This has to be your minimum provision.
- See if they offer a discount if you take extra measures.
- Seek out reputable suppliers to suit your pocket, and remember that locks and alarms are available from good DIY shops and easy to install yourself.
- Always look for the quality and standards marks – these are not products to even think about cutting corners on.
- If hiring a company to carry out installations make sure they are accredited.
- Never hide a key outside – thieves know all the tricks.
- Use a cheap ultra-violet pen to put your postcode on valuables.
- Don't forget to make sure sheds and garages are secure too.
- Shred personal finance and other sensitive paperwork.

Home security

Smoke alarms

Not having smoke alarms fitted is right up there with stupid, stupid, stupid. They are easily available in high street shops or from your local fire station, cheap and really easy to fit. As the fire service says, they are proven to save lives, so use them and use them properly. Here's how:

- Have at least one on each floor of your house.
- Halls and landings are the best places.
- Site it at least 30 cm from a wall or light
- Make sure you will be able to hear it from your bedroom.
- If you have a TV or other large electrical appliance in your bedroom place one above it.
- Test the alarm-test button once a week, vacuum the inside twice a year, once a year change the battery.

It goes without saying that your electrics should be safe and that particular areas, such as the kitchen, are more prone to fire incidents. Have your heating systems checked annually, especially gas-run ones.

Decluttering

I've said plenty on the stuff you *need* but there is also the throwing away of stuff to consider. When it comes to **rubbish collection** and household clearance, you best bet is to ring your local council and see what services they offer. There's increasing pressure on everybody to **recycle** now (see page 238) and my local council have just recently introduced a Garden Collection scheme – special biodegradable bags (that go to a composting rather than a landfill site). You can get rid of most things – fridges, washing machines, furniture – if you ring up and pay for a special collection service.

If you want to **hire a skip**, look in the phone book for private skip-hire companies. Depending on your local council, you may also need to pay the cost of the road permit if you want it to go on the street. The skip company apply to the council on your behalf and it takes three working days. You need to put lights on it and cones around it if it's in the street and it's worth bearing in mind you can't always have a skip outside your house – it depends on the speed limit and volume of traffic that passes – which is why the council sometimes need to do a site visit. They may suggest rear access or a side road. If you've got something nasty to get rid of, like asbestos, the skip company need to be told beforehand and sometimes you will need to have an enclosed skip. This all costs more, not least because the skip company have to drive further and pay more to offload toxic materials.

Home is where the heart is

Rather fitting that this chapter should end on how to get rid of junk as it was seeing people doing this that made me make the most momentous housing decision of my life. One Saturday morning before Christmas, when I lived in a busy commuter town near London, after grumpily queuing for ages to find a parking space near the shops, I was then caught up in a dreadful traffic jam going in the opposite direction a couple of hours later on my way home. This time it was hundreds of people queuing in their cars to dump stuff at the council tip – making room for everything they were buying and getting for Christmas, presumably. I looked at all their miserable faces and thought what utter madness it was. What were these people's homes like – just temporary depositories for disposable things, purchased on a whim? It was the clincher in helping me decide to downshift and move.

If you've got the money and inclination to make your house beautiful and stocked with gorgeous things that you will love and cherish, that is wonderful; but never lose sight of what it fundamentally needs to be. Look upon your home, or at least some part of it, as your nest. It might have to be functional and practical, it may not be pretty or particularly salubrious but the most important thing is to make sure that it, or one room, or even just a corner of the sofa, is somewhere you absolutely love to be, somewhere you can retreat to, to curl up in and be surrounded with things you cherish. They may all be a bit tatty, or peculiar to you but they are the things that will make your house your home.

Image

If life is a bit rubbish and big things are going wrong, you might not feel the time is right to invest effort and energy in your appearance. It might seem a bit beside the point to think 'haircut' or 'new boots' when your main relationship is floundering, you're not making a major contribution to world peace or your career hopes have just been dashed.

Think again. Sorting out your look and presenting a scrubbed-up fresh face to the world is an easy win and in the face of adversity can work wonders to recharge your dealing mechanisms and launch you back into the fray with renewed vigour. Conscious choices about the way you look are much more than skin-deep decisions. It's naive to say that looks don't matter or that you don't need to consider your appearance because you are happy and fulfilled without doing so. Who are you kidding – a compliment about the way you look, the cut of a jacket or your beautiful complexion send your spirits soaring even higher – don't they?

Appearances matter because they say something about you before you have even opened your mouth. Make sure that the message you give out is a positive one and your clothes and personal grooming aren't letting you down. Ask yourself these questions:

- *How would you define your look?*
- *What clues does it give others about the sort of person you are?*
- *Do you feel pressure to dress or look a certain way?*

Your wardrobe

You need to match your wardrobe to your lifestyle and weed out any offending garments that don't work or fit. Obvious, huh! But come on, we all know how easy it is to end up with a clothes mountain that fills up your cupboard space and over-faces you every time you go to choose something to wear. If clothes had sell-by dates just think how many would be chucked out or given away. Too small, too old-fashioned, too ghastly (always was, so why is it still there?). Your wardrobe may consist of items bought when you've been taken with a look regardless of whether it suits you or your lifestyle. Kipper tie, loon pants or lime-green stilettos? Absolutely nothing wrong with them as long as you have the base wardrobe covered first. If you can go to your wardrobe and know there is a passable ensemble for every eventuality you can anticipate, then you can give free rein to impulse purchases. But before the word 'fashion' even passes your lips you need to get back to basics and get a minimum wardrobe of clothes that work for you. And this doesn't just apply to women, the principles are the same for men – lime-green stilettos crop up in the strangest places.

How to be well-dressed

Susie Faux coined the phrase 'capsule wardrobe' in the 1970s when she was working in recruitment and couldn't get women into jobs. The philosophy at the time was – get the job, then buy the smart clothes to go with it but Susie knew these women would never get the jobs of their male counterparts if they didn't dress the part for the interview. They needed to be taken seriously and for that, they needed a capsule wardrobe – a few good-quality, key pieces that

Image

could be put together in a number of different ways. If they couldn't afford a jacket and a dress and a pair of good boots, then they should just start with the jacket. A really good jacket – well cut and in top-quality fabric – would see them through all manner of occasions and set them apart from the competition. So Wardrobe Susie's shop in central London, was born. It offers honest, one-to-one guidance on putting together an individual collection of clothes that are both time-saving and cost-efficient in terms of initial investment versus amount of wear. The business has been going for thirty-two years now and has more than six thousand customers on its mailing list, and while most of those people are professional working women, their budgets and lifestyles do vary enormously.

Susie is passionate about the quality of cut and cloth which distinguishes a good piece – say a shirt – from a shoddy one. She says it pays to pay when it comes to the key pieces in your wardrobe – a jacket, good black trousers, a pair of boots and a classic white shirt – and then you can economise if needs be on accessories and the fashion elements that are likely to change every season. Although Susie treats every customer on an individual basis, here is her suggested capsule wardrobe for a part-time working woman with kids:

Two decent pairs of well-cut **jeans**. You can slob around in them or wear them with a smart jacket.

White T-shirts. Expensive T-shirts do look lovely but cheap ones will do the trick and you can buy more of them.

A **good jacket**. If you can only afford to get one real quality item, then buy a good jacket. Whether it be tweedy, black or some other neutral colour, you'll be able to wear it with everything and get your money back in spades.

Boots – either ankle or long ones to wear with a skirt. Make sure they have a little heel and try elasticated ones if they're long – they're flattering and go well under jeans.

How to be well-dressed

Well-cut pair of **black trousers**. Indispensable. If they fit you beautifully, you'll feel and look fantastic.

A good **bra** that fits – essential.

As good quality a **white shirt** as you can afford. It really shows if it doesn't fit well over the bosom.

Basically Susie says, buying cheap shows. It's a false economy. If something is made out of good-quality fabric and hand-finished it will last well, wash well and you'll still be wearing it years later. It's about making a proper investment in yourself. (However, see page 222 for bargain shopping.)

The capsule principle

Obviously this list isn't going to apply to everyone – especially if you're a retired bricklayer – but think about how your wardrobe needs to work for you. Think in terms of your work life, your home life, your outdoor living and your night life.

Interestingly, apart from the 'good bra', the capsule principle applies to men too. The items in **men's wardrobes** are usually more understated than those in women's and certainly less prone to fashion whimsy that can make individual statements. Therefore everything should be chosen with just that bit more special care.

Your minimum capsule wardrobe should also include a **suit**, black or dark grey that will work for business and formal social occasions, **white shirts**, which work open-necked with jeans, a couple of **ties**, which are the most inexpensive way to reflect fashion, **Chinos** or **cords** in neutral khaki or camel, which work in virtually *any* situation, and **good shoes** – quality, well-cared-for shoes speak volumes about a man!

Most men view clothes differently to women. They tend to like a uniform that ensures they fit in with the crowd – whereas a girl would die if someone turned up to a party wearing the

Image

same frock as her, a bloke might well see someone else in an identical shirt as reassurance he'd got it right. Men are most unlikely to waste money on a pair of shoes that are too small, just because they're the right colour since, as a rule, they put comfort before cutting edge. That said, I also think that inside almost every comfy cardie-wearing bloke is a peacock waiting to get out and strut his stuff. Underneath it all, men aren't so different to the ostentatious males of lots of other species in nature.

Marcus, a teacher, completely changed his comfy corduroy look one autumn and confounded his pupils by turning up in a sharply cut pinstripe suit. 'I realised how much I like clothes and that just because my job doesn't automatically lend itself to sartorial elegance I shouldn't let that stop me enjoying what I wear. Liking clothes is not just a girl thing. I'm going to greater extremes now and I think the kids are enjoying it as much as me! It was red braces and yellow socks, and I've certainly got their attention in class. Although I heard one of them say I was cool – not sure about that!'

Do you spend your life in jeans but sometimes wish you looked a bit smarter? Then buy yourself **a really good pair of jeans** – invest the time and money in finding the perfect pair and you'll be amazed by how wonderful you will feel. Everyone's capsule wardrobe will be different because everyone's basic uniform will be for their sort of life and style. It's all about working out what small amount of key items will work for you, and certainly it makes sense to identify what the most important and oft-worn item you wear is and buy the best and longest-lasting you can find.

Jemima was adamant that she 'couldn't live without' a pair of Earl jeans – 'The cut is so flattering and they still look good after a year of constant wear and washing. I like clothes that fit well and celebrate my femininity. I wear my jeans with a black polo neck, black jacket nipped in at the waist and a pair of Jimmy Choo boots with a heel. I bought my first pair in a sale in New York and am adding to my collection when I can afford to! They just look fabulous and the design is so elegant. Also a great-fitting coat will see me through most of the year.'

And let it be said that no capsule wardrobe is complete without **comfort blanket clothes**, the sort of thing most of us own but may not want to go public with. Comfort-blanket clothing should not be underestimated. It's my 'black floppy thing', a loose fleece robe that is the first thing I put on most mornings while I make coffee and feed the animals and after a ghastly day is the one thing I long to get into to flop in front of the box and escape into the world of soap. What's yours? Cherish it.

Ben had a favourite jumper. 'I loved it, it was baggy and threadbare at the elbows and cuffs but it was really big and soft and warm. I even gave it a name, Jim. Jim the jumper! Always worked when life was s**t.'

And don't forget **'in case' clothes**; the black tie for funerals or a 'wedding hat' are classic examples.

So we've already established that it's worth splashing out on the capsule basics. Some other things are also worth spending a bit of money on if you can. Like **cashmere**. You can always spot someone wearing their first cashmere sweater. They keep stroking their arms and seem ever so slightly in soft focus. Once worn, a cashmere sweater becomes your favourite thing and no other wool will do. Susie may disagree and no doubt the cut isn't quite perfect but remember you can buy cashmere and silk separates relatively cheaply at supermarkets now.

Accessories generally are an area where you can economise but a really good leather bag or relaxed briefcase or man bag is worth shelling out on. Similarly a good watch will keep you very good company. Susie recommends you buy maybe one decent accessory a year, or whenever money allows.

It's also worth remembering that **clothes should be fun** – so beautifully cut trousers withstanding, don't forget to take pleasure in adorning yourself. Fashion is so personal that your idea of the perfect treat will be specific to you, but broadly speaking, if you know you simply have to have something, that's the thing that's worth spending on – just not every week! Enjoy shopping. If you like the high street, put aside time (preferably first thing in the morning before it all gets frantic) to have a good look and experiment in the changing rooms. If the thought of foraging through rails and communal changing make you feel faint, go online and shop for your favourite labels in the comfort of your home.

Accessories

With a basic capsule wardrobe giving you a pretty plain canvas you can change your look most quickly and cheaply with the accessories you choose. Think about belts, scarves, jewellery, bags, hats and sunglasses – they really do change the tone of whatever you're wearing. More practically, judicious use of accessories makes your clothes more versatile and (sorry, I hate this expression but it does say it) help you move effortlessly from workaday to evenings out! In recent years, really fantastic accessories have become inexpensive and accessible to all on the high street, so get out there and have a good look.

And shoes are, of course, key. For both sexes they make style statements, and for women heels are great, if you can walk in them, flattering your legs and making you look confident, while flatties are practical and can be neat and cute.

Ongoing management

Reassess your wardrobe twice a year, pack away off-season items and create outfits to suit fashion trends and the seasons by matching separates and accessories differently. Always start with your capsule classics and identify things you need to buy to replace or update. Cull things you haven't touched for six months. Watch the fit of clothes and which areas of your body you draw attention to if your weight and shape changes. Look after your clothes by hanging them, cleaned and repaired, on wooden hangers with moth deterrent sachets or cedar blocks.

Design company CEO Salli follows a formula that always works. 'I buy things three at a time and throw out anything black if it goes "grey". I only really have one "set" of clothes – jeans, black trousers, black V-neck jumper, white T-shirt, black T-shirt, white strappy, black strappy, black jacket, black long bias-cut skirt and a black halterneck top – and a pair of high-heeled boots . . . most of the clothes change subtly over time . . . T-shirts get longer or shorter, jeans get lower rise or a different leg, the heels on the boots change shape and the cut of the jacket might change – but otherwise I have worn the same "look" for a very long time. (God, how boring!) The only thing I wouldn't change is the cut of my skirts – only one "cut on the bias" will do. I buy a few expensive accessories – and tend to wear them to death. If I buy anything in any other colour I wear it – usually only once – everyone says, "Oh that looks nice". What they really mean is "That looks different!" I spend the whole day feeling really uncomfortable and self-conscious and so it goes into the wardrobe and doesn't see the light of day again. I tend to buy one "fashion piece" a "season" – it is usually expensive (I am crap at finding bargains) and I wear it at every opportunity – this summer it is a black skirt covered in sparkly bits around the waist – when I wear it I feel like a million dollars.'

How to make your clothes flatter you

You can give the impression of adding or losing pounds simply by the clothing choices you make, so if your size is a weighty issue take heed of the following. In any event read the tips through to make the best of your shape, whatever it may be, and minimise your weak points. Women first.

If your body has gone **pear-shaped**, make the most your top half with more flamboyant or colourful clothes. A beautiful wrap or piece of jewellery will do the same trick as will areas of bare skin that will draw the eye upwards, so bare shoulders, or a wide neckline will help give an illusion of breadth and balance out your shape. **Thunder thighs** need bias-flared skirts and longer lengths. Look for soft, loosely woven fabrics that fall well in wide-leg trousers, or swishy, floaty hemlines to distract from

Image

your heftiness and draw attention to slim ankles, which you must show off if you've got them in pretty pumps or elegant heels. Never wear gathered waists, pleats or flounced skirts.

Much of the same applies to **apple shapes** except that as well as accentuating your top half and shoulders and using tricks to draw the eye upwards, you can also elongate your shape by using vertical lines in the form of long scarves draped around your neck and long loose jackets. A belt hung on your hips underneath will give the impression of a waistline. Never, ever, wear a one-piece, one-colour loose tunic – you'll look as though you are wearing a sack and it will draw attention to your problem area.

If you've got a **grand bosom**, celebrate your womanliness. Buy good bras, with the central fabric seams fitting snugly against your breastbone to flatter your wonderful natural cleavage. Wear will-fitted tops or neatly layered camisoles and cardigans that will show off your shape simply without thrusting your chest up and out. Leave that to those who need to make more of what they've got. You really don't need tops that shout out with loud patterns or dramatic plunging necklines. If you have a good waist, wear wrap-around tops and dresses in stretchy fabrics to ensure a snug fit and to emphasise your curves. A-line skirts and boot cut trousers below will help to balance you out.

If you **bum looks big** in *everything* be brave and, instead of hiding it under full skirts, wear trim tailored numbers that skim your hips, hit the knees and are set off with some high heels to lengthen the look. Go for streamlined and seamless, making sure your iron knickers give your cheeks lift and control and show no VPL. If you feel too self-conscious about it or vulnerable in some situations, slip on a loose shirt or jacket left open over the top. But try to think J-Lo rather than lay-low!

If you are **straight and flat** as a pancake, create curves with nipped-in waists and big belts, wide-legged trousers and flirty floaty skirts. Pad out your shoulders and your bra with investment tailoring and lingerie. Don't do streamlined, break up your outfits into different coloured separates. Always wear heels, however small, they'll give your calves an illusion of shape and make you walk in a more 'curvy' way.

If you are very **tall and angular**, you have hundreds of wardrobe options and a glance at any catwalk will give you all the inspiration you need as super-models are chosen for *your* shape. So it's pretty much all good news – you can carry off patterns and flounces, separates and long fluid clothes too. If you are conscious of your height be more concerned about your posture. Lanky girls can look dreadful if they stoop or slouch. But at least you don't need heels to walk tall; colourful flatties and swinging skirts with belts and layered tops will break up your long lean look – damn you!

If you are **petite**, many of the fashion ranges cater specifically for you, and if you look at how they adapt looks it's easy to see what will work best for you. Don't choose anything with acres of fabric, such as full skirts or swing jackets: you'll get swamped. Stick to simple fitted shapes in classic cuts. You can wear beautiful dresses and neat suits like no one else. Save heels for under trousers and then wear as high as you dare. Invest in tailoring and jewellery.

The rules are similar but simpler for fellas. If you are a **tall chap**, major on horizontal lines and features such as your shoulders, pocket flaps, and even turn-ups. You can carry off a double-breasted jacket beautifully as you also can tweeds and checks. If you are **short** go for subtle pinstripes or dark solid materials for suits and single-breasted jackets with long lapels and slim-cut trousers. Wear striped shirts with long collars and ties with small knots. If you are **thickset**, avoid bulky or textured fabrics and choose plain dark or pinstripe. If you are **jowly** avoid button-down collars and always make sure your collar size is generous enough! Wear your ties long and your shoes narrow rather than round-toed or squared-toed.

Terry had never given much thought to styling himself to make the best of his good bits. 'My wife really got into the whole body shape thing and had a real hang up about how my suits fitted. So eventually I agreed to let her buy me a new one and I

Image

have to say lots of people comment that I look as though I've lost weight, so it was worth spending the time in the shop trying different styles on.'

How to have style

Style is a difficult thing and creating your own even harder. We all know someone who looks effortlessly fantastic in their clothes. They aren't slaves to fashion, but neither are they conventional or 'safe'. They are invariably dressed for the occasion but their clothes are always individual enough to say a little bit more about them. Don't be mistaken in thinking that they just shrug things on and by luck an outfit comes together – these people really think about what they wear. Karen, a publicity director, always looks great but look how clear and focussed she is. 'Fit is important. I'm quite slim so anything shapeless looks awful. If I wore a kaftan I might as well wear a sack. I always ask myself: Does it look elegant? Is it flattering? I don't follow fashion trends unless I believe they suit me. Most of the boho look, which I loved, would have looked completely wrong on me (too old). But that season, I did find a beautiful green gypsy-style skirt in Kookai which, topped with a beautifully cut white Nicole Fahri T-shirt looked OK. I have to look smart for my job so the bulk of my wardrobe is smart suits or dress and jacket. I spend as much as I can on quality and restrict myself to a few outfits I can mix and match. I get very little time to shop so I have to buy things I'm really happy with and that will be timeless. I wear my clothes for years. I also go to a good hairdresser regularly. For casual, it's jeans, M&S men's merino-wool sweaters, flat brown suede boots in winter, Gap cut-offs, usually white or tan, men's shirts worn over white T-shirts and flip-flops in the summer.'

Your relationship with your clothes can be as complex as that with food and is often related. Fatties will know what I'm talking about – eating too much of the wrong sort of food is a head thing, hunger doesn't come into it. Same with clothes. Fashion won't be in the equation if you are unhappy with your sense of style, or lack of it, or the body you're dressing. Your clothes choices will be about providing decency and protection, camouflage not fashion. As with getting to grips with a diet to lose weight, you may need to force yourself to change your attitude to your wardrobe and see your clothes as more than just pieces of fabric sewn together.

Think creative, think what they can add to the sum of you, get excited by the sort of subliminal messages you are going to send out each day by what you wear. We often choose clothes to make others comfortable with our presence, or to impress them, but these messages don't even have to be for other people. They could just be for you, to re-inforce how you feel about life and your circumstances or maybe how you need to make yourself feel. Heave yourself out of your rut and the constraints of your current wardrobe and visualise in your head how you wish to look and want others to respond to your appearance. You don't have to replace your whole wardrobe but start thinking in shapes and colours and don't forget make-up and those accessories. My friend Margot swears by the magical confidence-building power of applying some amazing red lipstick. 'It makes me feel fantastic and instantly I look better too, even if my look is falling apart everywhere else.'

If you find yourself playing it safe or opting for camouflage rather than clothes, look around at other people to get ideas. Magazines or pictures of celebrities are a good research tool – try to work out exactly what it is you like about an outfit. As long as it makes sense on your body shape, don't be afraid to mimic slavishly!

Famous people have dedicated **stylists** who 'create' looks for them but the service is not exclusive to the rich and famous. Department stores and private consultants can provide exactly the same service for you.

Fashion Age

Goodness, there seem to be a lot of taboos and assumptions about what one should and shouldn't wear in order to age with style. I suppose it's the terror of ending up looking ridiculous, mutton dressed as lamb. I pass the following on in case you want to know the formal form. If you've always hankered to be chic, older age is definitely the time to do it with single neutral colours working best and pastels being kindest to older skin. Skirts should be worn on or below the knee with sensible heeled shoes and boots, and observe the less is more rule in terms of accessories. There – that's said! If you love clothes it could make you want to kill yourself.

The truthful message from *real* people I've met is quite different. Universally, it seems to be that the older you get the more relaxed you become about your fashion look, for one main reason – you stop caring! Either you really don't care any more about style, and comfort and utility take over as the main considerations (in which case, of course, you won't be reading this), or you stop giving a monkey's what other people think of you, but continue to love clothes and dress as you like – in a style that you have evolved over time, cherry-picking current trends and mixing them with beloveds or classics of the past. How fantastic is that? Bring on the purple!

Grooming

Grooming is quite simply maintenance. Make-up and beauty styling are something else, but grooming, well, that slightly old-fashioned word is about presenting yourself, clean and tidy and well maintained. It applies as much to men as to women, maybe even more so because without the help of make-up, men have to make what they've got naturally work harder and look better for them. I don't think many men are sensitive now about looking after their skin and hair, and most salons offer men the same treatments available to women. This chapter takes the same approach although some sections may be more gender specific than others.

The world of uber-grooming has a zillion products to choose from and working out which to use can be the hardest part. The products are intended not only to help your body but also to massage your psyche and soothe the insecurities most of us have about our bodies. For example Philosophy's range all have witty titles, such as their 'Hope in a Tube' eye-firming cream with the sub-title 'Believe and it shall be yours.' They make me laugh but they also rather irritate *me* but a friend loves them, partly because of the empathy their names show. For me, meanwhile, Chanel's packaging does it, making the contents inside the gorgeous pots worth every penny. So be aware what it is about a grooming product you *really* like.

Advice and inspiration are abundant in magazines and newspapers, but remember that beauty and make-up brands have big budgets to spend on marketing and PR and make it their business to get their products mentioned. Think about why you covet some marvellous potion you've heard or read about. Listen most to personal recommendation from a friend you trust, ask for a sample and if you really, really want it, then buy.

Treatments and procedures

There are professionals who can help you sort out any flagging bit of your body and there are increasingly exotic procedures (Fraxel, Thermage, Mesotherapy, Isolagan!) for the high-maintenance woman who wants non-surgical treatments to shrink fat, slow down ageing, remove thread veins or fade stretch-marks. If you are considering any radical work, surgical or non-surgical, really do your research first and always talk to someone who has had the treatment and see for yourself if they look better and younger.

Trying to halt or disguise the effects of ageing can be part and parcel of body grooming. Men have it lucky – greying hair and

Image

facial lines lend them an air of distinction and even a middle-aged spread can look . . . intelligent. Whereas on a woman – well . . . it's harder! But women are increasingly giving scant nod to ageing, incorporating their grooming routines with busy vibrant lives and refusing to automatically opt for the dullsville grey perm or dab of compact powder. A fifty-year-old woman is now something to be reckoned with and more than likely beautifully groomed and at her sexual peak. Honestly!

In this section the main areas of the body to be groomed are covered with some advice on basic procedures and some information on products, including any time-saving or DIY versions that do the job too.

For tool box read tool bag, basket or drawer. You should have several – portable and permanent. If you always do your nails (we're talking filing and painting *finger*nails not clipping *toe*nails, please) in the sitting room while watching TV put all your nail stuff in a basket and keep it near where you sit on the sofa. Because I'm on a time-saving mission and hate scrabbling around in bags, I keep all my things in see-through ones that have handles and can be hung on bathroom doors, drawers, etc.

Bathing

Mrs Beeton recommended that a bath twice a week was needed to keep clean, but I don't think there are many people who don't now see a daily bath or a shower as essential. Showers save time and water but a bath can offer something more . . . It can be restful and relaxing, refreshing and energising, or stimulating and brisk depending on temperature and what you add to it. The warmer the water the more restful and relaxing the bath will be. Try adding the following under the running tap to make sure of dispersal in the water.

- A couple of drops of essential oils – lavender or sandalwood for relaxing; rosemary or mint for refreshing; pine, eucalyptus or lemon for stimulating.

- You could add these either to a tablespoon of ordinary olive or sunflower oil to lubricate your skin (if you use oil, really clean the bath afterwards and make sure the surface isn't slippery for the next person) . . .
- Or to a cup of powdered dry milk that will soothe and soften your skin . . .
- Or to a tablespoon of baby shampoo.
- A bunch of mint and rosemary, caught up in a square of muslin and tied to the hot tap will be energising.

The longer you can lie in a warm bath the more effective it will be with the heat opening your pores and making your skin more receptive, your muscles relax and tensions disappear.

Hair

Long hair needs trimming every six weeks, short hair even more frequently, so diary it in now and you'll never have another one of those mornings looking in the mirror before an important occasion and realising that it has gone too far. Isn't it weird that one day it can look the best it ever has and the next, really grim?

When you are thinking about a new hairstyle, keep it simple and consider the shape of your face. As with clothes, you need to emphasise the good points and minimise the poor ones. In other words if you've a long lean face, long straight hair either side with a centre parting is going to emphasise that so go for a choppy cut with a side parting.

A long layered cut around the face will disguise a square jaw or chubby cheeks. A fringe will emphasise big eyes, as will wearing your hair up or behind your ears; and adding layers on top or flicks or curls at the ends will create volume in either area if you need to balance out your features.

Think too about the texture of your hair and your ability to manage it, when you're choosing a style. When you cut out a picture of a look you like to take to the hairdresser, be sensible. Don't go in asking to look like Claudia Schiffer if you've got dark curly hair; and be honest with yourself about what the haircut you're proposing is *really* going to look like on *you*.

Wash your hair as often as you want, less vigorously if daily. There are shelves and shelves of different shampoos and conditioners for different hair type. It's worth reading what they promise, to volumise, to remove yellow tinges from grey hair, to cure split ends, etc., and be critical about results. Don't get locked into permanently using one brand; change every couple of months.

Hair treatments work best the longer they are left on the hair and if you have time you will get great results if you massage a great dollop in, pat your hair close to your scalp and wrap cling film around your head with a warm towel on top of that for a couple of hours before rinsing off.

The only hair product that I have seen in every professional hair and make-up stylist's bag is Elnett hairspray, which is available in every chemist and department store. It does what it says on the tin and then brushes out.

Speaking of brushes, they're like kitchen knives and there is one for every job. It's all pretty much common sense although there are loads of endorsements for Mason Pearson's paddle brushes, which are fantastic for long hair and tangles. Best bit of advice is probably to watch what your hairdresser uses and then buy your own.

These home-made versions of haircare work brilliantly, although my hairdresser will probably never speak to me again.

- Washing-up liquid or shower gel for shampoo! It's true. Almost every time I have used either of these someone has commented on how shiny my hair is and I've had enough reports from other people to know it's not just me!
- Warm some olive or almond oil in a glass placed in a bowl of hot water and use instead of a branded hair-conditioning treatment.
- A large jug of warm water with a cup of vinegar or the juice of one lemon in it as a final rinse will add shine.
- Flat beer in a spray bottle will work as a styling spray.

Hair

- A couple of shakes of talcum powder rubbed into roots and left for a few minutes before brushing out works well as a dry shampoo.

Balding

Just a brief word on balding. While there's no treatment available on the NHS (as it's not a disease, but is invariably genetic and part of the normal ageing process), there are hair regrowth treatments available. The two which are generally recognised as the most effective are minoxidil, marketed as Regaine and finasteride, sold as Propecia. Both have to be taken on an ongoing basis for the benefits to be permanent. Hair transplants and scalp flaps are also available and just like other major grooming operations, such as plastic surgery, it's important to do your research and most important of all to meet someone who has had the procedure done. A private clinic may also offer you treatments that might help – but the consensus seems to be, among those I have asked, that balding men do much better to come to terms with their hair loss, trim short what's left and smugly celebrate that they and their compatriots seem to have an extra dose of sex appeal. Don't, whatever you do, try to disguise your hairless pate by draping the remaining hair over it.

Eyebrows

Perfectly shaped eyebrows are possibly the most important facial-grooming thing you can achieve. They will make your eyes appear bigger, open up your face and make you look – groomed.

Establishing the perfect arch that suits your face is something that is best done in a salon if you are not confident about doing it yourself. Ask friends with well-shaped brows to recommend their beautician or visit a salon that specialises in brows. It's just too important to get wrong. There are three eyebrow-shaping methods; plucking, waxing and threading. The first two are self-explanatory; threading is an Asian method which pulls the hairs out by catching them between criss-crossed threads. Once a shape has been created it's fairly easy to maintain it yourself with some good tweezers. This applies to men and those horrid hairs between the brows and the long curling ones that grow out at extraordinary angles. Get plucking and ask your barber for an eyebrow trim when you next have your hair cut.

Sit in a good light with a magnifying mirror. It's easiest to pluck eyebrows after a warm bath when the pores have opened. Brush or comb eyebrows upwards and lightly brush across the top edge. You can remove any untidy hairs there but don't spoil the natural line. Use tweezers to remove hairs between the brows. Then, alternating between eyes to maintain balance, carefully pluck out any errant hairs between the eye socket and the brow, working your way to the outside brow end. Use a very soft pencil or powder on a fine brush in the same colour as your brows to fill in any imbalance or to lightly extend them. Finally use a little eyebrow gel and gently stroke your brows with it to keep them in shape all day.

There are special eyebrow-shaping kits, stencils, scissors and gels on the market and most of the major make-up ranges have eyebrow palattes, but as far as implements go, front-runners by a mile are Tweezerman products, especially their slant tweezers.

Shaving

A good shave is very satisfying but elusive without the right equipment and products. A poor shave feels horrid, looks dreadful and can lead to ingrowing hairs which are unsightly and unpleasant. Electric shavers suit some and are convenient although most prefer the effect of a wet shave. If you can, have an electric shaver for when time is tight or you have a five o'clock shadow that causes your problems.

This is definitive advice on how best to do a wet shave according to the people at Geo F. Trumper in London – perfumers and barbers since 1875. The key seems to be water and warmth – for the best results keep the skin wet and as warm as you can throughout the operation.

How to shave

- Hair absorbs hot water and consequently becomes softer and easier to cut. And the heat makes your skin and facial muscles relax so the whole thing becomes much easier.
- The best time to shave is in the shower or bath but if this is not practical, drape your face with a flannel that has been soaking in hot water for about thirty seconds.
- If you have sensitive skin or want a really smooth shave, apply a glycerine-based skin food at this point. Massage it in against the growth of the beard.
- Lather up your shaving cream – ideally with a good-quality, badger-hair shaving brush. If you're using a shaving cream, rather than soap, put some in the palm of your hand, dip the brush in hot water and then, using a circular motion, stir the cream into a rich lather with the brush.
- Wet the face and apply the lather to the beard, again with circular motions, so the brush lifts up the individual hairs.
- Then to actually shave – run the blade or your razor under hot water and shave your face in the direction of the beard growth. Go with it, not against it. If you're in a cramped spot, for instance under the chin, you could go sideways but if you go against the growth you'll more than likely cut yourself and get in-grown hairs and shaving rash.
- When you've finished, rinse with cool water and pat dry.
- Afterwards use an after-shaving moisturiser or skin food – to protect your newly exfoliated skin from the elements. Don't use anything containing alcohol as this will dry out the skin and could inflame it.

Depilation

Whatever you do, be regimented about it. As with the hair on your head, things can go from fine to out of control pretty quickly. One minute your legs, underarms, upper lip, bikini-line will be smooth as silk the next you're bristling like a yard brush. Treatments are shaving, waxing, sugaring or creaming, electrolysis or laser. All but the last two are self-do-able from kits and equipment found in most chemists – there are bleaching products too if actual hair removal isn't necessary. Make sure you follow kit instructions to the letter, especially when it tells you to do a patch test; but let the experts do anything you might make a fist of because that will look worst of all. For the record note that super-models are inclined to shave wherever they need to be hairless because they can't afford to wait for any regrowth between treatments.

For hair removal elsewhere for blokes, first-hand reports say it's really worth going to a salon for waxing or sugaring, which will leave you much smoother, with less regrowth less quickly. Waxing involves warm wax being painted on to the skin and then removed quickly with a piece of fabric, taking the hairs and roots with it. Sugaring works on a similar principle but uses a sticky sugary paste, and some people say they find it less painful. Back waxing, followed by chest waxing are the most popular treatments offered by most salons.

Skin

It's the biggest single organ of your body and is the first-line defence against the elements so the obvious best advice is to protect those bits that are exposed with high-factor sun protection creams. Drying skin is a process of ageing, so diligently combine high SPF with moisturiser from an early age and bingo – you will have discovered the secret of eternal youth; well, nearly. The principle is solid, the reality, of course, is slightly different. Finding an elixir that will plump out wrinkles, smooth a crepey neck and get rid of age spots is a huge industry that spends a lot of money on research.

Some products undoubtedly do make a difference, but there is also an unassailable truth that your skin is likely to be more a product of what you put into your body than what you apply on to it. So drinking water is one of the best beauty tips there is, while the consequences of smoking, drinking and chocolate binges will be more evident than the results of smoothing on any wonder gel.

But moisturising your skin, both face and body, definitely does make it feel more comfortable. You don't have to spend a lot of money for that. Many of the world's beauties use basic creams such as Nivea, Vaseline or chemist-prepared aqueous lotions. Your choice will depend on your pocket and what sort of *feel* you like from your moisturiser: either gloopy and creamy or a more liquid lotion. Different parts of your body will require different sorts of cream and the light lotion you tap around the delicate area of your eyes is not going to make much impact on crusty elbows or horny heels, which may require slathering with heavy-duty petroleum jelly. Give every cream you try several weeks before evaluating its worth.

Having good circulation and exfoliating dead skin cells is also important because the skin renews itself every month. Use granulated scrubs and buffing sponges in your bath or shower. Try these simple tricks for improving your skin-care regime.

- Mix together rose water and witch hazel (both can be got from the chemist) for a great, really cheap toner. Adjust the level of witch hazel depending on how oily your skin is.
- Mix oatmeal with an egg yolk (for dry skin) or egg white (for oily skin) and apply as a face mask, with a couple of slices of cucumber over your eyes and lie down for at least quarter of an hour for it to draw out impurities and refresh.
- A face flannel will make any face cleanser work better with its buffing qualities.
- A brisk body rub-down with a towel that has *not* been fabric-softened or tumble-dried will make you glow.
- Olive oil mixed with granulated sugar makes a great exfoliator before showering (see 320).
- Fill a plastic freezer bag with ice cubes, fasten the top with a tie and then put it in a full sink of water before plunging your face into it and holding it there for a few minutes.

Skin care for men

Whilst many men have pretty straightforward and simple skin care regimes, according to Sally Moore at Space NK, the men's grooming business is booming. There is now a vast quantity of products, all of which come with the same sort of promises as are made by products for women. With a dedicated line for men, Sally reports that straight men make up the vast majority of her customer base. These are the things she recommends all men do:

- Use a face wash (slightly gentler than soap) and if you're going to do it just once a day, wash your face in the evening rather than in the morning, to get off all the filth of the day.
- Don't confine your attentions to your face. If, for example, you are prone to a spotty back, which many men are, make sure you scrub up well there too, using an antibacterial wash if necessary.
- Exfoliate, either before you shave or every other day. You get a closer shave if you do it beforehand and use a scrub with man-made fine grains rather than natural crushed bits of apricot or whatever, as the grains are rounder and gentler on the skin.
- When you shave, use a good shaving product – a cream or a more substantial foam. And a special tip: don't eat before you shave as apparently your blood will circulate more as you digest your food and you will consequently bleed more.
- Use an aftershave balm – rather than a traditional alcohol-based aftershave – which is the worst thing you can do to your skin.
- Moisturise (instead of balm).
- And finally use an eye-cream. Men tend to age much more slowly than women because their skin is thicker and more oily, but eyes always give age away. An eye cream can do much to get rid of the effects of a hangover and reduce shadows and puffiness. Don't stick it right in your eye (as apparently many men are wont to do). It's not like Golden Eye Ointment! Put a tiny, tiny amount on one finger, rub it on to another finger and then pat the cream around the line of the socket. (Same applies to women's eye cream.) The cream will travel to the lines all on its own.

Skin care for men

Hands

Use hand cream daily, especially after your hands have been in water for any time, massaging it down over your wrists. Obvious – but use gloves whenever you're doing housework or gardening. One very easy and effective treat is to pour a dessertspoonful of olive oil into the palm of one hand and then the same of granulated sugar and massage your hands for five minutes for a great softening rub. Use this too for any other part of the body that needs some natural exfoliation.

Nails

Neatly shaped, clean and healthy-looking nails really shout that a person is well groomed. False nails, either salon-applied or DIY'd, mean everyone can have long nails but having a regular manicure done professionally, if you can afford the time and money, is a wonderful way to ensure your natural nails look great. It is the most charming grooming routine for men, as well as women.

If you don't want falsies and have poor nails, better to keep them short and neat and give them daily attention. It's easy to do them yourself, and if you are shaky-handed with the varnish get someone else to do it.

How to give yourself the perfect manicure . . .
- Make a cup of tea, pour a glass of wine – make sure your book, magazine, remote control are all close at hand.
- Remove old varnish.
- Shape nails with an emery board using long strokes from the side to the centre.
- Massage a rich cream, almond oil or cuticle cream, into the nails.
- Soak in warm soapy water for up to ten minutes.

Image

- Pat dry and gently push back the cuticles with an orange stick wrapped in a wisp of cotton wool, using cuticle cream if necessary, and carefully clipping away any dead skin.
- Massage your hands and nails with hand/nail cream and/or using a gentle nourishing scrub.
- Gently wipe over the nail area with some nail varnish remover to take off all grease.
- Buff your nails gently in one direction, with a nail buffer, for one minute. Use buffing paste if you aren't going to use varnish.
- Apply any nail strengthener then your varnish, using a base coat if the treatment varnish doesn't do the job. Two coats of colour and a clear top-coat sealer.
- Sit back and relax with tea/wine and reading material/TV and let the varnish dry.

Feet

I think most feet are ugly and, if that wasn't bad enough, because they are such a hard-working part of the body and not the easiest of things to get at, they are often made to look worse by wear and tear, neglect and being stuck into unsuitable shoes. Then the more neglected they are the more distasteful they get with hardened skin and mis-shapen toes. OK, I sound like a foot fascist, but seriously, it really is worth taking care of your feet, for health reasons as well as aesthetic ones. A professional pedicure is a good idea if you have neglected your feet for a while. Once someone's done the hard work, it's so much easier to do the maintenance yourself.

. . . . . *and the perfect pedicure*
- As previously, make sure all comforts are close at hand and take off old varnish.

- Soak feet for ten minutes in a bowl of warm soapy water.
- Scrub well with a nail brush and then use a pumice stone or foot file on hard skin.
- You can buy many different hard-skin removing creams and implements. Basic but effective if your heels are really hard is a bladed foot-scraper which requires careful use to shave away the hard skin gently.
- Rub in a granulated scrub and rinse off in the water.
- Clean under nails and down the sides with an orange stick wrapped with a wisp of cotton wool.
- Clip nails straight across and then file to smooth.
- Gently push back the cuticles with an orange stick wrapped in a wisp of cotton wool, using cuticle cream if necessary, and carefully clipping away any dead skin.
- Massage with foot or body cream using a more heavy-duty unguent if necessary.
- Gently wipe over the nail area with some nail varnish remover to remove all grease.
- Buff your nails gently in one direction, with a nail buffer, for one minute. Sweep the buffer along the top edge too to help prevent flaking. Use buffing paste if you aren't going to use varnish.
- Use toe separators or wind a doubled-up and folded twist of tissue in between the toes to separate them.
- Apply a base coat of nail varnish, then two coats of colour and a clear top-coat sealer.
- Sit back, relax and let the varnish dry for at least an hour before putting shoes on. Sounds like a long time but, trust me, it takes ages for nail varnish to dry fully, especially the cheaper brands, and there are few things more annoying than ruining all your work at the last moment.
- Peppermint, eucalyptus or lavender essential oil, added to your footbath, is very soothing for aching feet.

Image

Make-up

'A good face doesn't need it, a bad face doesn't deserve it,' was what the nuns used to preach at my schoolfriends and me as we were sent to wash off the offending lip gloss or mascara. How harsh is that and how entrenched it ensured our lifelong love of slap became. Making up your face is not only about highlighting your best bits and concealing or minimising the flaws, it's a ritual that many of us need to carry out to make us ready in more than just looks to face the day. I know from personal experience that, when applied properly, it can transform your face from very ordinary to, well, OK plus. For fifteen years I was made up professionally almost every day to present the news and other television programmes. I know exactly what make-up can do because I still remember the reactions of people when I came out of Make-Up. They couldn't get over the difference and said so! So I have a deep respect for the power of make-up but am also, like many people, still nervous about getting it wrong because I, and I'm sure you, have all seen people who've done just that.

So what should you use and how should you apply it? I recommend either booking a make-up treatment at a salon or seeking out a friendly consultant on a beauty counter which stocks your favourite brand and asking them to make your face over with their product so you can see their technique and what they use. Don't be embarrassed about asking if you can hold up a hand mirror to watch the transformation.

If you don't know what to buy and want some guidance on products as well as some make-up tips, head for one of the Space NK apothecary chain of beauty shops. They have the very best range of skin care, make-up, fragrance, toiletries and accessories, and because they sell so many brands under one roof, they can offer proper, impartial advice. Their makeover service is complimentary and every makeover can be tailored to suit your particular requirements, so it can be a five minute 'quickie' to find the perfect lip colour, or a full hour's skin and make-up overhaul. Although walk-ins are generally available, they recommend that you telephone your local store to book your makeover in advance to guarantee a place. In terms of the right way to put things on, this is the professional way, courtesy of Space NK.

How to apply make-up

Moisturise, then do your hair or get dressed, by which time the moisturiser will have sunk in.

Use a skin primer if you have a very porous skin.

Then apply either, or a combination of, concealer, foundation or tinted moisturiser – just to the areas where you need it so that your skin tone is evened out. You shouldn't slap it all over or your face will look like a mask with that tell-tale line round the edge.

Most people benefit from a bit of blusher, just on the apples of your cheeks, or blended back up your cheekbone; it will liven up your face and make you look younger. If you use your fingers to apply it don't rub too hard or you'll make the blood rush to the surface and give a false impression.

Bronzer is a great enhancer but is often misused and people can end up looking very odd and not sunkissed at all. Brush it along your cheekbone, under the jaw bone and down the centre of the face – where the sun would catch you. As with everything, less is more and apply all of these basics in good, even, natural light. If you want to – a light dusting of translucent powder will set everything and keep it all in place.

Think of your make-up as a capsule wardrobe with things like lipsticks and eye shadow providing the seasonal colour and fashion element.

If you're using lip liner, match it to your lip colour, not your lipstick. Either apply it all over or feather the line. If you eat off your lipstick, try one of the long-lasting brands and just reapply gloss during the day. These can be especially useful for thinning lips or lip lines fading with age. The rule, less is more, applies most of all to eye shadow, especially the

Image

older you get. Make-up in general needs to be lighter and subtler as we age.

Fashion changes as to where eye colour and lines are used to highlight or shadow but whatever trend you follow, blending the shades is the most important technique to master.

If your lashes droop, use an eyelash curler.

Apply your mascara rolling the brush from the roots to the tips with one coat on the top of the lashes before dealing with the underside. Several thin coats are better than one thick one and if your mascara smudges or flakes, change it for a different one!

Make-up maintenance and removal

In terms of how long make-up should last, you should change your mascara every three months but everything else should last eighteen months. You can smell when something has gone off – it smells musty, and things like foundation separate. Obviously if you're sticking your fingers in something every day, the potential for bacteria is greater so it may not last as long.

As with everything else make-up-wise, there are many different sorts of products that will remove your make-up: oils, emulsions, creams, foaming cleansers and, of course, soap and water. They all do the job if used properly and your choice comes down to what makes you feel most cleansed. If it's soap and water, make sure you moisturise; if it's oil, you may need a toning liquid to spritz away the residue. If you have sensitive eyes or wear waterproof mascara use special and appropriate removal products.

Love your image

Finally, talking to Life Auditors about Image has been interesting. At first I had to make all the conversational running because

Love your image

it obviously wasn't something people wanted to be open about in relation to their concerns or interests. In fact there was positively a reticence to talk about it at all, as though, in the scheme of things, it was an irrelevance and not worthy of much thought compared to life's BIG issues. However, do you know – when I sent out an email asking for any advice and experience about clothes or grooming that people could offer, I received loads of feedback, all of it beautifully detailed. People passed my request on to others and I heard back from these complete strangers, too, about the attention they give to their style. It was all quite shaming, receiving and reading their emails, sitting, as I do when writing, in dog-slobbered trackie bums and my son's old rugby shirt. But it just goes to show that image is important, that grooming makes a difference and that there are lots of people out there who know it and are making it work for them.

Image

Mortality

How each of us deals with death is very personal. Whether it's facing the prospect of our own demise, caring for loved ones who are dying, or being bereaved and coping with loss, death is probably the most challenging aspect of life. It's an inevitable shuffle we will all do, kicking and screaming or silently heading into the good night . . . How prepared are you? Life Auditors considered these questions:

How terrified are you by the prospect of death?
How often do you think about it?
Do you think about the process of dying or death itself?
Are your affairs in order?
Do your family know your wishes?
Do you spend time worrying about how they'll cope?

I believe, and the experience of Life Auditors bears this out, that planning for, and thinking about your own death, as well as what you feel about it in general, is an incredibly worthwhile thing. I suggest you consider your emotional response to this enormous and challenging subject and also that you address the many practical aspects of settling your affairs, making your wishes clear and leaving your estate in order. Researching this section and talking to others has left me astonished at how much choice we all could have about different aspects if we were only better informed about them.

This chapter on Mortality is predominantly about the reality and practical processes of dying. If you have emotional and spiritual questions, you may find that the section on Soul (see page 82) will help resolve them or at least point you in the right direction to seek some answers, and if you are sensitive about some of the physical eventualities you may want to skip the first part of this chapter and move on to the organisation and administration issues.

There is a lot about death that is taboo and a lot that gets tiptoed around, leaving most of us pretty ignorant about it until we have to deal with someone close to us dying. Then we are likely to be at our most vulnerable and least equipped to make painful and important decisions. How much better if the facts and practicalities of death were pragmatically explained early on, along with other facts of life. But for most of us they're not and here we are, dealing with death, some chapters on from tea-making and pillowcase-ironing. It is not macabre to face up to the issues surrounding death and to say it is, is up there with other bizarre human conspiracies, such as childbirth doesn't hurt. So let's bust this taboo open and first get straight about what does actually happen to our bodies as we die.

What actually happens on the deathbed

The first thing to stress and to bear in mind about everything to do with death is that everyone is different and no two deaths will be the same; so much depends on the individual, their circumstances and whether or not acute illness or trauma is involved. However, there are some common occurrences that are distinct stages of the process.

When death really is imminent there are several things that can happen to indicate it, although it's also possible that none of them will. They can take a few minutes or last a matter of days – again all dependent on the circumstances and person involved, and it's absolutely not always like it is on TV or in films. Some people may be aware that they are going to die soon and be calm and resigned. Others may be very agitated or hallucinate, and often people may slip into a coma-like state.

Physically, as the body begins to shut down, the major organs slowly stop working. As the heart is affected there will be decreased circulation which might be evident in cool, dis-coloured hands and feet and sometimes blue lips. The brain's message to the lungs to take breaths will get less strong and so breathing becomes weaker and erratic. As the breaths get more shallow and slower so the body slips into unconsciousness because oxygen is not getting to the brain. Sometimes there may not be a breath for about twenty seconds and it might seem the person has died. At such a critical moment, however, the brain can send an urgent message to the lungs to breathe which may result in a large breath, often followed by a sigh. This may become a pattern of breathing over a period of time and is called Cheyne Stoking, a pre-terminal state of breathing. It can be very irregular and sometimes (not always) noisy, which is why some people call it the death rattle. At this point the person is deeply unconscious and their organs are shutting down. Eventually the blood supply to the brain decreases and it stops responding to the low levels of oxygen, and breathing ceases.

The practice of giving the Last Rites, is predominantly a Roman Catholic one. Strictly speaking, if someone is dying they should have a last Holy Communion – the *Viaticum*. Sometimes, though, this isn't practicable so more often a priest will give them the sacrament of the Annointing of the Sick, which isn't necessarily for those who are dying but for anyone who is ill and needs religious succour. Some Protestants perform the Last Rites too, while other religions have their own version.

However out of it they may seem, it's possible that the dying can sense people around them and hear speaking up to the very end, although no one really knows. Certainly, other people's presence will help the dying feel less alone and it's important to be supportive and loving. Simply holding their hand and staying with them on their journey is likely to be a comfort to everyone. The Dalai Lama says we should try to provide the dying with a warm and relaxing atmosphere without wailing grief from loved ones being too evident. At the very end things can progress very quickly and it's sensible not to put off visiting someone near death. Friends and family should take it in turns to stay at the dying person's side so they are never alone in their final hours. That said, it's often the case that someone 'chooses' to actually let go and die when people have left the room and they are alone. I have heard of this a number of times.

Some people die with their mouth and eyes wide open and even if they were closed at the moment of death they may open again afterwards. It's all to do with chemical changes in the muscles causing them to contract and stiffen. This is rigor mortis which occurs over the next twelve to twenty-four hours and will affect the whole body, beginning with the smaller muscles, such as the eyelids. You should straighten the limbs of a dead person within a few minutes as rigor mortis can begin to set in quite quickly. But don't worry about removing false teeth. Leave them where they are. If you turn a dead person there may be a sudden rush of air out of their mouth that can sound like awful groaning. Sometimes stomach fluids can seep out. Blood can pool on the underside of the body turning it dark blue and mottled-looking and is called liver mortis. The face and lips may also go blue.

What happens afterwards: Dealing with the admin

It goes without saying that this a distressing time. Take things slowly and get as much support as you need. Although it can seem hellishly complicated, the fact is that apart from a couple of formalities, there is a lot of freedom of choice if you give your-self time to make the right enquiries. Things vary, depending on where the death occurred – at home, in hospital or in some other institution. It's also more complicated if the death is sudden.

Just as with birth and marriage, there are formalities to

observe and that means forms that will need filling in. Depending on the circumstances there can be quite a few, but all have a place and logic to them so don't be over-faced by the paperwork. Here are the main ones.

In the first instance after a death you need to tackle the practicalities. You will need a **medical certificate of death**, which will give the cause of death, and then you must decide what is going to happen to the body. The two things to do if someone dies at home are: call the doctor, then, when he or she has been and issued the medical certificate of death, call the undertaker. It may be that you know you're going to have an unconventional ceremony (and we'll deal with all the options later) but bearing in mind that it usually takes about a week between a death and a funeral, you will probably want to have the body taken away. In the UK, there's nothing to stop you keeping the body at home, but unless it's been off to get embalmed, it might become a bit unpleasant after a couple of days. So you need to ring an undertaker and ask them whether they might keep the body for you while you make alternative arrangements, or take it away with a view to doing the whole 'job'. Some undertakers will be more sympathetic than others about the storage-only option – so again, it's good to know these things in advance. If somebody has been at home, ill and dying, more than likely you or the dying person will have given all of this some thought. If someone dies at home suddenly, the doctor will want to refer it to the coroner anyway, in which case he or she will arrange for the body to be taken away to a public mortuary.

If **death occurs in hospital**, the hospital staff or the police, if it's been an accidental death, will contact the next of kin to identify the body and, if necessary, to give permission for a post-mortem to determine the actual cause of death. By the way, the next of kin doesn't have to be a relative if the deceased had named someone else. If the circumstances are appropriate, hospital staff may make an approach to the next of kin to ask about organ donation even if there is no evidence of a donor card. The hospital will organise the medical certificate of death and the body will be kept in the hospital mortuary until arrangements are made to take it away. You can request to see the hospital chaplain.

If the death of someone is **unexpected** or sudden, but not suspicious, you should immediately contact a doctor and next of kin. The police can help you find the latter. You may also want to contact the deceased's minister of religion. If there are any unusual circumstances about the death or evidence of any violence or unexpected accident, you should avoid touching anything at the scene and contact the police immediately.

A **death abroad** has to be medically certified and registered in the country where it occurs; and if you are with the deceased, your holiday company or the local police will help if you can supply them with as much documentation and information as possible, including passport details, warning about any infectious condition such as HIV or hepatitis, and contact numbers for the next of kin. If a relative or friend dies abroad you need to ensure the details have been passed on to this country's police who will have contacted the next of kin. Consular staff will liaise with the deceased's family about their wishes regarding the body and burial or cremation or of getting it home.

Registration of Death

By law all deaths must be registered and the funeral arrangements can't proceed until this is done. The address of your nearest registrar will be in the phone book under Registration of Births, Deaths and Marriages.

You will need to take the medical certificate of death and birth and marriage certificates. The process will take about half an hour and you will need to tell the registrar the deceased's full name, last usual address, date and place of birth, whether they were married and their spouse's date of birth, their occupation and that of their spouse and whether they were getting any state pension or benefit. The registrar will then give you the **Death Certificate**. You may want to get several copies of this as other

Mortality

institutions and agencies, such as banks or Social Security, may want to see it. You can order extra copies at a later date. You will also get a **Certificate of Burial or Cremation** which is needed before either can take place.

Coroners

The doctor may report the death to a coroner, who is a doctor or lawyer charged with investigating deaths, if the deceased was not attended by the doctor during the last illness, or had not seen him or her in the last fourteen days before the death; or if there are violent, unnatural or suspicious circumstances, or if the cause of death is unknown. There will also be a referral to the coroner if death occurred during an operation or there was failure to recover from anaesthetic; if death was caused by an industrial disease, in police custody or in prison.

The coroner may require **a post-mortem** to be performed on the body, which does not need the next of kin's permission, although they can be represented at the examination by a doctor. If the post-mortem doesn't reveal anything untoward the coroner will issue forms that will enable you to register the death and arrange the cremation or burial. There will be an inquest if there is any uncertainty about the cause of death, and the coroner will hold this in public, with or without a jury, depending on what he or she feels will best serve the public and the family's interest. Relatives can attend an inquest and question witnesses, but only about the medical cause and circumstances of the death. If there is any question of compensation it's advisable to consider being represented by a lawyer.

If the body is not needed for further examination the coroner may issue forms to allow its burial or cremation even though the inquest is not completed. A letter confirming death may also be issued for National Insurance and Social Security purposes. The coroner will send a cause of death certificate to the registrar after the inquest to allow the death to be registered.

Arranging the funeral

After the formalities of registering the death you have to decide what is to happen to the body and arrange the committal. You don't have to use a funeral director at all but there's no doubt that a good one does take away a lot of the distressing aggravation. Whatever you choose to do, think of someone who could help you with phone calls and share the burden of sorting everything out. You need to consider any particular requests the deceased might have made. It may be they arranged it all beforehand and have even pre-paid – have a look at their will. It may all be detailed there. Otherwise you will need to get quotes for the range of services an undertaker offers, and ask for this in writing. You don't have to have the full funeral package: there may be aspects of the arrangements you want to do yourself. You may find an undertaker who will help you organise the funeral yourself and charge a fee based on an hourly rate to do so. Remember, your funeral director is a facilitator and only 'in charge' as much as you want him or her to be.

Ask these questions of the undertaker:

- What special services can they offer, for example female undertakers, or to bring the coffin to your home for a while, or to allow it to be viewed at the funeral parlour?
- Do they follow a trade code of practice – if so, which association are they affiliated to? This body will police the funeral director and their premises and would address any complaints you have.
- What are the payment arrangements?

You need to think about the viewing of the body, which some find a comfort; whether you want the body embalmed with preserving chemicals; what clothes the deceased should be buried in, anything from a supplied gown or shirt and tie to a best suit or a dress to sports clothes; what items you wish to place in the coffin; and whether you want the body laid out in a Chapel of Rest or brought home.

Burial

There is tremendous pressure on space in churchyards and cemeteries so if the deceased was associated with a particular church you will need to contact the officiant there to see if they have reserved grave space. Other cemeteries are municipally owned and non-denominational and have the same space pressures. You are likely to be buying only a leasehold on a burial plot with the remains being moved elsewhere within the cemetery when that expires. You may need to arrange for a family plot, if you have one, to be reopened before the funeral. You will have to check on the availability and price of burial space and consider reserving other plots or a larger space if family members want to be buried close by.

There is a wide variety of **coffins**, from the very expensive, polished fine wood with velvet padded linings to ones made from woven willow or recycled newspapers, and reusable ones available for cremation where a wooden outer box hides a cardboard inner that slides out of one end into the furnace. Some funeral directors will make it possible for you to decorate a plain coffin with painting, photographs of woven flowers or garlands, or you can cover it with fabric, a drape or a quilt for the ceremony.

Most cemeteries have rules about the sort of **headstone** or memorial that can be placed at a grave and will even have a list of accredited masons. Check before you commission the headstone, especially if you want a more individual design.

Natural burial sites

And remember – you don't have to use a funeral director at all. Increasingly people are opting for alternative funerals with eco-pods, or even shrouds instead of coffins, and woodland sites with trees planted instead of cremation or cemetery burials and headstones. There are hundreds of natural burial sites and many eco-coffin suppliers. It's important to make sure the alternative burial site is appropriately managed. Ask these questions:

Funerals

- What are the long-term arrangements for the site?
- What happens if the land owner or managing company ceases to own the land or goes out of business?
- What ecological principles are observed?

You can also bury someone on **private land** as long as you own the land, and in fact it doesn't require anything like the amount of permissions and legislation of many home-building improvements. It does, however, lower the value of your property and you should consider what you will do if you have to move. All you need to do is fill in an authorisation form from the Environment Agency and ensure the grave is sited more than 10 metres from standing water and 50 metres from a drinking-water source and be deep enough to deter foxes or other animals digging the corpse up. The exact location of the grave will need to be detailed on the deeds of the property.

If you wanted to arrange a **sea burial** your choice is likely to be much more limited, with specified sites pre-determined, and you will need a separate authorisation from the coroner and a licence from the Marine Environmental Protection Agency.

Cremation

If you are opting for a cremation you will need to consider what is to happen to the ashes. You need to decide if and where they are to be scattered or buried, and supply a particilar urn or other container for them. The crematorium will use a temporary urn which is the size of a small shoebox that will weigh approximately 2–4 kg in weight. You needn't question at all that the ashes you get are those of your loved one. There is an urban myth that they might not be and a grim reason why you can be reassured. The incinerator is so hot that everything literally goes up in smoke except for the ashes left from the larger bones of the body just cremated. These are easily collected and contained for collection and the furnace cleared for the next cremation.

Ashes are scattered in all sorts of places from football stadiums and golf courses to public parks. Some local councils have strict views about when and where this is permitted, so check first with relevant authorities.

There are other options. For example you could have them made into a 'coral reef', have them fired into space, made into fireworks or even a yellowy-coloured, certified, high-quality 'diamond'. The exact colour depends on the quality of your loved one's carbon – they only need about 8 ounces of remains (you could make about fifty stones from a normal adult-sized body).

The Ceremony

There is no legal requirement to hold a ceremony although most people do hold one, usually religious in tone, before the committal. This can be held at the crematorium, or at the funeral director's if they have a special room for it, or at a place of worship, or even at your home. You should speak to the officiant about arrangements for the service.

Whatever you decide, you will need to think about:

- The time and place of the funeral.
- What sort of service or ceremony should be held.
- How you can follow the wishes of the deceased if you know them.

If you are reading this and haven't made your own wishes clear – you really should think about it! What a nightmare of decisions you are leaving behind for those closest to you.

If you have opted for a non-traditional burial site, you can, of course, completely organise the ceremony yourself at that location. Or if you are opting for a cremation you might decide to hold the ceremony at the location of the scattering of the ashes. You might include some music and readings and perhaps have people talking about the person who has died. Give the event a

Cremation

structure and order and think carefully about how it will conclude and go on to the committal. Or contact the Humanist Association who will be able to put you in touch with secular officiants.

There will be other issues too, connected to the ceremony, such as these:

- Who would wish to attend?
- Who is going to notify them?
- Do you want to put a notice in the newspaper?
- Do you want to have an order of service printed?
- Would you like there to be a photograph or some personal memento of the deceased visible at the funeral?
- Does there need to be some sort of seating plan with some seats reserved for the closest family and friends?
- Do you want people to send flowers or to make a donation to a named charity?
- If there are flowers, consider making arrangements for them to be sent to an old people's home or hospital afterwards.

The will or any paperwork left by the deceased might contain instructions and it is usually a near relative or the executor who will see this and make any necessary decisions. They do not have to observe the instructions left in the will about the funeral.

You may want to ask for specific readings. If the service is being conducted by an officiant who didn't know the person who has died, it can make all the difference to personalise proceedings with a friend or loved one of the dear departed making some sort of individual tribute. Music is also something you must consider. There may be secular pieces of music or popular tracks associated with the deceased. If the funeral is held in a church it is usual for at least one hymn to be sung. You may want to choose a favourite hymn if it is known by the organist. Remember too that as most funerals happen during the day on weekdays, a church choir may not be available, so the delivery will be dependent on the gusto of the singing of the congregation. If meagre attendance is expected their valiant efforts may make this sadder. If you can get a choir they may make a charge for special services, although if members of the choir were going to be attending the funeral anyway this may not be the case.

Think too about other music playing during the ceremony, which might help in quiet contemplation of the deceased. An organist will suggest pieces that can be played and you can, of course, use recorded music although you may have to provide the equipment to play it on and possibly pay a copyright fee; this will need checking with the vicar. You may also need an order of service printed.

 It's important to remember what the purpose of the funeral is – it's really for the bereaved, for the living, to say farewell to the deceased and to remember them. You may decide to have a standard funeral and then organise a separate memorial service or event. The funeral director will be able to advise on most aspects.

Different faiths

Different faiths have different funeral practices and it is important to flag these up early in making arrangements. For example most local authority cemeteries are non-denominational and so a Muslim preference for a grave to be facing Mecca may not always be possible, which, according to the faith, would mean a breach of Islamic law. Hindus traditionally are cremated with the son lighting a pyre. Some authorities can accommodate different wishes, such as having a remote ignition button for the cremator.

After the funeral

It's customary to invite mourners to join with the bereaved for some refreshment after the ceremony. All the major religions have some form of after-funeral gathering, usually with some form of food and beverage provided by either the bereaved or friends and family of the deceased. This is important for many people as they may not have had a chance to talk to the family or other people, and it can be a comforting part of the grieving process. This can be as basic as a simple tea or something more ambitious, and in many cases can be as much part of the funeral farewell as the committal itself, with an opportunity for people to make speeches and reminisce. However, there is no formal expectation on anyone to observe any social niceties. If you can, give the responsibility of organising this to someone else.

Linda and Judy both had elderly parents in poor health. When Linda's mother died, Judy offered to make the sandwiches and get everything ready back at the house for the mourners after the funeral. Several months later Linda did the same for Judy and her family when her father died.

Wills

Everyone should make out a will, and probate or 'confirmation' is the official process of validating and approving wills which occurs after a death (or in the absence of a will, it allows for someone to be granted representation to distribute an estate as well as paying bills and paying off any debts). Before the contents of the will can be actioned there must be an application for probate made to the local probate court and that can take several weeks. Without a will the process can take much, much longer. If there's a will, the person to administer the estate is called the Executor. If there's no will, the personal representative is called the Administrator and normally the next of kin would apply for this role. While a solicitor need not necessarily be involved it's wise to seek legal advice.

It's helpful to deal with the solicitor who drew up the will in the first place and important to ensure that close contact and regular communication is kept up between him or her, the executors and the beneficiaries. If a person is depending on funds from the estate of the deceased person and has a legal tie, it may be possible to release some money early to pay for immediate incidental costs.

Most people will see a solicitor to draw up their will although there is no reason why you shouldn't do it yourself. There are DIY will packs available at stationers and as long as you make sure certain information is included your own version should be valid. Make sure you will is identified and dated as being the last will and testament of yourself, and include your full name and address; state that you revoke all previous wills; name and give the addresses of at least two executors, with an extra person who could act as a substitute if necessary; list specific gifts or legacies and say where you want the remainder of your estate to go. Then sign it with two witnesses, both over sixteen years old, who will date it and also give their signatures, names and addresses. A will is a good place too to add your funeral wishes and whether you want to be buried or cremated.

Other practicalities

As well as the administration and paperwork concerned with the death, the funeral and will, there are other practical issues that need to be thought about.

For instance, someone will need to contact the deceased's bank, building societies and credit card companies (even if the accounts are in joint names), their employer and the tax office. Licences, the Utilities, phone company, Social Security and local government offices will need to be notified to cancel any services, payments or benefits. Passports need to be returned to the Passport Agency to be cancelled. You can ask for them to be returned to you afterwards. And outstanding hospital or other appointments will have to be cancelled and any loaned equipment returned. Companies concerned with insurances and investments will also need to be told about the death. Premium bonds are not automatically transferable and some paperwork from the post office will need completing.

Wills

You will need to sort through the deceased's personal paperwork and notify any agencies of the death if monthly or annual subscriptions or memberships are paid. If the person who has died lived alone there may be a need to have mail redirected by the post office. When leaving the property in this instance check that it is secure and consider leaving some form of heating on low if it is wintertime. Make sure a neighbour has a key if you live some distance away.

The challenging bit: Choices about dying

Now then, much of the above is specifically relevant to those who are with a loved one while they are dying and immediately after, but now you know what is involved and the decisions and choices there are, you might want to consider how you feel about the facts in relation to your *own* death.

- For instance do you have a specific wish to be at home or in a hospice or with particular people?
- Conversely are there people you most definitely don't want around you?
- Is there a particular way you want people to behave around you or a way you want to be treated as you die?
- Do you want to make an advance directive or think about making a living will which will specify what type of care you would like if you become unable to make decisions?
- Are there any spiritual or religious people or practices you would like involved either at the time of your death or after you have died?

Consider now too whether you want to **donate organs**. The donation of one person's major organs can help many others to stay alive. You will need to make this intention clear and it will help both your family, friends and medical staff if you register your wishes and carry a donor card.

Mortality

It's an unfortunate reality when doing this to be mindful that most organ donors are patients who die as a result of a severe head injury, brain haemorrhage or stroke and who end up in a hospital intensive care unit where death is finally diagnosed by tests on the brain's stem. They are called heart-beating donors and a ventilator keeps their hearts beating and blood circulating after death; without this their vital organs would deteriorate quickly. Both heart-beating and non-heart-beating donors can donate their corneas and other tissues, such as skin, bone and heart valves. Another option is to leave your body to medical science, which means it can be kept for several years. Again you will need to make your intentions clear.

If you are leaving instructions for **your own funeral** make sure they are left to someone who has some organisational skills or that the instructions are very clear to avoid additional distress. For instance consider the music and reading choices you'd like and indicate where they can be found if they are in any way obscure. You might want to name the people you want actively involved for the readings, or if the body is to be carried other than by the undertakers, think about anyone who would act as a bearer.

Single mother Annie is only thirty-one with two sons, but she has made her funeral arrangements. 'Should anything happen to me I don't want the boys having to deal with it so I've found a scheme where you make all the decisions about the funeral and pay for it in total now. It's a fixed price and all the boys will have to do is make one phone call for everything to be sorted out.' Annie's parents have also made similar arrangements and several 'age' charities have links with funeral services that offer monthly instalment payment schedules to spread the cost.

Bereavement

Poor us, left behind. Many people say that the realisation and subsequent grief only really kick in once the business of arranging the funeral and dealing with the practicalities is over. Then we can feel, suddenly, very alone. In fact there is a tremendous amount of support out there for the bereaved, from children to the elderly left widowed, and they can offer some comfort and practical help about things such as bereavement benefit, even though you may feel inconsolable and reluctant to deal with formalities.

The thing is – you are likely to have been knocked sideways on both an emotional and practical level if the person you have lost was a member of your family or a really close friend. Therefore you will be going through a period of intense adjustment, and just coping with that on a day-to-day basis is bound to be very stressful.

This stress may manifest itself physically too and give you yet more to deal with when sleeeplessness leads to exhaustion, panic or anxiety attacks, lethargy and loss of appetite. It's important to be kind to yourself and to look after your most basic needs in order to help you deal with your grief as best you can. Be wary of reaching for false crutches, such as alcohol, which will ultimately plummet you further into despair.

You'll run the gamut of emotions – anger, guilt and yearning – and must take each day at a time as you come to terms with what has happened. You'll be distressed at feeling so sad and yet if the sadness lifts for a minute you'll feel that you shouldn't let it. Try not to suppress your feelings or be unnecessarily strong in front of others. If people are prepared to listen and you want to talk about the dead person, then do. Likewise, if you are a friend of someone bereaved, be prepared just to listen. You are unlikely to be able to say anything that will materially alter the way they are feeling because nothing will bring back the loved one they have lost. But so many people are frightened not only of death but of another person's grief (I suppose it's an obvious reminder of their own mortality). The greatest thing you can do for a bereaved person is to stand firm and be there, in whatever guise they need you to be. Don't cross the road just because you don't know what to say. Follow their lead. If they want to talk nonsense, keep them company and talk nonsense too, but be ready for the tears should they fall.

As the bereaved person begins to adjust it might be helpful to think of somehow positively addressing their feelings of grief. In the same way that memorial services can be a wonderful way to celebrate a person's life and give some comfort to the bereaved, so can a kind of informal, remembering occasion. Get together with family and close friends and bring along photos and fond memories to talk about. Perhaps hold it on a day that the loss will feel most acute, such as a birthday or anniversary. This sort of gathering can make it easier to share your grief and be comforted by others. It's especially helpful for those who might be feeling a loss intensely and privately and not feel as able as others to articulate it, so isolating themselves even more. Remind each other that the person who has died would not have wanted his or her loved ones to feel desperate and unhappy, and they owe it to them to support each other and keep the good memories alive.

Or maybe think about a memorial for the person. This doesn't need to be anything grand – it could be planting something special or commissioning a painting or engraving; something that will celebrate the person they were.

I wonder where you are right now reading this? Trying to make sense of what to do after someone you loved has died? Determining to set out your wishes and wanting to know some options? Or, trying to burst the bubble of deep fear you have inside about your own death, with some concrete facts?

I'm frightened of the uncertainty of death, as most of us are. Just as I was frightened of childbirth and, more surreally, I'm sure I would have been terrified anticipating *being* born if I'd had any conciousness then. It's the unknown, both of what happens and then what is going to happen next. The only universal certainty is that fear of something inevitable is destructive energy that will sap your living hours. My advice is to deal with the practicalities, file them away under D for Death and then let your fear-full confrontation act as a spur to make every minute count – for the living and your life. (See all other chapters for help doing that!)

Conclusion: Life is for living . . .

Finally then, here we are at the end of the Handbook which I hope will shore up your own resources and reserves and empower you to make your personal choices. Adapt the principles and information in it to make your own bespoke Handbook for Life; create checklists and contacts file for each area of *your* life. Even if some of the items on your lists are just wishes and will do's at this stage, that's fine. A wish list is a starting point, whether it notes the threadcount of the sheets you want, the pursuit of an interest or the nurturing of a friend. Compile a checklist of essentials, the core of self-knowledge that will inform everything else. Know these things about yourself so that when you have the time or the money or are in just the right circumstances, you can make good decisions and plans.

In **Relationships** – who are the ones you love, have you a full complement of friends, some easy-going chums, a mentor, a bosom pal, a shoulder, an honest broker; who are the professionals you trust to carry out your business and support services?

How best can you give your **Soul** succour and nurture the inner you? What is in your file of cherished memories that makes you happy? What music lifts your spirits? What criteria does your **Work** life have to fulfil? Do you harbour unrealised ambitions? What would you need to achieve to make them happen? What **Leisure** pursuit lets you switch off? How much time do you give it? What do you need to do for optimum **Health**? Are you doing it? What *exactly* is your net worth in terms of **Money** right now? How financially organised are you –

how long would it take you to work out that figure? Can you count the ways you have done your bit for good **Citizenship** to make the world a better place since you woke up this morning? What are the nesting materials and ingredients you need in your **Home**? When you think of your **Image**, what is your signature look?

And have you thought properly about your **Mortality**? Are you as ready as you can be for whatever comes next, including knowing you're living your life now to the full?

Dip in and out of this book to find out more about the things and issues that matter to you and go to the website www.the-lifeaudit.com to drill down and find out even more detail.

It's a cold, rainy autumn morning and, as I write this, I am sat in my car looking out over a windswept beach in south-west England. It's mostly deserted but there are a few people. Three women, wrapped up in thick jackets and hats who I thought were beachcombing, but who I now notice have clipboards and are obviously recording the flotsam and jetsam washed up by the tide. They are clearing up all the plastic and debris as they go. How good of them and how interesting a project. I wonder who it's for? There is also an elderly couple, retired I suspect, flying kites. How extraordinary. How lovely. Their laughter has made me look up a dozen times. Now here's a businessman who has just pulled up beside me in his car. He looks like a rep, his suit jacket is hanging up and there are loads of samples on the back seat. He's eating a sandwich and looking out at the view. Seems very cheerful. And here's a walker, a young backpacker, a traveller, looks a bit lonely, but as he passes I can hear him humming along to whatever is in his earphones. He nods hello and smiles.

We are all wearing jumpers in these different lives in this moment. All different. All alone. All together. We are incredibly lucky in so many ways. Life can be really quite simple – it's just us that makes it complicated.

Index

Index

Index

Index

Acknowledgements

Goodness, where to start? Family, friends, colleagues, acquaintances and members of The Life Audit website have been so generous in giving advice, information and support. The irony of me writing this book will not be lost on those who know me well, I suspect. I am grateful to them all; they include the woman with the cleanest house, the man with the healthiest lifestyle, the couple with the most style and the wisest man. They have variously tried to help ease my chaotic lot by offering to clean my house, giving me style guidance (having described my dress sense as '*Top Gun* meets polo match') and taking me to task about living more healthily. They also applauded my generally optimistic demeanour as an obvious reaction to the fact I have much to be depressed about! They will know who they are and I know are too modest to want to be mentioned here but I treasure having them in my life and couldn't do without their affectionate interest in my wellbeing, even if I sometimes ignore their advice. (I do still wear pearls with black leather.) Similarly, no names, but many thanks to the hundreds of people I've talked to outside my immediate circle, most found via the internet and too many to mention individually. The research for this book was daunting, especially when looking for information on the web and being presented with many millions of sources. But thank you anyway, Tim Berners Lee, who invented this fantastic tool. As he said, 'The original idea of the web was that it should be a collaborative space where you can communicate through sharing information.' How right he was and is!

I'd also like to thank Jenny Day, who told me the saying: 'put a jumper on and get over it'. It was at a time when I needed more than just a catchy heading for a section. It worked!

Finally, thank you everyone who has worked with me on this book, especially Charlotte Barton, Helen Coyle at Hodder and my agent Jane Turnbull.

Acknowledgements